D1492229

TYNDALE-BISCOE
OF
KASHMIR

A KNIGHT'S PRAYER

My Lord, I am ready on the threshold of this new day, to go forth armed with Thy power, seeking adventure on the highroad, to right wrong, to overcome evil, to suffer wounds and endure pain if need be, but in all things to serve Thee bravely, faithfully, joyfully, that at the end of the day's labour, kneeling for Thy blessing, Thou mayest find no blot upon my shield.

ONE WAY OF LEAVING SCHOOL

To overcome the prejudice of parents against their sons being taught to swim, fees were doubled each year for those who persisted in their prejudice. And so it was that the timid and weakly creatures who entered the school gained strength and the courage to use it in the service of others.

Tyndale-Biscoe of Kashmir

AN AUTOBIOGRAPHY

With Forewords by

THE EARL OF HALIFAX, K.G., O.M.
Viceroy of India 1926–31

FIELD-MARSHAL LORD BIRDWOOD OF ANZAC
G.C.B., G.C.S.I., G.C.M.G.

SHEIKH S. M. ABDULLAH
Prime Minister of Kashmir

THE RIGHT REVEREND GEORGE BARNE
Formerly Bishop of Lahore

LONDON
Seeley, Service & Co. Ltd.
196 Shaftesbury Avenue

CANON C. E. TYNDALE-BISCOE was educated at Bradfield and Cambridge where he took his B.A., and coxed the Jesus College boat, head of the river for three years, and coxed the Cambridge eight to victory in 1884. He was awarded the Kaiser-i-hind medal 1st class and bar for his services to India.

❧ ❧ ❧

Steve Fairbairn, the great Cambridge oar, wrote of Canon Tyndale-Biscoe, in *The Times* of June 30, 1932: "I won the College Pairs with the cox (of the Cambridge eight), and knew that he had done the better performance in our boat. I was not ashamed of having done worse than a man 8 stone lighter than I. I was proud of him. I have often said of rowing, 'As you meet your stretcher so you will meet your God.' That cox, Tyndale-Biscoe, met his stretcher perfectly, and throughout his life, in his missionary school in Kashmir he has done wonderful work —a real Empire-builder."

❧ ❧ ❧

General Dunsterville of "The Dunster Force" & *Stalky & Co.*, wrote: "Tyndale-Biscoe is a born optimist who regards dangers and difficulties as so many hurdles to give the racer the pleasure of leaping; a strong, forceful character with unshakeable ideals and an unswerving determination to move without hesitation towards those ideals; a striver with a strong sense of humour and good sportsmanship, and an indomitable courage, both moral and physical; such are, briefly, the traits that have enabled this indefatigable missionary to realize the remarkable success that has attended his lifelong efforts."

Foreword by
THE EARL OF HALIFAX, K.G., O.M.
Viceroy of India 1926–31

MUCH has been said and written about Canon Tyndale-Biscoe and about his remarkable work and influence as a Schoolmaster in Kashmir. From this book, carrying as it does the impress of his personality, many who never had the privilege of knowing him, will be able to see for themselves what the secret of that achievement was.

Unconsciously, as I suppose, the boys in his school breathed the atmosphere of his own life and conduct. His standards instinctively grew into theirs. A sense that there was always a sharp distinction between right and wrong; a loyalty to principle, and fearlessness in standing up for it; generosity of judgment; the recognition of obligations, expressing itself in service that boys and men were happy to give; these were some of the things that his boys learnt from him and that, as they went out into the world became the foundation of their citizenship.

Thus will the work that he did continue to live and speak through the lives of many of his old boys, and whenever the value of it is discerned, the name of Canon Tyndale-Biscoe will be held in honour.

HALIFAX.

Foreword by
FIELD MARSHAL LORD BIRDWOOD,
G.C.B., G.C.S.I., G.C.M.G.

I AM asked to write a few words as a foreword to the late Canon Tyndale-Biscoe's autobiography. This I do with great pleasure, for during my forty-seven years of Indian Service there was no man for whom I had greater feelings of admiration and indeed affection than I had for him. I know I can say that his whole life was spent in doing all he could for the well-being and happiness of his fellow beings.

His great joy must have been the knowledge that when he left the schools, over which he had presided with such signal success for over fifty years, he had performed a really great work in making MEN of by far the greater number who came to his schools (as I think I can say) with the effeminate feelings of rather miserable creatures. Such work will stand to his memory with far greater honour than any memorial of stone or metal could do.

May his memory as a great man be held in honour for many a long year in Kashmir for which he gave his best life's work.

BIRDWOOD.

Hampton Court Palace.

SHEIKH S. M. ABDULLAH
Prime Minister of Kashmir

THE death of Rev. Canon Tyndale-Biscoe has indeed been a personal loss to the people of Kashmir. Canon Biscoe came here at a time when Kashmiris were steeped in ignorance and apathy which are generally attributes of a backward community. A callously unsympathetic system of administration lasting for centuries on end, had reduced them to barbaric conditions of living which stultified their imagination and brought about their intellectual stagnation. Amidst this darkness, Canon Biscoe set out to kindle a spark of enlightenment and liberal knowledge, and immediately came up against prejudice, superstition and social taboos. He was misunderstood by many and these reactions at that time were natural. But he did not feel discouraged by these initial setbacks. His was an inspiring way of winning the people whom he had come to serve from across the four seas. With sympathy, love and understanding he associated himself with them and shared in their joys and sorrows and thus overcame one prejudice after another, till in the end he succeeded in creating for himself a place in their hearts.

Canon Biscoe patiently and persistently tried to instil in our youth the spirit of self-help, *esprit de corps* and social service. The institutions with which he was connected were places where young Kashmiris not only were taught high and noble ideals, but were imbued with enthusiasm to

strive for them. It is a source of regret to me that I have
not had the good fortune of passing through his school;
but those who have been under his care as students feel
joy and pride to be known as Canon Biscoe's boys. He
breathed his own idealism, purity of thought and action,
and love of service into all his students, and made them
models of uprightness, honesty and good character. He
was a teacher in the real sense of the word.

What makes his work all the more remarkable is the
fact that elsewhere in India the gestures of foreigners,
however friendly, were generally regarded with distrust
and suspicion. But Canon Biscoe set an example of how
true relationship between two peoples, seemingly quite
alien to each other, could be built on equal and human
terms. By sheer self-denial, courage and toil, he created for
himself goodwill and gratitude. He was regarded by the
people of Kashmir as their friend and sympathizer.

To-day Canon Tyndale-Biscoe is no more amongst us
but his memory lives enshrined in our hearts and the
traditions of selfless service that he has created will never
die.

S. M. ABDULLAH.

THE RIGHT REVEREND GEORGE BARNE
Formerly Bishop of Lahore

D URING the last two hundred years or so the British Isles have been famous for producing outstanding missionaries. The latest of these great men is Cecil Tyndale-Biscoe of Kashmir.

The following pages (more or less an autobiography written in action) will introduce readers to a remarkable character. They will remind old friends of sixty years of courageous rowing against the stream and will enlist many new friends. They will make all who read them convinced that the Biscoe tradition must be maintained.

It was my good fortune to be in personal touch with Cecil Tyndale-Biscoe for many years when I was Bishop of Lahore. I never visited Kashmir (that beautiful country of mountains and lakes, of valleys and rivers) without coming away exhilarated, not only by the air and gorgeous scenery, but also by the work in the Biscoe schools; and thanking God for the man who had founded them and poured his spirit into them.

What was he at, for sixty years, this great little man of Kashmir, this little man who had coxed the Cambridge Boat from Putney to Mortlake sixty-six years ago in the days of the great Fairbairn and then had gone out into the Mission Field to found a unique and remarkable tradition? What was his target. It was to *make men*. Men with bodies, minds and spirits fully developed and functioning as the Creator intended. Men of character and courage, serving their fellow-men, fighting for truth and justice, constantly engaged in killing dragons, valiant men in thought and action. Biscoe recognized no other way of hitting his target except through Jesus Christ. "In all things be men" says the Biscoe school motto. Christ might well have said the words; or Paul.

And what unpromising material to start on! So many Kashmiris the very embodiment of a way of life diametrically opposed to Biscoe and all that he stood for. From the very beginning Biscoe faced his task unflinchingly. Everything he taught was to make the Kashmiris better men, men of character and courage (this cannot be repeated too often) and thereby qualified to serve their fellow-men.

In the midst of rivers and lakes no one would touch an oar or paddle except the *máugi*, the man who made his living on the water. In time all the boys could use an oar or paddle and use them in the service of others. At the beginning few boys could swim. If anyone fell into the water the usual tradition was to run away in case the spectator might be considered to have a hand in the accident. In time all the boys could swim (many finely, miles across the lakes) and tales of saving life from drowning became woven into the fibre of the schools. A unique Honour Board occupied the central position in the school hall. It bore the names of those who had saved life at the risk of their own.

The tradition grew. Old boys came back as masters, anxious to hand the torch to others. I have a photograph of Tyndale-Biscoe and his staff taken at the time of his golden jubilee. Nearly one hundred men and only about half a dozen of them not Old Boys. Practically all in the group non-Christians. Biscoe has been criticized for this but he knew what he was about. He knew that the tradition of love and service was safe in the hands of his Old

Boys. Many of them are carrying it on still to-day. Sometimes I used to hear these men take their Bible classes. I can recall many a scene where I have heard the teaching of Jesus Christ as faithfully taught as I have ever heard it. I was continually astonished . . . but these were Biscoe's Old Boys. His spirit had entered into them and it was the authentic spirit of Jesus Christ. Some day, perhaps, Bishop Lefroy's prophecy will be fulfilled that from Hindu ashes and Muslim graves many Christians will rise and go into the greater life.

Unconventional? Of course Biscoe was as unconventional as he could be. When I offered him a canon's stall he at first declined to accept it as he said he was not fitted to be a canon. Afterwards he accepted my offer and if a canon's stall means a recognition of faithful, fearless and outstanding work, no one ever merited his more.

His work among girls and women must never be forgotten. He founded a girls' school which grew and prospered. They held the same traditions as the boys. Knowing something about the homes from which the girls came I always regarded this school as a miracle. And so it was; and is still to-day more than ever so.

Then Biscoe fought against the pernicious system which condemns young widows to virtual slavery and the impossibility of marrying again. He loved animals. Cruelty or indifference to their suffering roused his feelings strongly. There is a prayer which I often use which begins "O Thou whose divine tenderness doth ever outsoar the narrow loves and charities of earth, grant me to-day a kind and gentle heart towards all things that live." He was always in my mind when I used that prayer. "All things that lived" claimed the attention of his kind and gentle heart and he got his boys to work for their care.

All these things and hundreds of others you will find in

the pages of this book. As you put it down you will thank
God for an exceptional man, a man of untarnished faith
and simple trust, of pluck and perseverance of a very high
order, an educationist who regarded character as the
most important part of education. It is no ordinary achievement that to be known as a Biscoe Boy was often considered a much better qualification than a university
degree.

You will find in these pages references to Blanche, Cecil
Tyndale-Biscoe's wife. She stood by him all these years,
shared his problems and perplexities, supported him in all
his undertakings, and, like the good missionary she always
was all through her long life, bore her constant witness to
the Love of God as she knew it in Jesus Christ. Great
people these two, great in their simplicity, courage, faith
and love. May their paths be as the shining light that
shineth more and more unto the perfect day.

GEORGE BARNE.

CONTENTS

13

LIST OF ILLUSTRATIONS

CHAPTER ONE

Holton & Bradfield

IT was towards the end of the eighteenth century that
my great-uncle Elisha Biscoe sold his estate of Swallow-
field in Berkshire and bought the Holton estate in
Oxfordshire. Holton Park was one of the most beautiful
wooded parks in Oxfordshire and in it stood a fine old
castle surrounded by a deep moat. Inscribed on one of the
corner stones of the wall standing out of the moat was the
date 1307.

In the days of the Commonwealth, when the Parlia-
mentary party was at Oxford, Cromwell used the castle
as his headquaters and one of his daughters was married
in the castle chapel.

After a few years Elisha Biscoe discovered that the
castle was haunted. He was not partial to ghosts so pulled
down this beautiful old castle, not leaving one stone upon
another. With these stones he built a house in the centre
of the park making it somewhat like the old castle he had
pulled down.

Elisha Biscoe was a bachelor, and liking to live alone
and not be disturbed, he kept a ferocious bull in the park
in order to keep out pedestrians. About a quarter of a
mile from the house there was a small mound which he
named London. When he saw any carriage driving towards his house he would suspect visitors and go straight
off to this mound. The butler had orders to tell visitors
that the Squire had gone to London. He only remained
there until they had gone.

When my father, who had inherited the property, took
possession of the house it was soon discovered that the
ghosts from the castle had taken up their quarters in Park
House. The first news of their presence came from our

B

servants who wished to leave our service. My parents tried to calm their fears, telling them that they should not be so foolish, for up to that time none of our family had met the intruders. The subject of ghosts came up at intervals when friends and relations came to stay; several of them told us at breakfast how they had been disturbed during the night by uncanny sounds and an unpleasant feeling that strangers were in the room.

I happened to be the first of the family to be honoured by an apparition. I was about twelve years old. It was ten o'clock at night and I was standing with my back against a table looking towards a flight of stairs. On my left was a glass door leading into the front hall where a lamp was burning on the table. In front of me to the right of the stairs was a dark passage leading to the middle hall, in which also a lamp was burning. All of a sudden I saw a boy of about twelve running towards me very fast, I put out my arms to stop him as he turned sharp round the bottom of the staircase in order to go to the front hall. I noticed that his feet did not touch the ground, he ran straight through the closed glass doors, and when he had reached the front hall, first his head and then his body went up suddenly in smoke as if he had exploded. I then ran into the drawing-room, where several of the members of my family were, shouting: "I have seen a ghost! I have seen a ghost!" They answered: "Shut up, don't talk non-sense," but they could see how excited I was and that I was not fooling. The only explanation that I can give of this incident is that I may have fallen asleep while standing up and that what I saw was a dream.

The next apparition was seen by my uncle and aunt, both of them very sensible people. They were sleeping in the haunted room in an old-fashioned four-poster bed. My aunt woke up and saw a white figure standing close to the bed, so she woke her husband and whispered to him that someone was there. He answered sleepily: "Go to sleep," but she then shook him saying, under her breath, that there was someone close to the bed. When really awake he saw the figure and, thinking it possible that one of us was playing the fool, shouted out "Go away", whereupon the figure moved slowly across the room to the dressing-room which he knew he had locked, and that was that.

On another occasion our cousin Tom Tyndale, a lawyer, saw a boy whom he mistook for the footman. Then one morning we noticed that our butler looked ill for he had no colour in his cheeks, so my mother said to him: "You are ill, you must see the doctor," but he answered: "No, madam, I am not ill. But last night I saw a ghost. I was in my bed adjoining the pantry when, on hearing a noise I went into the pantry and there I saw a very big woman standing in front of me." "How was she dressed?" asked my mother. "She had a high collar and puffed sleeves, such as the pictures of your ancestors which hang in the dining-room." "Did you speak to her?" asked my mother. "No," he answered, "I was too frightened and fell against the wall, but if I were an artist I could have painted her." Later my mother saw a ghostly dog which the servants told her that they also had seen. My mother tried to catch this dog but it eluded her.

An elderly woman, a boy and a small black dog were the three spirits which appeared to us, and of course, many uncanny noises. We children, as we grew up got great amusement in frightening our guests by adding to the number of ghosts by artificial means. We also tried to discover the reason of their appearances but it was not until I arrived in Kashmir that I heard of a possible clue.

Our aunt, Lady Barrington-Kennet, who with her husband had seen the ghost already mentioned, met a Mrs. Whorrard in a Swiss hotel, who told her that her ancestors had owned Holton Castle and asked her if the Biscoes had ever heard of the murder committed in the castle, to which she answered in the negative. Mrs. Whorrard then told her the story, namely, that the eldest son of the family was murdered and buried by his governess.

It is possible that Park House had been built over that child's body, and hence the apparitions. But what the dog had to do with it was not mentioned. Anyway, we as children were thrilled to share our home with such interesting phenomena and only wished that they would appear to us more often.

My father William Earle Tyndale, born in 1813, was the eldest son of Rev. Thomas Tyndale, Rector of Holton, Oxon, who with persistent pluck, against much opposition put an end to bull baiting in Wheatley stone pits, which led to the abolition of this cruel sport in England.

My father became heir to Holton Park from his uncle, Elisha Biscoe, and in consequence had to add to Tyndale to his surname, Biscoe.

In 1850 he married Eliza Carey Sandeman, the daughter of Albert Glass Sandeman who was founder of the Sandeman Port Company. From this marriage there sprang a family of one daughter and seven sons, Stafford b. 1857, heir to Holton Estate, Frances b. 1859, Albert b. 1861 who became Colonel of the R.H.A., Cecil b. 1863, Edward b. 1865, a naval officer who later joined in 1890 the Rhodes Expedition to Mashonaland and had the honour of hoisting the flag at Fort Salisbury, Julian b. 1867 who became Colonel of the XI Hussars, and later commanded a brigade of cavalry in the 1914 war, Arthur b. 1872 took up market gardening and later commanded the Hants Regiment.

We were a most happy and devoted family from childhood and for all our lives. We were blessed with parents who taught us by their daily lives rather than by words, the meaning of Christianity. We all of us looked upon our parents as ideal and realized that it would be our own faults if we made a mess of our lives.

When visiting those ill in the cottages around, our mother always took one or two of us with her to carry the pudding or port or whatever it was, so that we might try to cheer up the sick, and learn the joy of service in a way which could never be learnt from books or sermons.

To give an instance. My mother sent our governess with her three pupils, Fanny, Teddie and myself to inquire about the welfare of a poor family. When we arrived, the family were at tea, and we noticed that instead of butter,

they were spreading lard on their bread. So when we returned home, we ran up to our mother saying: "Oh
mother! Do you know that we saw the family to whom
you sent us eating *lard* on their bread! ! Why don't
they eat butter as we do?" Mother answered: "Because
they are too poor to buy butter," so we at once said: "Oh
mother, do let us take them butter." "Certainly," answered
our mother, "if *you* pay for it." We had not thought of
that way out of the difficulty.

But we ran off to our tin money-boxes, and extracted
our treasured pennies. Then off we went to the dairy, and
asked the maid, who was churning, if we might help her
to turn the handle. When the butter was made, we paid
for it out of our *own* bank savings, and with joy went off
to that cottage and presented our gift. I date back to that
wise act of my mother the moment when the seed of
"joyful giving" was sown in our young hearts.

When I was about six mother took my brother Ted
and me to see our grandmother Tyndale at Oxford. On
the hall table was a missionary box with a nigger boy on
the top, standing with a broad-brimmed hat at his feet
with a slit in it. Mother said that if we dropped a coin into
the hat, the nigger boy would nod his head. So we
dropped in a penny, and the little boy did as mother said.
On our drive home we asked our mother about this little
boy and she told us of the African slave trade. When Ted
and I were in bed together that night, we promised each
other that when we grew up we would go to Africa and
set the niggers free. Ted did eventually join the navy, and,
when a midshipman, found himself off Zanzibar with the
East Indian Fleet catching the slave dhows and setting
the "niggers" free.

I was at Bradfield College when an old boy, D. W.
Lowndes of the U.M.C.A., from Zanzibar, gave a lecture
describing his experiences in Africa and the terrible sufferings of the Africans at the hands of the Arab slave
dealers. After the lecture my friend Harpur and I went
into a quiet corner and promised each other that we would
go to Africa and fight the slave trade.

Time went on and I was at Cambridge where I had the

great pleasure of arranging missionary meetings in my room. U.M.C.A. missionaries told of their experiences in Africa and of the slave market at Zanzibar with all its cruelties, and hoped to collect fellow crusaders. Later came the time when I could offer my services for work in Africa of which I shall speak later on.

On looking back to the days of my youth I can see plainly how God was preparing me for my steeplechase in Kashmir; especially by the untoward happenings of my life. I will take them as they came. When a baby, I fell ill with meningitis and was more or less insensible for a month and was only pulled through by our devoted nurse Eliza Seary. On account of this severe illness, I was for several years a weakling, always tired and bad tempered, and it affected my brain so that I could never learn by heart.

When I grew older and promoted to the school room, I was continually punished by our governess. She did not understand psychology and thought it was the devil in me and imagined it her duty to beat the devil out of me. So I continually had my ears boxed. Now this has turned out to be a great blessing in my work as a schoolmaster. For, contrary to the general rule of schoolteachers, I became far more interested in dull scholars than in "bright boys". So much so that my sympathies have always been more with those boys who fail in their examinations than with those who pass. Many a time, after a public examination I have lined up all those who have failed and congratulated them; cheering them up by saying they will score in the end, for they will have their subjects impressed in their minds by re-study. This line of action bucks up the depressed and puts life into them: for in India, boys take their failure very much to heart and sometimes even commit suicide. Then again, knocking boys about makes me see red, and the teacher whom I catch boxing ears receives no quarter from me. Hence I thank God that I had a bobbery governess, although I suffered with damaged ears all my boyhood.

Then on account of my dullness I had to endure more punishment than most boys. I am sure no boy in the school

had to give up more play time to write Compositions than
I. It has destroyed my handwriting, as all who receive
letters from me know to their cost. As the result of my
sufferings the Kashmir schoolboys have scored, for in all
my fifty years as a schoolmaster I have never given boys
lines to write, except when a boy has forged a teacher's
name or altered the marks given to him. Then I make him
write until he is truly sorry for having used his pen to
cheat his class fellows. He has to write a whole copy-book
of the forged name. We always in our Kashmir schools gave
punishments to fit the crime. If a boy talks after the order
of silence, he has to stand on a human parrot perch and
continue to talk. Or if caught smoking he has to stand on
the top of a monkey pole and smoke Burmese cheroots in
public. I have never had to correct a boy a second time
for smoking. We do not like punishing boys continually,
hence our system of punishing according to the crime.

Owing to illness I had myself a sulky temper as a boy.
This helped me to understand and tackle sulky boys.

In 1875 my brother Albert and I were sent to Bradfield
College, Berks. As I was leaving my home my eldest
brother, Stafford, who was at Harrow, gave this parting
advice: "Cecil, when you arrive at Bradfield the boys will
treat you roughly, but whatever they do to you, never cry,
but laugh." How I have thanked Stafford for this: it has
been my salvation over and over again.

That very day I had my first opportunity of following it. I, with other new boys had arrived early and were
in the classroom as the schoolboys came pouring in,
having driven in large wagonettes from Reading station,
eight miles distant. As soon as they saw the new boys they
all came round to test us, asking all the usual questions in
quick succession. "What is your name? Where do you
come from? What is your father? How many brothers and
sisters have you got? What are the names of your sisters?"
and then followed some unmentionably nasty questions.
Anyone who did not answer up at once received a blow
from the fist or a kick in his pants. Those who showed
resentment were at once set upon. At the first blast of this
whirlwind I was a bit flabbergasted, but remembered

Stafford's advice and whether it was a blow or a kick I tried to take it as a joke, so that the older boys shouted "Oh! Leave that young squit alone, he likes it." But although I escaped bodily damage I had daily to see all sorts of cruelties done to defenceless boys. They were held close to the fire to be scorched. Others were hung by a rope from a ventilator in the ceiling. The victim, blindfolded and with hands tied behind his back, would be made to stand on the top of boxes with the ventilator rope round his neck. The boxes were then kicked from under him suddenly so that the victim would swing in the air and was left until his face became discoloured, then they would cut him down. Or they would pull a small boy's trousers off and bind him to the master's desk and then beat him with a fives-bat or knotted rope.

The bullies were just about to bind me to this desk and I was quaking with fear, when by a miracle I was saved. Suddenly a brave boy, only twelve years old, stepped forward and cried out: "Who is going to beat Biscoe? for he will have to fight me first." At this challenge everyone fell back, and I was saved. He had fought one of the bullies the week before and still carried the marks of battle on his face. The boy was Napier, the grandson of Lord Charles Napier of Magdala.

On another occasion I was saved again as by a miracle. The bigger boys were intent on raping me. I of course fought furiously with fists and toes. As they bound me I used my nails and finally when they forced me on the floor, and I thought all was up, the chief devil's leg came within reach of my mouth. I was just able to raise my head and with all my strength I got his calf between my teeth, and I am sure he carried that scar until his death. The sudden pain changed passion to anger. In the dormitory matters were worse, if possible; no one was permitted to say his prayers or read his Bible before going to bed, and we small boys did not dare to go to sleep until the big boys fell asleep.

When I returned home for the holidays I begged my father to allow me to be taught boxing. My father gave leave, and for seven years I had my weekly lesson in "the noble art of self-defence". Mr. Blake, late of Queen Victoria's bodyguard, was the instructor. How I loved, honoured and blessed that dear man, for he was my salvation and the salvation of others; for when devils knew that one could plant one's fist in a split second on the right spot then bullying ceased automatically.

I was at Bradfield for over seven years and for five of these years, I say, I was in hell, and then the two last years were "heaven" compared with what had gone before, for Dr. H. B. Gray arrived, a MAN, not merely a scholar of Oxford. He could read character in faces and knew how to tackle devils. His arrival was like the break of day after a dark night.

There was also a master who was a help in these days. I was never in his form, and I do not remember that he ever spoke to me. But I knew instinctively that he was a godly man, so that when watching a football match, I would try to get next to him, so that I could touch his coat, and thus get some moral strength.

Years afterwards, I was passing a church in Redhill and I saw the name Canon F. Daniell, Rector, written on the notice-board. It was about service time, so I went in to the vestry and found an old white-bearded man. It was my honoured Bradfield master! I told him how his presence when in hell had strengthened me, and needless to say we kept in touch with one another and then later with his son until they both, father and son, passed on to the life abundant.

In these five years of hell, how often I used to ask God why He permitted such wickedness to continue and beseech Him for strength to fight. I received the answer about fifteen years later and was able to thank God for having permitted me to suffer for those five years as you will hear.

I learnt many things at Bradfield which have proved of the greatest use to me as a schoolmaster. One of them concerned the *art of cribbing*. The half-hour respite between breakfast and chapel was devoted to preparing for the construe lesson whether Latin or Greek. A clever small boy was made to stand up on a form and read out of the crib the passage from the classic that we had been ordered to prepare for the next day's lesson. This English translation was read slowly whilst the rest wrote it under the lines of the Latin or Greek, whichever it happened to be. They could thus go to the class in confidence, knowing that their master would be pleased with their translation of the passages given them to read. Which he was. But poor me! My case was different, for I refused to have anything to do with the crib, and although I had tried with dictionary to worry out the translation, I was never able to compete with the fluency of the crib, and hence was accused by the master of laziness, and ordered as usual to write out the lesson out of school. Thus I learned that dishonesty was rewarded and honesty punished.

It was the same with the daily repetition which was always heard before breakfast. The same small boy was made to write out in big lettering the piece of poetry that we had been ordered to commit to memory. Then, when the master entered and sat at his desk, one of the boys would show him his lesson-book and ask some important question which would need the master's attention while another boy pinned the paper to the front of the master's desk, but out of the line of his sight. The result was that the master was very pleased with the diligence of his pupils in committing to memory so accurately the work set him, whilst I, who had been swotting hard during the previous evening's prep was turned upon and ordered to write out the piece so many times out of school hours.

At the end of term examinations it was the same. Some of the cribbing was really clever. It was interesting to watch the examinees' plans to have the requisite knowledge at hand when in the examination hall.

The keen cribbers would be hard at work some days before the examination writing out notes and passages from the books on which they were to be examined, in diminutive writing on neatly cut pieces of cardboard. These they fastened to pieces of elastic and the other end they sewed on to their shirt sleeves at the shoulders so that when they put on their coats no one could see the cards. When they needed information they would pull down the card below the coat sleeve and read the notes, but when danger threatened they let go the card and up the arm it flew.

The most expert cribber was a boy for whom I had an affection, for he never wished to bully, he was too true a sportsman, but he looked upon fooling the masters as part of the game. He later went into the church to please his father and took the family living.

Well, it was Prize Day and some celebrity had been invited to distribute the prizes and make a speech. The parents of the boys sat in the front rows to see their dear boys take their prizes. There sat my friend's father, the squire of an estate nearby, and his sisters, delighted to see Alec go up three times for his prizes, and hear the eulogies poured upon him for his hard work and deserved success! As Alec passed me, sitting near the back at the end of the row, he pushed the arm full of books towards my face, and said softly: "Look, Biscoe, what you can gain by cribbing!"

Well! This lesson of successful cribbing was not lost on me, as you will see later, and I thank God that I suffered so much from this clever cribbing of my class fellows.

Why were schoolmasters such fools in those days? I suppose because the teachers were chosen on account of their knowledge of the classics, not for their knowledge of human nature or for their desire to build up character.

There was another trial at school for which I thank God. The school rules were legion, so that it was difficult to move without breaking a rule, and what was so senseless was that many of the rules were such, that no master could know if they were broken, and therefore these rules were only kept by boys who possessed consciences.

One particular rule which hit me hard was the prohibition of bathing in the river. The river flowed along our playing-fields. I believe that I loved the water more than anyone in the school, yet I could not have a swim in the river because of this school rule. I felt it terribly, especially on a hot summer's day, when I would see crowds of boys, all rather fatter than usual, for hidden towels were swathed round their waists. As they passed me they would say: "You coward, Biscoe, afraid to bathe for fear of getting a licking."

The masters knew where all these boys were going, but they did not wish to catch them. Well, I say again I am most thankful that I experienced this bit of rotten law-making, for I promised myself that, should I ever be a schoolmaster, I would never make a rule that I could not see obeyed, and I have proved for fifty years that a school can be run on such lines.

Now that I am on the subject of swimming, I would say, how utterly important it is that a boy should never be sent to a public school as a non-swimmer.

Shall I ever forget my first day in the Bradfield swim-ming bath? Saturday was the small boys' day, but no provision had been made for supervision, and big boys also were there, hence they were having the time of their lives in bullying the new boys who could not swim. But I escaped as by a miracle. A big boy whom I did not know, for some reason took pity on me, and said quietly: "You just keep near me, no one shall touch you and I will teach you to swim." I clutched that unexpectedly kind offer with such keenness, that I learnt to swim in three lessons. I always remembered my kind deliverer and hoped to meet him again.

It so happened that when I was in Calcutta in 1903 I discovered that Basil Dow, for that was his name, was in a business firm, Bird & Co., so I went off and found him, and reminded him of his great kindness in delivering me a weak little boy of eleven years old. I found him the same kind-hearted fellow who without doubt was cheering and strengthening those who needed his help in the great city of Calcutta.

While at school I collected a wonderful lot of trusty friends who had suffered and fought with me through those days of hell and came through unscathed to do their bit in the Greater World, of protecting the weak and put-ting pluck into the weak-hearted. I think of three who were in the first football team, Henry Bonsall, Andrew Forbes and Frank Humphry who left school about the

same time as I did. Two went into solicitors' offices, and
one, to an engineer's office. All three found themselves
landed among clerks who made the office filthy by their
talk. Before the week was out all three offices had been
cleaned out, and in one, the head of the office thanked the
new clerk from Bradfield for his pluck.

One of the three had had a very narrow shave of being
expelled from school. His form master for some unknown
reason took a violent dislike to him, and sent him up to
the Headmaster every Monday morning to be beaten. At
the end of the term this master told the Headmaster that
either he or Frank Humphry must leave the school, and
so the boy had to leave.

I did not hear of this tragedy until I had reached home
for the holidays. I at once wrote to the Headmaster and
told him the truth, saying that I as a boy in the classroom
knew more of the character of the boys than a master
could possibly do, and told him what a power Frank
Humphry was for honour and purity. Dr. Gray answered
my letter by prompt action, for on my return to school
Humphry was there to greet me and his form master had
departed, so Frank Humphry was able to carry on his
gallant life for another term.

Hitherto I have spoken of the dark side of school life
which certainly did cloud the sun. But I did enjoy the
school sports, above all the yearly steeplechase which was
quite a sporting course of about two miles. We had to
cross the river twice and pass under the open sluice gates
which, for small boys was decidedly difficult, and over
various fences and hedges. I being not more than five or
six stone in weight had the advantage over the ploughed
fields as I ran on the top of the clods whilst the heavy
fellow sank in the mud. When it came to hedges I was
unable to jump, but I always found a hole made by a fox
or some animal through which I crawled; the scratches
from the thorn hedges left their marks on my skin for
many a day, but what did it matter so long as one had the
joy of defeating every obstacle? It was not until the seventh
year that my efforts were rewarded by passing the winning
post first.

This Bradfield steeplechase taught me to love obstacles. There is always some way of conquering them. Little did I imagine that these Bradfield steeplechases were preparing me for one lasting fifty years in a country of which I had then never heard.

At last the day came for me to leave Bradfield which I had learned to love, on account of the terrific change that Dr. Gray had wrought in turning a hell into heaven, for I can truly say that during my last term (in the lower fifth, for I never reached a higher form) one never heard filthy talk. I used to say it was like being in one's drawing-room at home. But nevertheless I left Bradfield wondering why I had been put in hell for five years.

From Bradfield I went to Mr. John Gibson a very good sort, a Crammer at Bromley, Kent, for six months. From the lower fifth I would not have been fit to pass the "Little Go" at Cambridge.

I had hoped to go to Oxford where my father, grand-father and other ancestors had gone, but to pass "Smalls" at Oxford I should have to pass in Latin prose, which I could never do. Cambridge did not require a pass in that subject, so there I went and spent three glorious years of freedom, making heaps of friends for life.

I chose Jesus College as I had heard about that college from two men at Bradfield for whom I had great affection. One was the Rev. John Powley, the choirmaster, who taught me to sing. I was one of those who had to stand in a row and sing a long Latin grace before and after every meal in Hall and start the evening Psalm on the note of G. How I funked it! For I always feared I should make a bosh of it before the whole school.

The Latin grace was anathema to me for two reasons. Firstly, I could never remember the words and had to substitute sounds something like them. Secondly, one of the headmasters of my time, a great classical scholar of Oxford, said that we wasted too much time over our meals, so he always touched the bell while I was still hungry. I used to cut two lumps of bread ready to pop into each cheek, to finish after the Grace had been sung, for to be caught putting food into our pockets would have meant a caning from the head prefect which was more severe than that administered by the masters.

The other beloved friend was the Curate of Bradfield Parish, Tommy Hughes, who used to befriend me and other little boys and give us tea in his rooms when the spirit moved him. In consequence I had a regard for the college in which they had been taught, so to Jesus College I went.

CHAPTER TWO

Cambridge & Whitechapel

BEING undersized I was pitched upon for holding the rudder strings of racing boats, and had the honour of coxing our college boat head of the river, for three years in succession, and winning the Grand Challenge at Henley Regatta and also of coxing the Varsity boat to victory in the Oxford and Cambridge boat race at Putney in 1884. I also stroked one of the college boats, but as I was only just over eight stone in weight two inches were cut off the end of my blade. I had the good fortune to have Steve Fairbairn as my instructor, for what he did not know about watermanship, no one else did. He taught me to steer the boat in the many races from start to finish without touching the rudder so that the pace of our boat was never slackened by its use. My voice was the rudder, as I shouted orders to the oarsmen in the bows, or the stern oars to pull hard or to go easy, as need requires. One would see other boats sending up fountains of water as they negotiated the sharp bends in the river whilst the Jesus College boat sped round the corners without any fuss.

One's life on the river was full of amusing and exciting incidents. It was the day before the Lent races, and we were ordered to row the racing course from start to finish, in order to test our pace. I was rowing stroke. It was snowing and also just getting dusk so the visibility was bad. We were rowing full out, when I noticed that the coxswain's face was very agitated and guessed there was danger ahead. So I glanced over my shoulder, and saw fire coming out of the funnel of a steam tug a few yards ahead. In a second I felt a bump, the cox had lost his head and did not know what orders to give, the men began taking headers out of the boat, and I followed, diving to the bottom of the river keeping my body scraping the mud, for I feared that the screw of the tug would catch my back as the Cam is not deep. I took care not to come to the surface until I reached the bank. When I did get on the bank I saw to my surprise that the eight-oar had not been cut in half or sunk, but was still floating and three of the men were still in the boat shoving the boat off the tug, with the cox still in his seat. This was one of the coldest swims I had experienced. Well, all's well that ends well, and it did not prevent our boat doing well in the race next day.

In this sporting college, like most others, we had what was called the "pi set". We had a weekly religious meeting in one another's room and generally tried to do some bit of Christian work, such as to help some parish padre with his Sunday School and the like. I joined up with this "pi set".

Now, the man in rooms exactly above mine happened to belong to the alcohol set. One evening this young gentleman had been drinking and as he passed my door he was talking to himself or to his supposed friends, saying what fun he was going to have to-morrow night, when he and his friends would pay the pi-cox a visit and smash his furniture.

As no Jesus College men could be found to make hay of my room he had to go to other colleges to collect brave men to attack one man weighing eight stone. Having been forewarned, I naturally forearmed by inviting a party of my rowing friends to coffee that evening.

It was about 8 p.m. when we heard a tramp of feet passing my door on their way to the room above, and later we heard much laughter and noise, as they prepared themselves for the attack by much drinking. In about half an hour they considered themselves fit for the job, and downstairs they came in great spirits. But these braves did not get nearer than the outside of my door, for they heard voices and laughter and they thought it wiser to wait on a more opportune occasion, which never eventuated.

In the year 1883 Moody and Sankey visited Cambridge and hired the Corn Exchange Hall for their meetings. Many odd stories were told of these two American evan-

c

gelists, so out of curiosity Frank Ince, an old school friend, and I decided to see what was up. On our arrival at the hall we found it crowded with over one thousand undergrads and a few women in the front rows. On the platform we counted seventy undergrads who were singing hymns lustily, and I noticed some rowing-men among them. I said to Frank Ince: "I would not join that lot for £200."

When the seventy men had finished their hymns Moody stepped forward and gave out that Mr. Sankey would sing a solo. He sang the hymn "Nothing but leaves" beautifully. Directly Sankey ceased, there arose loud cries of "Encore! Encore!". Moody stepped forward, holding his hand out for silence. He then said: "Gentlemen, this is a religious meeting, so please do not encore," but the audience continued until Sankey sang another hymn. Moody then said: "Gentlemen, we will pray." He knelt and made an extempore prayer. I was much surprised, for I thought that parsons always prayed from a book and also wore black gowns or surplices. Directly Moody finished his prayer there were loud shouts and stamping "Encore! Encore!". Moody then repeated: "Gentlemen this is a religious meeting, please cease," and the stewards in the hall tried to quiet the rioters, but this only stimulated them. First the Moody and Sankey hymn books were used as ammunition, then the hassocks, and lastly the chairs were flying all over the hall and on to the platform. Some of the ladies in the front rows fainted. Then appeared at the main door the Proctor and his bull-dogs, wearing their top hats, but they received short shrift and were shoved back through the door. Later the police arrived with their batons which they used freely and finally cleared the hall, with the exception of about forty undergrads. Frank Ince and I decided to see the show through. Presently when calm followed the storm, Moody asked us to stay for an "after meeting". He, Sankey and his helpers came amongst us to ask us if we were saved. This was a new experience for us.

I was told afterwards that Moody had said that this meeting at Cambridge was the most distressing he had ever experienced but also the most fruitful. He had never heard of so many lives changed at a single meeting. Amongst them was the "Cambridge seven" who agreed together to go as missionaries to China. The seven included C. T. Studd, Captain of Cricket, Stanley-Smith, stroke of the Cambridge boat, and Sir Montague Beecham, who was No. 7. Many others afterwards became friends of mine—Hector McLean of the Oxford crew, Sydney Swann, who rowed four times in the Varsity boat race and went to Japan as a C.M.S. missionary, Douglas Hooper, a rich racing man, who later worked for the C.M.S. in Central Africa, until he passed on, and crowds of others who gave themselves for Christ's service, not only as clergy but who worked in the service of their country and also for the Kingdom of God.

A few weeks after that meeting a certain Irishman, a man whom I had never seen before, walked into my room, apologized for the intrusion and asked if I would do him the honour of breakfasting with him next day at eight o'clock. I accepted, and arrived at his rooms in Market Square, to find an elderly lady the only occupant. After wishing one another good morning, a voice came from the bedroom (also the noise of splashing water) for our host was in his bath. "Let me introduce, Miss Weston, Mr. Biscoe," said the voice. Later the owner of the voice, Mr. F. C. Sutton of Dublin University appeared, apologizing for his unreadiness to receive us. I soon learnt that the lady was the Miss Weston who was setting up Sailors' Homes in all our naval ports.

Later, in walked a tall thin young Trinity man, the Master of Polwarth, President of the Cambridge University Debating Society, so I found myself in good company. Polwarth asked me to lunch with him next day at a well-known hotel.

On arrival there the following day I was directed to a large upper room with a long table at which were seated some twenty undergrads and one elderly man in a smart grey suit, who asked me to take the seat next to him. He was Mr. Edwin Arrowsmith, a great worker for the Children's Special Mission Service. He had come to

Cambridge to gather a band of helpers for his summer campaign, concerning which I was profoundly ignorant. I thought him a queer sort of fellow for he talked so much on religion that I began to fear a trap, and thought of escape. However, he persuaded me to watch the boat races with him that afternoon to tell him what was what. So to the river we went, but I soon found that Mr. Arrowsmith was far keener on talking religion than listening to my answers regarding the various crews.

Well, before the races were over, he had made me promise to come to his rooms, to hear more about his beloved C.S.S.M. That evening I had managed to persuade two of my boating friends to share this ordeal with me. And, in the end, we all three promised to join his C.S.S.M. party at Llandudno. Mr. Arrowsmith was a clever fisher of men, for he made me see that as a Cambridge blue I could be a great help in attracting public school boys to his services on the beach. I quite saw his point for when at school I had great reverence for Varsity blues, but I made him promise that he would not ask me to preach. I would gladly play games and teach the boys to swim; anything in the athletic line but no preaching. To this he agreed.

Term was over; I was at home enjoying life to the full with my brothers in our lovely home at Holton Park, but as August drew near my courage began to fail, as I thought of this children's mission and all its publicity. I hoped I should catch scarlet fever and rode a bobbery horse hoping that I might break a leg or something. My horse bolted with me in the Park and took me under a low-branched beech tree which swept me clean off the saddle. As I fell, I thought, now at last I am in luck, but to my grief I picked myself up without damage. A day or so later I had to set off for Llandudno. When I arrived, there was a jovial crowd to welcome the late-comers; Arrowsmith had collected thirty Oxford and Cambridge men to help him. Amongst them were Sydney Swann, Hector McLean, and Cecil Boutflower who later became Bishop in Japan and afterwards Bishop of Southampton. A cheerier crowd it would have been difficult to meet.

We were set to work at once. My duty was to wear my light blue blazer and go scouting for schoolboys and bring them to the eleven o'clock service on the beach. I was fairly successful at this sport, and amongst the many I collected were Arthur Waistell, who became Admiral Sir Arthur, K.C.B., Lennox Russel and Hope-Simpson, knighted later on for their good work in India.

Among them also were the three Burges brothers who invited me to their home in the Christmas holidays. They lived in Birmingham where their father was vicar of a parish of 16,000 people and working himself to death, so keen was he to win his parishioners for his Master. When the invitation for a certain day arrived from Mrs. Burges, we had news from my brother Edward that he would be arriving home from sea that very day. He had been away for three years with the navy, fighting the slave traffic off Zanzibar and the Mahdi in the Sudan, so naturally I longed to see him. However, my conscience bade me not disappoint the boys in Birmingham, so I left home sadly, little knowing what was to befall me in Birmingham. It was there I met the youngest sister Blanche, who was later to become my wife.

In 1886 I took my B.A. degree, to my great surprise. How I managed to satisfy the examiners I did not know. I thought that possibly my college dons had made the examiners kind-hearted. I then went to York to read theology with the Rev. E. A. Lane and lived in Monk Gate Vicarage with his most delightful family whom I to this day love to remember. Later, I was accepted by Dr. Vaughan, Dean of Llandaff and Master of the Temple.

I am always thankful that I went to Dr. Vaughan to read for orders as everyone who had that privilege has been, for Dr. Vaughan was a truly outstanding Christian gentleman, who influenced every one of his pupils and left his mark on them for life. He thought far more of character than dogma. He expressed himself at one of his daily Greek Testament lectures in this way. "What pleases me at my Trienniel meetings (when three hundred old pupils meet at an Oxford or Cambridge College) is to see their diverse clothing, some with soft hat and white ties, some with hard hat and stiff dog collar, some with hard hat with tassels and some in cassock and biretta. I don't care what you are, so long as you are Christian gentlemen."

How different is this outlook to certain Theological Colleges which turn out one particular brand. It may be strict Evangelicals or rabid Anglo-Catholics thus manufacturing disunity in the service of Him, who prayed that we might be *one*. Surely there are enough Christian sects all preaching different doctrines without the Church of England dividing itself into opposite factions. It is not *Christian* whatever else it may be.

If those who call themselves Christians would turn their attention to practical Christianity instead of bothering themselves with dogmas, we should be drawn together as brothers and hence be true disciples of one Master even Christ Jesus. Do they never realize how the Devil rejoices to see Christians fighting one another.

In 1887 I was ordained by the Bishop of Oxford, John Fielder Mackarness, a father in God to his diocese and with a delightful family whom we knew well, for Cuddesdon Palace is only two and a quarter miles from Holton Park. I, of course, failed in this Deacon's examination and the Bishop told me I knew nothing, which I knew to be the truth, but he said he would ordain me on my past record. I fancy that it was my uncle, Henry Tyndale, Rector of Holton, who influenced the Bishop.

My first curacy was at Bradfield Parish. I accepted the offer of Rev. C. H. Owen to be his curate as I wished to get in touch with the boys at the school, whom I thought I might be able to help. Dr. Gray kindly allowed me to poach on his preserves and hold a Bible Class for them in my rooms at the farm where I was living. I remember his words on my arrival as curate. "Cecil," he said, "you have come into a hornets' nest, for your predecessor was most unpopular and had his windows smashed by his parishioners." I was thankful for that warning.

Fortunately for me, when at the school, I had made friends with the village blacksmith, who was on the Committee of the Radical and Free Thinkers' Club and was therefore agin the parson. Also I had made friends with the village shoemaker, a dear little man to whose workshop I used to go for a quiet chat, away from the noisy class-room. He was the Methodist minister. The young "toffs" of the village thought the new young curate was fair game and started their games straight off, but the unexpected happened.

There was a fine handsome young ploughman who was one of their leaders, whom I met one day coming out of the pub rolling drunk. I, fearing that he might fall and be run over by a cart, went up and put my arm round him to prop him up and he put his strong arm round my neck. So curate and drunk had a nice little friendly walk down the main road. Ever after that this handsome ploughman and I were sworn pals so that whenever I came upon him ploughing, he would pull up his team, and take off his hat and salute me.

To save the young men from wasting their week's earn-ings in the pub on Saturday evening, I bought a set of handbells, and was fortunate in securing the services of an expert handbell ringer, a hotel keeper in Reading and a delightful man. I also provided cocoa and biscuits.

The result was that the local publican, a huge man with a lower chest to match, gave out that he intended to give this young meddlesome curate a horse-whipping. This desire of the publican was not known to me at the time, nor the fact that my bell ringers had arranged a bodyguard to see that the curate should not feel the whip, which they effectively did. The publican having been checkmated over the horse-whipping, succeeded in upsetting the hearts of some of my friends for he wrote an account of my death from a cycle accident in the *Reading Mercury*. There are some very steep hills at Bradfield down which I used to coast, and people often predicted my death, so the publi-can picked on this way of killing his enemy on paper and had the joy of reading it in print.

The postman on his rounds was always glad of a cup of tea at my rooms. He was a Plymouth Brother and liked to talk on religion more than I did. One morning as he was about to leave me and get on with his duty, he asked: "I hope Mr. Biscoe you are one of the one hundred and forty-four thousand." "I hope not," said I. (He gasped, opening his eyes and mouth wide.) "Because if I were one of the hundred and forty-four thousand, I should be keeping out someone else from salvation." He left my room, thinking I knew not what.

Every Wednesday some twenty Bradfield boys would come to my rooms after football, when I was able to talk to them freely. They knew that I knew their difficulties in living a Christian life at the college. So we had great times together, and I kept touch with a number of them all through life. One was an especially dear fellow, who later became Bishop of Peterborough.

There was one very interesting case. This boy, the son of a peer, was known by the nickname of "Sin" because he had gone to the Devil. Well! One day he turned up at my lodgings, asking me if he might join my Scripture Union Class. I had seen him several times, though not to speak to, and had spotted him as a difficult customer, though I had never heard anyone mention him or speak of his character. I was much surprised, when he made this request.

After inviting him into my rooms and having a straight and friendly talk, he opened his heart saying that he had gone to the Devil, but wanted to be like my brother Arthur, his fellow classmate who was a straight, clean fellow and not afraid to show his colours. So he joined the weekly Bible Class crew. As he had made a clean turn round, he naturally had to undergo some weeks of persecution, as all men do when they break away from their old life and start climbing upwards. Later he went to the Varsity and after that was ordained to the ministry, and I guess he has been a great help to those who like himself were once blind but now can see.

My life as curate was a great joy except for the weekly sermon, for in those days there was no school chapel and the college boys attended the parish church. Shall I ever forget my first sermon which took me sixteen hours to prepare and write out. In a blue funk I mounted the pulpit, with the parishioners, plus the whole school, facing me. Having been a boy myself I knew how they hated sermons and how they were on the lookout for any slip or untoward behaviour of the preacher. And then there were the masters who knew that I knew nothing! For the first few seconds I only saw a blue mist, and later faces began to appear. In my terror I made a stupid slip in pronunciation of a word and expected to see the boys nudging one another, but no, nothing happened. At last the eight or ten minutes' purgatory was over, and I was down on terra firma again.

My Rector exchanged with a Rector from Yorkshire, a hunting parson who said he did not need to keep a curate since, with an extra horse, he could do the curate's work. I was thus free to take a curacy elsewhere.

I was staying at Maidstone with Rev. W. H. Hewett, a beloved college friend, who was just off to London to interview the Rector of Whitechapel about a curacy in his parish and suggested my going with him, with the result that the Rev. Arthur Robinson offered me the third curacy. So in the month of July 1888 I found myself in the clergy house of St. Mary's, Whitechapel.

I happened to arrive at a most notorious time, for the whole of that part of London was stirred to the depths by the terrible murders of women by a man known as "Jack the Ripper". Five women of the unfortunate class had been murdered in or close to our parish of St. Mary's. One corpse was found on the steps of St. Mary's Church and one just outside our clergy house. The result of this succession of murders was that the people lost their heads, so that when they saw a man carrying a bag they would call out "Jack the Ripper". In a second the poor fellow with the bag would be running for his life with a crowd at his heels shouting "Catch him". I have even seen a policeman on duty join in the chase.

On one occasion I stupidly was carrying a bag in which I kept my canonicals. When the cry was started, "Jack the Ripper", I fortunately did not lose my head and run for it, but stood still and looked my would-be chasers in the face, as a dog does when he is attacked by several dogs, with the result that after smelling around me they looked foolish and walked off. It was not easy to carry on our duty of visiting from house to house as our custom was, because the women would not let us in.

Often I had to thank God for my time at Bradfield. It taught me to be cautious. Among my experiences in Whitechapel was one when I was returning, tired, to my lodgings after an afternoon's visiting. I must have been using my brains and not my eyes for I walked straight into a rough crowd of young men and women horse-playing in front of the London Hospital when, all of a sudden, I found myself a prisoner, with the strong arm of a young lady fast round my neck. She was wearing a large blue ostrich feather in her hat. She drew my face to hers until our lips all but touched, and said: "Give me a kiss, dear," and as she held me as in a vice the crowd around shouted: "Go it, 'Arriet." I was powerless, but my eyes were free and I looked her straight in those glistening eyes and trusted her, with the result she waived her strong arm off saying: "You may go, my dear," and the crowd set up a cheer as I continued my way to my lodgings.

On another occasion, through the strength of a drunken woman's arm I was forced to dance with her round a barrel organ, to the cheers of the delighted Whitechapelers. Once in a doss house I was saved miraculously from being dragged out by my hair by a super lusty drunken wife, mistaking me for her poor husband.

How often I had to thank that dear boxing master at Bradfield for teaching me to box and other important matters that go with it. Mentioning the London Hospital reminds me that the house surgeon was Wilfred Grenfell of Labrador. A more gallant man never lived. He left his Mark in Whitechapel as in every place he ever went. His tackling of drunken men and women, and scoffers at Christianity, and his great efforts in turning young hooligans into gentlemen, was an inspiration for all Christian workers.

I would mention another man who made his mark amongst the East End men in those days. He was Winnington Ingram, later Bishop of London. It was great to see him with his men at the Oxford Mission House with its four hundred members. There was also that king of evangelists, General Booth, who had started his mission close to our church, a few years previously, getting hold of the down-and-outs whom we failed to reach.

My special jobs were to look after two Sunday Schools, a Band of Hope, a boys' club and a mothers' meeting, plus a district of four thousand people. I found the Sunday Schools and Band of Hope anything but well disciplined, for my predecessor had been ill and unable to tackle the youngsters. I saw that action, not words, was needed, which at once changed the atmosphere, for the teachers were splendid and they only needed a captain.

In order to teach the youngsters what we meant by Christianity I bought a bath chair and a double-seated perambulator, and set the older boys and girls to seek out decrepit old folk and crippled children and take them for joy rides in Victoria Park and generally to cheer them up. The children took on this job with delight and it was inspiring for the East Enders to see the youngsters using their health and strength for the afflicted.

For the elder boys, besides the usual gymnastics and boxing, I started a swimming club in the public baths, and a boat club on the Thames. Every Saturday afternoon we would take a penny steamer from London Bridge to Battersea Park where we embarked in our boats and rowed up to Putney or elsewhere according to the tide. On return to the boathouse, I introduced them to a cold bath, unknown to them previously. My chief reason for getting them on the river was to get away from the smells of the streets and alleys, the coarse life around them and the general drunknness, and filthy language.

Among those whom I taught to swim was Jack Cue, son of the church verger, a splendid specimen of an Irishman. Jack Cue learnt quicker than any of the scores I have ever taught to swim, for he was launched at the third lesson. He was a delightful youth, good at gymnastics and boxing. He contracted tuberculosis and was sent on a voyage to Australia. Later he was ordained and later still became a Canon. He wrote to me saying: "They have made me Canon. I don't know why, but Canon or no Canon I shall always remain your poor boy Jack." In the Great War he went to France with the Australian troops and was loved by them.

The spell of this delightful life of service was broken by my having to sit for my priest's examination. I felt like a lamb being led to the slaughter, and a slaughter it was, for when called up to face his lordship, Fredrick Temple, then Bishop of London, at his palace, I did not feel like singing.

The Bishop was suffering from partial blindness. As I neared his table, he asked me who I was, and told me to sit down. On his table were my examination papers, and as he turned over the sheets he exclaimed loudly: "Shocking! Shocking! You don't know anything, Biscoe." "I know I do not," I replied.

Bishop: Then how do you think you can teach anybody if you don't know anything yourself?

Biscoe (scratching his head): Well, sir, perhaps there may be *some* people in the world almost as ignorant as I am.

Bishop: I doubt it! I doubt it! You are only fit to teach the blacks, there now!

Biscoe: Sir, if you can only persuade my parents and the Church Missionary Society to send me to Central Africa, I shall be most grateful.

Bishop: Ah, then you'll do! You'll do! But I can't ordain you on what you know, for you *don't know anything*, but I am going to ordain you on your work at Whitechapel, so you can go.

And I left in a very different frame of mind from when I entered.

Of course the reason for His Lordship's making an exception in my case was my beloved Rector Arthur Robinson's pleadings. I knew Bishop Temple had the greatest respect for Arthur Robinson for he was a man after his own heart. They were both MEN.

My next step was to visit the C.M.S. headquarters at Salisbury Square to offer my services for any part of the world but if possible for Central Africa, as Bishop Hannington had lately been murdered there and Mackay seemed to be working alone near Lake Victoria. The slave trade was in full swing, so there would be plenty of work to be done even by an ignoramus. I guessed it would be *action* rather than *talk* that would be needed.

The Rev. Mr. Wigram, the General Secretary, received me most kindly and for him I always had affectionate regard. Later I was called before the great C.M.S. Committee mostly grey-haired padres and colonels. Wigram tried to help me in answering searching questions, and then I left the room. What happened I knew not until fifty years later, when Dr. Sutton who happened to be in that Committee Room in 1890 told me. It was this. After my departure, much talk ensued and it was finally put to the vote, and I was voted *unfit* to be a missionary of their Society. Then up rose the Rector of Whitechapel and made such an impassioned speech that my name was again put up, and this time I was voted a fit agent for the C.M.S.

A week or so later I was called to C.M.S. House and told that they could not send me to Africa as the doctors forbade it (I had twice suffered from sunstroke in England), but that I would be sent either to North-West Canada, Persia, or Kashmir and I should hear in three days' time to which country I was to go.

Three days later I was at tea with my family at Holton Park, where I read out my marching orders. "You are to proceed to Kashmir to help Rev. H. J. Knowles at his school." On this announcement there was a loud peal of laughter from all the family. "Fancy Cecil being a schoolmaster!"

My next thought was, where is Kashmir? So I went up to London to the Royal Geographical Society for information about Kashmir and how to reach that far-off country.

The day came for me to leave my many friends in Whitechapel, my beloved rector, and his dear wife, who though a semi-invalid, was a true helpmate to her husband, my fellow curates and voluntary helpers, three hundred of them, for my rector believed in Christianity in action and roped in all those willing to render help in church or parish.

Let me introduce to you one of them, Mr. Silber-schmidt, a converted Polish Jew, a Scripture reader who loved striving to reclaim the down-and-outs in the doss houses, and the professional thieves to whom he gave an annual tea. To this tea party I had the honour to be invited, but with the warning to leave my watch and money at home as they certainly would not be in my pockets when I left the tea party. These thieves so appreciated Mr. Silber-schmidt's interest in them that they formed themselves into a bodyguard to protect him, when they knew he was visiting, after dark, in unhealthy streets or alleys.

The last week or two before leaving England was spent in farewells to friends and relations. My parents invited Blanche Burges, to whom I was now engaged, and her mother to stay at the Park and my parents congratulated me on my choice.

CHAPTER THREE

Kashmir in 1890

THE day of my departure for an unknown land arrived. According to the C.M.S. rules furlough was not allowed until after ten years' service and marriage after three years, if the necessary language examinations were passed. So the parting was especially distressing with my father and dear old nurse, both nearly eighty years of age. I could not expect to see them again, but my mother not having reached seventy I did hope to see in the future.

It was hard on my father as he had intended that I should accept the family living of Holton, like my uncle and grandfather. But my father had no difficulty in filling it, as he received seventy applications.

How clearly I remember that journey. The farewell at that country station, my last look at beloved Holton Park with its beautiful old oaks and elms which my brothers and I had so often climbed, the cattle and the fallow deer browsing beneath them.

It was a November evening in the year 1890 that I left from Victoria. The station bright in the gas light, and then suddenly, darkness, for I was alone in a carriage without a light. It fitted my thoughts, taking a header into an unknown sea, for I could picture nothing; not unlike what we all have to meet as we pass from this life into the greater.

At Calais I found myself in a carriage with three C.M.S. missionaries bound for the Punjab, Rev. E. Guilford, David Davies and Kennedy, from whom I heard the joyful news that the C.M.S. had just altered their rules from ten years' service to seven before furlough.

At Marseilles we had an amusing episode. We had found out from Thos. Cook how much we ought to pay the French porters for handling our luggage from the omnibus to the quay. The porters refused the right payment and crowded round us, as if to force us. So we four padres stood back to back and with our fists faced these gentlemen who danced and gesticulated around us. While we were in this position the S.S. *Locksley Hall* glided up to the quay which caused great amusement to the crew and passengers who crowded at the bulwarks to see the fun.

The captain permitted Guilford and others to preach to the Lascars, and have morning and evening prayers in the saloon, for the passengers. He also permitted us to take exercise by climbing the masts and rigging, for ships in those days had sails as well as steam. Arriving at Karachi, the captain and all the ship's officers came to the station to bid their passengers farewell.

Leaving Karachi for Rawalpindi I was entertained at various places by C.M.S. missionaries and met my cousin, Sir Robert Sanderson, who had ruled Baluchistan so successfully.

At Rawalpindi, the chaplain, Mr. Griffith, and his wife received me. The dear couple tried to keep me but I was anxious to get on to Kashmir. From them I departed in a two-horse tonga for the 200-mile drive through the mountains, changing ponies every five or six miles. On the third day I reached Baramulla. It was a hectic three days as I would not put up with cruelty to the tonga ponies.

From Baramulla a three-days' cold journey in a native boat called a doonga, up the River Jhelum, brought me to Srinagar. My nose introduced me to Srinagar before my eyes did. The British Government had sent a sanitary expert to China to see what could be done to cleanse the cities there, and from thence he came to Srinagar which, he said, was even more insanitary and filthy than any of the cities in China. So there was plenty of work ahead of me if there is any truth in the saying that "Cleanliness is next to Godliness".

I little knew as I passed in my boat up the three miles stretch under the seven bridges what a campaign there was before me, for the moral filth was even greater than the

THE AUTHOR: A MAKER OF MEN

He imbued his Hindu and Muslim staff and the hundreds of boys who attended his schools with a
dynamic spirit of service. Communal differences vanished in the common purpose. They fought cruelty
and humbug. In fires, floods and cholera epidemics they were magnificent. Some gave even their lives.

physical. But my experience of five years of hell at Bradfield was to help me.

The Rev. J. H. Knowles, Principal of the C.M.S. schools, met me at the river bank, and took me straight up to the hospital to see the brothers, Dr. Arthur and Dr. Ernest Neve, in whose house I was to live. Their hospital was famous far beyond the boundaries of Kashmir.

The day after my arrival, Knowles and I walked through the city to the Mission School near the third bridge, a walk not to be forgotten. I recall what attracted my attention most. The stench, the utter filth of the streets, notwithstanding the thousands of pariah dogs, starving donkeys and cows trying to get a living from this foulness.

Most of the houses had thatched roofs. I was astonished to see not a single chimney, and only one house, that of the Governor, had glass windows. Many of the houses were off the straight, often leaning one against the other, like two drunken friends supporting each other.

We at last reached the school, a rented house overhanging the river. We climbed to the hall on the third story where there were 200 bundles on the floor. As I entered, the stench almost knocked me backwards. It was winter; therefore all the lattice windows covered with paper were closed. Every boy was covered up in a dirty blanket and under the blanket a fire-pot (live charcoal in an earthenware pot encased in a basket called "Kangri"), so the hot air passed through the filthy blanket, damp from snow or rain. In the winter, bathing is at a discount, so you can probably realize something of the atmosphere which greeted us. As Mr. Knowles introduced me to the bundles I was able to study their faces. In the front row I saw many beards and whiskers, for practically all were married and some of them fathers.

They were nearly all Brahmans and so had the large daub of red and yellow paint on their foreheads which extended often down the bridge of their noses. The more holy they were, the longer was this daub. As I scanned the faces of these bearded ones I received a shock and I pinched my right leg to discover if I was awake or having a nightmare, for I was back at Bradfield.

D

As I saw evil written on their faces I said to myself: *"Now I know at last why God allowed me to go to Hell."* Then I was a weak, helpless child, now I am a man and top-dog. Thank God!

I was told that several of these boys wished to become Christians. They could quote a great deal of the Bible by heart, far more than British schoolboys could, but my first look had told me the truth. Kashmiri boys' expressions and British were the same, and before long I was to discover that the city of Srinagar was a city of Sodom and this was how I discovered the fact.

One day a party of hooligans came on to the football ground and attempted to catch and carry off good looking boys. In the fight that ensued, the leader of the gang was knocked down and a book was taken from him which proved to be the minute book of the Srinagar Sodomy Club in which were written the names of the officers of the club, President, Secretary, Treasurer, &c., and of 140 pretty boys with their addresses and other particulars. I compared this list with our school roll and discovered that about half these boys were in our school and the rest in the State School.

I called on the Headmaster of the State School and asked him if he would join me in attacking this devilry. He answered, that he had no bad boys in his school, they must all belong to the Mission School; so I wished him good day.

I realized that a small army would be needed for the campaign. The police were in with the devils, so until my staff and decent elder boys became handy with their fists not much could be attempted, as I knew from my Bradfield school days.

An unforeseen difficulty presented itself at once, boxing gloves were made of leather which a Brahman must not touch. But by a lucky chance I was able to jump this obstacle (I made the boys box, wearing cloth gloves), and boxing became part of the school curriculum. We had the city and even the Brahman priests against us, because pretty boys were needed to attract worshippers to their temples; as in other parts of India, girls were needed in their temples.

I had maps made of the city, with houses of refuge marked, as in days of old there were "Cities of Refuge" in the land of Canaan. A map was hung in every school (there were three C.M.S. schools), so that when boys were attacked after dark they would know where to call for help.

To cut this story short, let me say we caught the President of the club three times at his devilry and handed him over to the police, but on the first two occasions the police let him escape from their custody. The third time I was able to frighten the police officer, so that this devil was brought to trial.

I visited the Judge, a Brahman who tried to frighten me by telling me that the city was very angry with me and that I should be careful what I was doing. However, I finally persuaded him to condemn the President to two years' hard labour and his three accomplices to six months' imprisonment. The Judge was much upset as he said no one had been punished for this offence before.

When the time of imprisonment was over the President of the Sodomy Club came straight to me, thanked me for having been the cause of his imprisonment, as he had thus learnt what a devil he had been and asked me to allot him any work I thought fit. So I put him on to help in protecting our boys, and he did so bravely until I went on furlough. The police then caught him as he always feared they would, and on my return to Kashmir, I found he had been in prison for six months without trial. I hardly recognized him, so brutally had he been treated in prison. It was only by taking strong action that I eventually succeeded in getting him set free.

The upshot of our long campaign has been that the Bench have adopted the English law, punishment of seven years for this crime, and young boys are safe in the city of Srinagar after dark. If it had not been for those bad years at Bradfield, how should I have been able to know a devil at sight? Through the Bradfield steeplechases, one had learnt the joy of tackling obstacles. The words of Joseph in Egypt often came to my mind, spoken to his brothers who had tried to kill him: "But God meant it for good."

To go back to my first months at the school, it was to my sorrow that the C.M.S. had sent me to Kashmir, for I had never heard of slaves in that country.

However, when I arrived at the C.M.S. school in Srinagar I found it full of the sons of the Hindu ruling class, the top-dogs in this Mohammedan country. Over 90 per cent of the Kashmiris are Mohammedans. Those sitting before me in the schools were the sons of the slave dealers, not the slaves, for the Mohammedans did not send their sons to school as all Government service was closed to them. They were there to prepare themselves more efficiently for the work that their fathers had been carrying on. So what better stuff to tackle? What these bipeds needed was not brain training but heart changing. This could not be done by books but by action and plenty of it. So I set to work driving them out of their classes with a stick, to the fires in the city, there to save humans and property from the police and other thieves, to rescue animals in distress and later, to save women and girls. This is what the C.M.S. schools have stood for for years. Boys and teachers both have known what it is to bleed in these fights. Now some of these slave dealers' sons are in office and doing the opposite of what their parents had loved to do. May this living education not be changed again to biped and monkey education as of yore.

It was in June 1891 that I heard that my dear mother had passed on. On that day, fortunately for me, I was fully occupied, for, as Captain of the Boat Club, I was responsible for the Regatta on the Dal Lake—yacht races and rowing races as well—and a very pretty show it was. The Maharajah had lent us three of his gaily painted houseboats, with the State Band on the roof of the largest one. It was propelled by sixty-eight boatmen. About the same time I received news that the C.M.S. had waived their order about having to wait for three years after passing the language examination before marriage. If they had held to this, I could never have married as languages were not my *forte*. Mr. Knowles had induced the C.M.S. to waive it for me.

On November 1st, 1891, a P. & O. liner bringing my fiancée, was due to arrive at Bombay.

I started in October in an ekka on the 200-mile journey to the railway station at Rawalpindi, which took me five days. At Bombay I joined my brother Albert, he having made the long journey from Madras to act as my best man. On November 2nd, Blanche and I were married in the C.M.S. church at Girgaum.

Next day we started on our journey to Kashmir, which we broke at Jeypore where we stayed and were made most welcome by Colonel and Mrs. Abbott at the Residency. There we met Sir Swinton Jacob, a delightful man who wielded much power in the state. At Delhi we dined with the Cambridge Mission Brothers, who never spared themselves.

At Amritsar we visited Rev. & Mrs. R. T. Wade and their two little daughters, Daisy and Lilian. The latter became the world famous Mrs. Starr, who so courageously rescued Mollie Ellis, kidnapped by robber Pathans on the frontier.

At Pindi we stayed with the Rev. and Mrs. Spens, a dear old couple and met at supper Robertson, then a Scots Greys corporal, later to become Colonel of that regiment, and finally a Field-Marshal. Blanche had taught him in the Sunday School at his village of Welbourne in Lincolnshire. We left Pindi in a two-horsed tonga. On the second day we reached Uri 130 miles from Pindi where we spent Sunday. On account of having broken our journey we lost our right for the tonga which was taken by Mr. van Someren, Superintendent of Post Offices, and his servant. As he had a spare seat he offered it to my wife and off he went with my bride. I, not wishing to be left behind, ran the third stage to Rampore, fifteen miles farther on, and arrived there before the tonga. I was able to do this by making a short cut down a deep ravine, crossing the river at the bottom and up the opposite side, thus saving nearly two miles and also by gaining time while the ponies were being changed at the five-mile stages. Arrived at Srinagar we started our married life in quarters called the Barracks on the banks of the River Jhelum in the Munshi

Bagh, the only place where Europeans were permitted to
live.

The C.E.Z.M.S. ladies lived next door; Miss Hall,
Miss Reinsford, Dr. Jane Haskew, Miss Newman and
other notable people who shared the barracks with us,
including Sir Benjamin and Lady Bromhead with their
daughter who at that time became engaged to Lieut. Birdwood, later to become Commander-in-Chief of India and
Field-Marshal Lord Birdwood of Anzac, Colonel Bruce,
the famous mountaineer, Knight, the correspondent of
The Times, who was just starting with the troops for the
Hunza Nagar campaign, and author of *Where Three
Empires Meet*.

When the Raja of Hunza was brought prisoner to
Srinagar and lodged in Hari Parbat fort for seven years,
his five sons were sent to our schools. Absolute young
savages they were. I was climbing a mountain with the
eldest boy and when we rested he said: "You know,
sahib, my father is a very brave man." "I expect he is, but
in what way?" I asked. "I will tell you," said he. "My
father took his brother, my uncle, out hawking: later on
they stopped for food and when they had finished and
were mounting their horses, my uncle came forward to
hold my father's stirrup, but my father said: 'No, you
mount first', and insisted on holding the stirrup for my
uncle to mount. Then as my uncle was lifting his other leg
over the saddle, my father up with his gun and shot my
uncle, his brother, in the back, and killed him dead! Oh,
my father is a *brave* man, but not only because of this
incident. I will tell you another." (His eyes were then
sparkling with pride over his father's bravery.)

"My father had an old mother, my grandmother, a *very*
old woman, sahib, who had no teeth. Well, my father went
into the Zenana to see his old mother. She was sitting on
the floor and my father wished her good morning and
then asked her to look out of the window, and as his old
mother turned to look out, my father up with his gun and
shot her in the back and killed her dead! But you see my
grandmother was only an old woman and had no teeth,
sahib. Oh, my father is a very brave man."

I tell you this incident so that when you read of the C.M.S. schools later on you will appreciate what we mean by education. This boy when he first started boxing was true to his parentage, for if his adversary got in a direct blow, he would chuck down his gloves and go for him with his nails which were like the talons of an eagle.

I must admit that this savage we never really tamed, although he came to heel outwardly. We never taught him to honour old women who have no teeth.

CHAPTER FOUR

Fire, Floods & Cholera

THE Munshi Bagh is situated up the river above the city. The distance to the C.M.S. school in the city by river is from two to three miles and by land about two miles. There were no roads as there was no wheeled traffic. When I mentioned the word "wheel" to the boys they asked what a wheel was, so I called for a blackboard. When I drew the spokes they pointed to these and asked what use they were.

We usually went to school by boat until I brought the first bicycle to Kashmir, which caused even more astonishment than did the first motor-car many years later. My first cycle ride was at night. As I passed a coolie carrying a load, I heard a shriek and on looking back saw him on his back, shouting in terror: "I am dead! I am dead!" Poor fellow, he had heard much of djinns and had at last seen one with his own eyes. What a grand tale he must have had to tell when he reached his home!

I had now been at work in the school for more than a year, and had learnt more and more that what the Kashmir youths really needed, was not books and talk, but *action*. They had read the Bible daily and listened to religious addresses and learnt many chapters of the Bible by heart but it had not entered into their hearts. A walk through the city and anyone with any sense of pity would be stirred to action. But could they understand the teaching of our Lord if their hearts were dead?

We began by tackling cruelty to animals. Our first job was a cow, a sacred animal to a Hindu. At that time I had, on a visit to the jail, counted seventy Mohammedans in prison for life, for having killed, or been accused of killing, cows. One day when it was winter, with one to two feet of snow in the bazaars, there was an emaciated starving cow, fallen in the snow, with pariah dogs tearing at its hinder parts and hungry crows at its eyes. The distressed animal was trying to shake off the birds. There was this ghastly sight in full view of all passers-by. No one took any notice of it, as it was a common sight.

I at once sent for the owner of the cow, and to the school for teachers and boys. The owner who was a Brahman turned up first. "Is this your cow?" I asked. "Yes," said he, "it is no use to me." "But," said I, "look how it is being tortured." "Ah," said he, "it will die all the quicker."

Teachers and boys arrive. I tried to shame the crowd that had gathered around. I of course failed, as this was a common sight for the citizens of Srinagar. But the teachers and boys were under my command, so I arranged that this dying cow should be saved from further torture from the dogs and crows, by putting on three guards at a time, changed every three hours. All through that day and night with snow falling, they were kept off until in the morning it passed out of its misery. Unhappily we might not kill it as it was unlawful in the Kashmir State to put a cow out of its misery; the penalty for such an act being life imprisonment.

That was the Brahman boys' and teachers' first lesson, namely, to have mercy on their God-like animal. Since that day hundreds of animals have been rescued from pain by the boys of the C.M.S. schools.

The next practical lesson taught was again not in their reading books but at a fire. I was teaching my class in the top room overhanging the river, when I heard a bugle call and looking up saw a figure on the roof of a house about half a mile away. I asked the boys what that meant. They answered that he must be a policeman blowing a bugle to warn the people that a house was on fire. The boys not being interested went on with their writing. Within a few minutes I saw a flame and smoke rising from the place where the policeman was standing. I ordered the boys to stop writing and come with me to help at the fire, but they said that it had nothing to do with them. They were not coolies but "safed posh", in other words high-bred gentlemen and they wished to continue their lessons. I then took action and drove them out of the classroom in front of me downstairs and into the street. At the double I herded them with my stick to the fire.

Arrived there, we found that scores of citizens had already taken their seats at every available place in order to enjoy themselves at an entertainment for which they would have nothing to pay. As the flames spread from one house to another they seemed highly delighted, shouting out "Hurrah!"

A woman came out of one of the burning houses, calling upon the spectators to come to her help. She told us that her husband was away, and she had no man to help her. Just in front of where I was standing was a long deodar beam. On it there sat five "gentlemen". They were taking snuff and offering it one to the other and took no notice of the woman in distress. The woman, seeing that her request was unheeded, rent her garment from the top to the middle, calling out: "Can you not see what trouble I am in," but those in front of her took no notice and took more snuff. She then raised her hands to her head and pulled out two handfuls of black hair and holding them out to the men (I should say "bipeds") in front of her said again: "Can you not see what trouble I am in? Come and help me." But nobody moved. She then said: "I will pay you for every pot of water you bring." (There were no buckets in the city of Srinagar in those days.) Some men asked how much she would give for every pot of water. When the price was mentioned they all lost interest. She then doubled the price and at that sum the bipeds moved off to search for pots.

I had, of course, ordered my boys to fetch as many pots as possible. Within a minute or so one of the boys came to tell me that there was a cargo boat coming up the river, laden with earthenware pots, so I told my boys to purchase as many as they could carry. Well, the boys came back saying that the boatmen were not selling their pots to-day, so I went down to the river bank and called to the men in midstream and ordered them to bring the boat

ashore, but they told me they did not wish to sell the pots.
So I called one of my big boys who could swim and told
him to swim out to the boat and bring the boat ashore.
When he climbed on board the boat he seized a paddle
and before long the boat was at our feet. I then said to the
boys: "Help yourselves." The boatmen were very angry
saying that they would report me to the Governor and
His Highness the Maharajah. As we heaped up the
earthen pots on the shore, I held out to the man in charge
twice as much money as the pots were worth, but in his
anger he refused to accept it. So I put it on the ground at
his feet and we left with our loot.

We had not been long on our job of passing pots full
of water to the burning houses when a boy came to me
saying that the police were stealing all valuable property
out of the burning houses. The police had impressed
coolies to do this job and were collecting the stolen
property into a barge lying in the river near the burning
houses, so I sent off a fast runner to the school to bring an
armful of single-sticks. When these arrived I handed them
over to my teachers and strong boys, whom I placed round
the salvaged property, to keep away the police and anyone
else who wished to steal. This was my first experience of a
conflagration in Srinagar, hence it has been indelibly written on my memory.

On a later occasion I was returning home by boat, fairly
fagged out, having been working with my staff and boys
for many hours at a really big conflagration with over a
hundred houses ablaze. As I travelled up the river, the
boat dwellers were shouting out praise, such as "Bravo!
Your smell has reached to Kabul and nearly to London."

As I was landing at the Munshi Bagh, I was met by an
elderly missionary who looked at me severely through his
glasses, saying: "Biscoe! Where have you been?" I thought
that question rather unnecessary, for my face and clothes
were thick with soot. And even in the Munshi Bagh, two
miles distant, the cries of the city must have been heard
and certainly the flames and smoke from one hundred
houses seen. I answered: "I have been at the fire." "Did
not you know", said he, "that Friday is the day for the

Prayer Meeting?" I did not answer him, but I thought: "Suppose, my dear man, your house was on fire, and I was passing and you called for my help and I had answered: 'Sorry, sir, but I am off to a prayer meeting.' "

On another occasion I was called to task by a lady missionary. "Do you think that it is the duty of a padre to go to a fire? Why at the Great Fire of London the padres went into their churches and read the Litany." Well, well!

I think we have got over this obstacle in our steeple-chase. It is many years now since I have received admonition for leading our schoolboys to help their neighbours. But in those early days I had to listen to much religious humbug.

There never has been a lack of opportunities in Srinagar for social service. One of the greatest was the cholera epidemics which visited Kashmir every four or five years and caused a death rate of from 500 to 700 per day. The first one I experienced was in 1892. All offices were closed and parents would not allow their children to attend school. I managed for a few days to collect some of our boys for cricket, but soon that was stopped. They would not take Western medicine, but only that prescribed by their priests, which was a piece of Kashmiri paper, on which the Modammedan Mullah wrote "Allah" or the Brahman priest inscribed "Shiva" or "Rama". This paper was swallowed down with river water full of cholera germs.

Later, the people began to believe in Western medicine and so our school staff were kindly supplied with medicine from the mission hospital and were able to save the lives of many. In one epidemic I think we saved seventy. This bit of social service required more pluck than fighting the flames, for our men knew the danger they ran from handling the cholera stricken.

One day I was returning from my inspection of games on the cricket-fields (we had playing-fields at various points round the city) when I met Tara Chand Padi, who was on his way home. He said the boys had had a pleasant game and we parted. At 11 p.m. that evening I was called by a messenger to say that Tara Chand was dying of cholera, so I set off at once and got to his house in half an hour. There, to my dismay, I found Tara Chand in the third stage of cholera, out of his senses.

Bala Koul and Gana Koul, members of our school staff, were massaging his arms and legs, endeavouring to relieve him of terrible cramp. I had brought brandy with me to stimulate his heart; as I put a spoonful into his mouth, he gave a sigh, and Bala Koul, who was holding his head, asked me to leave the room. I thought he asked me to go because of the Brahman women in the room objecting to my presence.

Early next morning Bala Koul was at my window with the sad news that Tara Chand had passed from us. On my asking when, he replied: "At the moment when you put the brandy into his mouth; I asked you to leave the room lest the women should think you had poisoned him. Gana Koul and I kept at our job massaging him all night." "Why did you do that?" I asked. "Because", said he, "I did not wish the women to know that he was dead, in order to save you from being thought a murderer, and also because you know that it is better for women to hear bad news in the day, rather than at night, so we kept on massaging our friend's corpse until sunrise."

Now these men knew that cholera is very catching, but they did not think of the danger to themselves. Their only concern was to save first their friend's life, then my honour, and last the women from fear and sorrow.

The house surgeon of the mission hospital was an Indian named Thomas, who after visiting cholera patients in the city and trying to persuade them to take his medicine, was himself stricken. He unfortunately did not send at once for Doctor Neve. As soon as Dr. Arthur Neve heard, some five hours after his seizure, he called me to accompany him to the hospital, and there we found Dr. Thomas insensible, in the third stage of cholera. The only thing to be done then was to put blood into his veins, which Dr. Neve did by opening a vein in his own arm and transferring it with a rubber tube into Dr. Thomas's veins. Neve and I spent that night at the hospital and hoped for the best, but it was not to be. The dear fellow passed on in the early hours of the morning.

When I arrived at school I heard that one of our Brahman students had been stricken, so went at once to his house, which I found deserted, everyone had run away except the stricken boy and his mother, whom I found lying on the floor, left by their relations to die. As I was speaking to the boy I heard an unearthly row outside. Men were shouting, a motor-horn blaring, and the din was terrific. On looking out of the window I saw fifteen holy Sadus, their faces and bodies covered with ashes and long daubs of red paint on their foreheads and noses. They were marching in single file, holding iron tridents in their hands, also wooden bowls which they held out, and shouting in unison as they stamped their feet: "If you do not give, you will die" as they went from house to house frightening the terrified women, thus forcing food from them. I went down and asked the ringleader what he was doing. He answered: "Collecting food." So I naturally said: "Can't you see what trouble the people are in, come and help them." He answered: "That is not my job." "Who are you?" I asked. "A holy man," said he. "You look it," said I. I had a stick in my hand, so I waved this and ordered those fifteen holy rascals to "right about turn and quick march". As they did not like the look of me and my raised stick, they thought it best to obey. I then went to a State Dispensary close by for help, but the Indian doctor refused to come and sent the medicine with me by a servant to the patients I had just left.

Shortly after the cholera had finished carrying off its thousands of victims we experienced the first great flood. Fortunately I had watched the unusually rapid rise of the river and thought it might top the embankment which encircled the Munshi Bagh, though the old inhabitants said such an event was unknown. Nevertheless I had made hasty preparations.

I had with the help of Geoffrey Millais (the son of Sir John, the famous artist) and some servants, put the American organ on to the roof of our little wooden church and my monkey and black bear on to the roof of my cook-house, when I heard a great roar. While standing at the front door of my house, I saw great waves dashing against the trees and then against the garden fence which fell flat instantly. I had just time to shut and bolt my front door, when bang, the first wave struck it. Soon the waters burst in. In a few minutes the whole of the European quarter was inundated.

I still had time to rescue some property out of the house. Dr. Arthur Neve came to give me a hand. He pluckily got into the nearest boat; it happened to be an iron bath tub, which he handled most skillfully. I fortunately had my canoe handy and in these craft we entered the house but we saw that we should have to be quick, as the flood was rising rapidly, and we should be marooned. As we paddled through the door, we had to lie down to get under the lintel. I then paddled to the study, and arrived in the nick of time to see the big bookcase on the point of falling over. On the top shelf were Mr. Knowles's most valuable translations of the Bible into Kashmiri, on which he had spent many years. I shoved my canoe against the bookcase and held it there until I had placed the manuscripts in my boat, and, as the canoe left the study, the ceiling-high bookshelf fell over into the flood. Neve and I just managed to get out of the house before all exits were closed, leaving behind our new piano, floating, and all our property submerged.

Next morning we were out in boats to pick up refugees on roofs or up trees. As I rowed with two of my schoolboys, in my dinghy, down the poplar avenue seven to eight feet above the road, we saw an altercation proceeding between a boatman and a coolie who was up a poplar tree. I asked the coolie why he did not come down and step into the hanji's boat. He answered: "I have not got Rs. 15 which the hanji demands." So we ran our boat to the poplar tree and said: "Come in our boat." "How much do you want?" said he. "Nothing," we answered, but still he would not move, saying he had no money. However, by laughing and calling him an owl he believed us, and into our boat he came. The hanji seeing that we were robbing him, gave us of his best Billingsgate, so we all three stood up in our boat giving him three cheers.

At this exciting time I was fortunately alone in our

one-storied bungalow, my wife being up in the hills twenty miles distant, at a lovely little lake called Nil Nagh in a pine forest. Dr. Arthur Neve had asked me to take his niece Nora Neve, Miss Judd and my wife away from Srinagar, as the city people would not accept the medicine or help of any Britisher in the terrible epidemic, and there was no point in their being in such danger, several Europeans having already died.

I was very glad my wife was not at our bungalow to see the destruction when the flood subsided, leaving the floor of our house under six inches of mud out of which I dug clothes, books, pictures, everything! I think my wife felt most for her pretty hat, and wedding trousseau articles, and the cottage piano. The monkey and bear were very thankful, when at last I was able to release them from the roof of the cookhouse. Fortunately they were friends; the bear would nurse the monkey and allow her to ride on his back.

Since those early days we have taught over 5,000 boys to swim and our boys have saved over 400 lives from drowning, so you will see the fight has been worth while.

Here are two instances where persuasion was needed. One of the principal Ministers of Kashmir requested me to prepare his son for Oxford University. He had already matriculated for the Punjab University.

I said that I would accept this responsibility on three conditions: No. 1, he would pay the tuition fee in advance. No. 2, he would permit me to teach him manners. No. 3, that I might teach him to swim. To these three conditions he agreed. So I said: "Send him along."

At 7.30 a.m. he arrived at my house in good spirits, saying that he was ready for work. "That is good," I said, "but where is the tuition fee?" "My father will send it. He is a rich man." "That I know very well," said I, hence my desire to see the money in advance. "No money, no tuition, so off you run for the money." I had previously had money transactions with his father. Within half an hour he was back with a bag of rupees which I counted carefully to see that all was square—no counterfeit coins. Fortunately for him all was correct. No. 2, manners, also

LIFE SAVERS

The C.M.S. Schools in Kashmir hold a proud record. The staff and boys have saved several hundred lives from drowning. Time was when swimming was considered ungentlemanly. Furthermore, if anyone fell into the river onlookers would run away lest the police should see them and trump up a charge against them,

satisfactory as payment had been prompt. Now for No. 3
—the lesson in swimming. "We will start at once for the
lake." To that he took strong exception, saying: "Sir, I
cannot learn to swim. I'm not a coolie, I am a gentleman."
"That is interesting," said I. "Suppose you and your
mother were walking by the side of the river and she fell
in, what would you do?"

"Oh! I would call a coolie and send him in after her."
"But suppose there was no coolie, what would you do?"
To this question he had no reply ready.

So I said: "Mount your bicycle. We must start for the
lake at once." We had only gone half a mile when he
called out: "Sahib, please stop, my bicycle is punctured."
This was a fact, as he had been riding behind me, had
jumped off, and certainly had punctured his tyre. "No
matter," I replied, "just shove your cycle against the
fence and we will walk the mile and a half to the lake."
We did this, the son of this very rich Minister, although
a "gentleman" received his first lessons.

Later on I saw the boy at Cambridge. He was then cox
of one of the Trinity boats and most thankful that he could
swim like all the members of his college "coolie" crew.

Years passed, the son now an M.A. of Cambridge, and
an LL.B. of Dublin as well, was back in his own country
in an important position with His Highness the Maharajah
of Jammu and Kashmir. In many ways he helped the
schools when in difficulty. He had become a gentleman,
indeed!

The other instance was of a boy who came into my study
asking for a discharge certificate. On my asking why he
wished to leave the school, he said: "My father is unable
to pay the school fees." "But," said I, "your father is not
a poor man, what fees do you pay?" When he told me the
amount, which was about four times the ordinary monthly
fee, I said: "Then you must be a non-swimmer," (our
school rule is that every boy must have passed the swimming test before thirteen years of age, unless under doctor's orders, and failing this, the school fees are increased
by a quarter every twelve months) to which he answered
in the affirmative. So I said: "I gladly give you a leaving

E

certificate, as I have no use for fools in this school." As he was leaving my study, I said as a farewell: "I hope you will die from drowning." Before he had shut the door I called him back, saying: "Will you please give your father this message from me, that I hope he too will die from drowning."

I laid stress on my wish for his father as I guessed that it was his father who had prevented him from learning to swim, he being a Brahman Babu. Before an hour had passed, a card was brought to me, the messenger saying a gentleman wished to see me. It was the boy's father, who very humbly asked me to take back his son's leaving certificate, as he wished his son to learn to swim, so the boy returned and in a very short time passed the swimming test.

Yet again I would thank God for having permitted me to suffer as I did at Bradfield. I learnt there, when a small boy, what harm bullies can do to youngsters in the water. Hence I watched like an eagle over the swimming lessons, when there might be as many as forty boys learning at the same time in the river, canals or lake. The shortest time in which a boy learnt to swim was three lessons, the longest was three years. This boy had been nearly drowned before he came to our school, and although I took special care of him, he only passed the test after the third year. He is now in the police force, and I trust he will make use of his knowledge in saving others.

In 1893 I fell ill with typhoid which knocked me out for eleven months. If it had not been for the devoted care of my wife, doctors and nurses, I could not have pulled through. I am thankful that I had the experience of what severe weakness is (how I dreaded any stranger who was kind enough to come to cheer me!), and wished I had experienced such an illness before I was ordained. Then I would have realized how often I must have tired sick parishioners when reading and praying with them.

I remember that queen of nurses, Miss Newman, saying to me: "Some of the missionaries are put out with me because I do not start by preaching to the patients when they come to the hospital. How would you or I like being preached to when we are in pain? I think it kinder to relieve them of their pain first, and then when they are at ease they are ready and willing to listen to what I have to say." Surely she was carrying out the teaching of our Lord to do unto others what we would wish others to do to us.

In this connection I should like to mention a few facts which I always consider had weakened my powers of resistance to illness, before the attack of typhoid. Certain missionaries had been upbraiding me as they did Miss Newman, because, instead of preaching in the bazaar, I was filling my days out of school hours with all sorts of "goings-on", calling out my boys at night as well as in the day, to fight fires and above all teaching the school staff and boys to use their fists and what not.

These "goings-on" had reached the ears of the then Bishop of Lahore, and he came to Kashmir to turn me out. In this instance I was saved by Captain Losack, a mutiny veteran to whom he had told his intentions. Losack, being my churchwarden and a soldier, was able to explain to the Bishop the state of the city and its needs, so I was left alone till next time. When accounts of my goings-on reached Salisbury Square I received a strong letter from the C.M.S. Secretary, especially about my teaching boxing, which he said led to public-house drinking (there was not a single pub in Srinagar city, and I never saw a drunken person in the city) and prize-fighting. But in this case I was saved by my courageous friend in Whitechapel, Mr. Silberschmidt, the converted Polish Jew. It is just wonderful how those two met by accident, Mr. Silberschmidt persuaded him to be a strong supporter of me and my "goings-on" and he became a subscriber to our schools until he passed into the life abundant.

I tell of these unpleasant incidents as other friends of mine have suffered in the way I have, viz. Sir Wilfred Grenfell, who as a young man in Whitechapel, was trying to make men of hooligans. Also one of my old schoolfellows, the Rev. Arthur Robinson, who did splendid work in Nigeria, and who wrote to me shortly before he passed on, telling me of his fight to stop immorality among the native christians and how the Home Committee believed their word against his. Arthur believed much in preaching, and nearly met his death in doing so, but he also believed in active practical Christianity.

I would like also to put on record that three of the C.M.S. missionaries who objected to my unorthodox missionary methods, after they left Kashmir wrote and apologized for their attitude and sent me money for the school's war-chest.

Here is an example of a lady missionary who believed in action as well as preaching. Mrs. X came out to India to study at first hand the preaching of the Gospel. She accompanied an Indian padre to his daily bazaar preaching.

As a European lady was by his side, the crowd was larger than usual. While the padre was preaching, a bullock cart was passing and the driver was twisting the bullocks' tails unmercifully, so the lady asked the padre to pause and stop this cruelty, but the padre continued. Again the lady asked the padre to take action, but to her entreaty he turned a deaf ear, so she closed her white umbrella which was sheltering her from the fierce sun, and, in righteous anger, implored the driver to cease the tail twisting, but as he paid no heed the umbrella came down heavily on the driver's shoulders.

History does not relate the result in the minds of the bullock cart driver, the padre or the crowd, though I guess it increased the audience for the preacher that morning.

Here is another case of deeds versus talk. I was travelling in a railway carriage with a Pathan gentleman and in course of conversation I discovered to my surprise that he was a Christian, so I asked him what caused him to change his religion. He answered: "Dr. Pennell." So I asked: "What did Dr. T. L. Pennell say to make you wish to become a Christian?" He replied: "It was not what Dr. Pennell said but what he *did*. I was attending a fair in the town of Bannu when I noticed a noisy crowd and saw a sahib standing on a stool. Some of the crowd were saying rude words to him and trying to annoy him, but the sahib did not lose his temper. An old woman was trying to pass through the crowd with a bundle of sticks on her head. When men barged into her the sticks fell to the ground and the people laughed. But the sahib at once stopped his preaching, descended from his stool and picked up the sticks and placed them on the old woman's head and then returned to his stool to face his noisy audience. That is the cause of my becoming a Christian."

In the year 1895 my father passed on to the fuller life. According to his wish his coffin was placed in one of the picturesque hay waggons drawn by his favourite team of chestnut-coloured horses, which proceeded through the Park along his favourite walk to the church between a long avenue of old elm trees, followed by the tenants and labourers on his estate. There in the old churchyard, dating from Saxon times, his body was lowered in a grave beside that of our mother.

The only members of the family who were not present at the dividing up of the household property were my sailor brother Edward, and myself, with the result that our shares were of more value than the shares of those who were present. Our sister and brothers were determined that we should not suffer because of our absence.

When everything was settled and our eldest brother and his wife and family settled in the Old Home, my sister Fanny, brothers Albert, Julian and George came to Kashmir to visit us and a great time we had together.

CHAPTER FIVE

The Sea Was Salt

IN the summer of 1896 I was invited by Captain
Chevenix Trench, the Assistant Resident, to accompany him and his party to Ladakh, which delightful
trip I have described in my book *Kashmir in Sunlight and
Shade*. During my absence my brother George took care
of Blanche and our two little boys, Harold and Julian.
Later, when my family and I went to England on furlough in 1897, George took over the superintendence of
the school as an honorary worker for a year and a quarter,
with great success. He endeared himself to both staff and
boys and was always affectionately remembered as Gog
Sahib.

On our way to Karachi we broke our journey. Blanche
and the boys stayed at Murree with my brother Albert's
wife, whilst I joined my brothers Albert and Julian's
camp, outside Peshawar, as the 11th Hussars and Albert's
R.H.A. Battery were on active service against the Afridis.
I had a most enjoyable long week-end with the officers
and watched the 11th Hussars chasing after the Afridi
gun-men.

My chief deputation work while at home was to try to
interest schoolboys and I did a lot of it. I made friends
with many headmasters, and among them that great Headmaster, Doctor James of Rugby, generally spoken of by
the boys as "Bodger".

I was invited down to Rugby on two or three occasions,
one of them being on a school festival, when I had to
preach in chapel to a crowd of old Rugbeans as well as the
boys.

Deputation work is strenuous with its much travelling
and talking, but one meets a crowd of pleasant folk, and

one's hosts and hostesses are often wonderfully kind. I made several friends even in the railway carriages and also had some queer experiences with gentlemen who were over-full of strong drink and with cardsharpers who thought they were in luck's way when I entered their carriage.

On one occasion I scored in quite a different way. The train was crowded, and on trying to find a spare seat I noticed that several people had looked into a certain compartment and immediately walked on. I went to see the cause, thinking it might be a sick person or a lunatic, but no! it was a solitary Salvationist in his full war paint, with Salvation written in gold letters on his red sweater, having a whole compartment to himself. So I entered with great pleasure, and he gave me a hearty welcome. We had a delightful hour and a half together undisturbed.

On our return journey to Kashmir, I started two weeks before my wife and party consisting of the children, Harold and Julian, their governess, Miss Hilda Bonsor, and also Augustus Tyndale and Rev. Charles l'Estrange Burges, my wife's brother, who most nobly had offered their honorary service to the schools.

My brother Julian was returning to India to join his regiment, so we arranged to see something of Italy, Greece, Turkey and Palestine en route. A most interesting time we had. I found this visit to Palestine of the greatest help later on when trying to interest our staff and schoolboys in the life of our Lord, for so many seeming difficulties were cleared up and questions answered at sight.

Palestine was certainly "the East" forty-odd years ago, when the Turks were in command. We saw numbers of Russian pilgrims, mostly old men and women dressed in furs from head to foot. They were being driven along like sheep by Turkish policemen who waved a whip over them telling them to move on; they looked very weary. I was told by our missionary friend that these poor peasants had been paid by rich Orthodox Greek Church folk to do the pilgrimage of the holy sites for them.

When we were visiting the Church of the Nativity at Bethlehem we were greatly bothered by guides wanting to show us round the church, although we had a missionary friend with us, Mr. Sedgwick, who knew this church as well as the guides did. We asked them kindly to go away as we did not require their services but they refused to move. So I asked them if there were any underground rooms in this building. They were delighted at my question, so down we went into the vaults, they going in front with candles and we three following. I quietly whispered to my brother and Mr. Sedgwick to return upstairs, while I told the guides that I wished them to show me more vaults. They were very pleased and went on ahead to light my path. When their backs were to me I dashed upstairs and when we three were outside I quickly bolted the door behind us, so that we might have some peace.

When buying our tickets at the station we noticed a policeman at the booking office door who would not let the poor people pass until tipped. Then again when we were in the railway carriage which was a long saloon carriage holding about thirty passengers, a Turkish policeman entered just before the train started and made everyone tip him with the exception of my brother and myself.

It reminds me of an amusing episode which happened to me at Amritsar railway station at midnight.

I was on the platform close to the crowded third class carriages, watching the passengers struggling through the carriage doors with their cumbersome packages, when to my surprise I noticed a policeman *helping* them by shoving them and their packages through the doors. I was delighted to see so kind a policeman. But after they were settled in, he stood with his back to the carriage window and screwing his arm backwards and holding out the palm of his hand turned his head towards the inmates and hissed through his teeth the word "jaldi", i.e. look sharp! I wondered what he was at, until I saw the hands of the passengers go up to their turbans and out came coins, which they placed in this kind gentleman's hand; and so he went from window to window, collecting as a church-warden hands the plate in church. As the passengers were parting with their coin so easily it suddenly struck me that I might share some of their bounty.

So I followed the example of this arm-of-the-law. I placed my back to the windows of the next carriage, twiddling my moustaches with my left hand, as the policeman had done and twisting my right hand into the carriage window hissed through my teeth "jaldi", with the same success.

I soon found that I was the centre of attraction. I continued at my lucrative job, twiddling my moustaches and collecting at the same time. The policeman suddenly was made aware of my "goings-on", especially when he saw me turning to the passengers and returning their money with the laughing remark that I was not a policeman.

The face of that policeman was a study as he walked away still twiddling his moustaches. He kept looking back at me over the heads of the crowd, for he was a tall gentleman, with "who the devil can that man be?" expression. Whatever this little act did, it made all the crowd who watched forget their troubles for the time being, in laughter and jabber.

At Port Said I joined my family on their ship. My brother Julian had missed the trooper he was to have sailed in, but fortunately was given a berth in a passing British cruiser to Bombay.

On our arrival in Kashmir we were met by numbers of the school staff some forty miles from Srinagar. My brother George had filled the twelve-oared school cutter and rowed to Baramulla over forty miles and then walked over a hill some six miles and met us in our tongas. So excited were some of the school staff that they not only embraced me, but one Brahman teacher made a bad shot at my neck and embraced Miss Bonsor instead; much to her surprise and dismay.

When we neared our house we were met by hundreds of boys and old boys who unharnessed the ponies and dragged us home after the fashion of the extra pious Hindus who drag along Jagar Nath's car. I trusted our friends would not throw themselves under the wheels in order to gain salvation quickly, as the disciples of Jagar Nath did.

Our school staff now looked like a family affair with l'Estrange Burges, Augustus Tyndale plus my brother

George. L'Estrange was a wrangler and became a great help in instructing our staff in higher mathematics, and Augustus an M.A. keen on history, and a proficient carpenter. We soon had a carpenter's shop going, though it was a hard fight as the Brahmans said it was against their high caste to handle a tool of any sort. For that very reason I was keen to have a workshop got going to conquer this nonsense, as we had conquered opposition against football, boxing, swimming and much else. Also the carpentry in Kashmir as regards furniture was bad, glue and nails being used instead of mortices; in fact furniture was just knocked together.

One of the first carpenter Brahmans to face the anger of the Orthodox Brahmans is still living and is one of the best furniture makers in Kashmir; not only has he learnt to be a master carpenter but he has learnt to laugh. When we took him on we could not persuade him even to smile; he had a perpetual scowl. Augustus cured him and later he became carpenter instructor to British schoolboys.

The Rev. J. H. and Mrs. Knowles went on their furlough to England, and Rev. C. E. and Mrs. Barton with their children came in their place, and a very happy party they were.

In 1901 I was summoned with all the diocesan clergy by the Bishop of Lahore, George Lefroy, a man amongst men, to the Lahore Diocesan Conference and was invited to stay at Government House by Sir Mackworth and Lady Young.

There I met Bishop Welldon, Metropolitan of India, and later Headmaster of Harrow, who eventually invited me to stay with him when Dean of Manchester. He said he wished to be introduced to a headmaster whom he had heard punished members of his staff. In England headmasters punish members of the staff by dismissing them. But I found it more profitable to keep my teachers and train them to be honest and trustworthy men, rather than to bring in new men who would probably be worse than those I dismissed. It saved much time and energy.

We were faced on one occasion with a really difficult proposition. A youth aged twenty, an old student and a teacher, all three Brahmans, persuaded a pretty young Brahman wife to go in a boat on the lake for three days and there seduced her. In consequence this girl was thrown out of her home to become an outcast for life. Here was good news for the enemies of the Church Mission School!

What angered me also was, that the school which had put in the forefront of their activities the uplift of women, was publicly disgraced. Dr. Henry Holland, now Sir Henry Holland, was working at the mission hospital at that time, so I asked him to give the staff and boys a straight talk on purity and to speak very plainly. This he did. When he had left, I called up the three scoundrels to be beaten before the assembled school. I chose a strong municipal sweeper to do this because the culprits, as orthodox Brahmans, would feel the disgrace more than if I beat them, and I wanted the whole city to know what I and the C.M.S. school thought of a girl being ruined by a pupil, an old student, and a teacher.

When the chastisement was over, I told the teacher that he must suffer more than the two others on account of his position. He was to march to Gilgit, a military station on the frontier, 236 miles distant and carry such a weight on his back as I thought fit, so that he would have time to think over his sin and repent.

Well, he carried his load which was food for the officer's mess at Gilgit and his return load was dried fruits. The journey took him a little over a month and he returned bronzed and fitter than I had ever seen him. The punishment had done what I had hoped. He was a changed man. He was grateful to me for the punishment and worked faithfully in the school until he retired and later passed on a longer journey than to Gilgit.

That was not the end of this distressing business. Our work must be constructive so I put on members of the staff to do all in their power to save that girl from perpetual disgrace. A year afterwards the glad news came that the husband of the seduced young wife had forgiven her, made all square with the Brahman priests, and taken her to his home. We all felt that we could once more hold up our heads and be ready to face the next storm.

In the year 1901 we had another visitation of cholera which, as usual, carried off thousands. After it was over we thought it would be well to stir up the municipality to clean up the city, but the officials did not seem to be interested so we thought it would be a good idea for the C.M.S. schools to try their hand at it. We first of all canvassed the city to see how many citizens would like to have their compounds cleaned. The result was that seventy asked for our help. We then approached the state officials to supply us with spades, shovels and baskets for moving the filth and also for a fire engine to swish down the streets. They agreed so we were able to start at once. The river being low at that time enabled us to fill our boats with sand from the sand banks, which we brought down to the city and filled up filthy compounds and cesspools.

All had been going well for some time when one morning at school I found both staff and the boys had lost their happy expressions and interest and were looking glum and frightened. On asking why I was told that the Brahman priests were very angry with us for undertaking such unholy work and that those who persisted in it would be excommunicated. Fortunately for us the Tehsildar of the city, who is the chief executive officer, heard of our trouble, and although a Brahman gave us his full support. Furthermore he asked me to see that his son, who was a pupil in our school, rode home from school on his pony carrying a spade across his shoulder so that the city should see that he was not ashamed to dig. Our masters and boys came in for a great deal of cursing and unpleasantness but they bravely stuck to their work right through the winter months, when something else happened.

A British official who had just come up from Jammu asked me what mischief I had been up to during the winter, for my wickedness had been reported to Mrs. Annie Besant in Madras and she had arrived in Srinagar as a guest of His Highness the Maharajah in order to look into the evil doings of the Principal of the Mission School in making his Brahman staff and boys do sweepers' work in the city.

The fact of Mrs. Annie Besant having arrived was news

to me so I decided at once to make her acquaintance. I called on her at the Palace which the Maharajah had lent her during her stay at his capital, but I am afraid the interview was not very successful. My headmaster also visited her and invited her to visit the mission school in order that she might discover the untruths that she had heard concerning the institution, but she declined.

The next thing that happened was a mutiny in our school. Three of our staff left suddenly, taking with them three hundred boys to a building on the opposite side of the river where Mrs. Annie Besant had opened her Theosophical School and put in charge an Australian and his wife, who were theosophists.

The Australian was not happy in his work and left. Before leaving, he called on me and apologized for having taken on this job as he had been told lies about me and about the work being done in the mission school.

The next man to be appointed was a scholar from Cambridge, who, after a few months, discovered how things really were and, instead of fighting against the mission school, he became my friend, so that we were able to work together for truer education in the Kashmir State.

At the time of Mrs. Annie Besant's arrival our roll numbered 800, then dropped to 500, and people predicted that our schools would disappear. Two years later our school roll numbered 1,600, so we hoped that Mrs. Annie Besant would again pay a visit to Srinagar. As she had promised her Brahman friends to be reborn a Brahman boy, we hoped she might find herself in our school so that we could teach her the joys of cleaning a filthy city.

When teaching physical geography one often came across strong objections. The boys told me that my teaching was contrary to their holy books. For instance, they said that their priests taught them that the world was as flat as a plate, whereas I tried to make them believe that it was round like a football. And again I had told them that the sea water was salt. In their holy books it was written that the sea was made of melted butter and sugar. So I thought that the best way for them to discover who was the liar, was for them to go down to the sea and drink the water.

I promised to pay the expenses of any three of the staff who would make the journey of discovery, but no one was willing to accept my offer until the year 1901, i.e. my eleventh year at the school. The three brave men who were willing to taste the sea water were Mr. Shanker Koul, Mr. Mahamand Razdan and Mr. Din Mohammed. I arranged for them to go to Karachi and from there by sea to Bombay.

Shortly after their return I asked them if they had visited any Brahman priests since their return. "Yes," said they. "We told them that the sea water was salt. But the priests replied that we could not have been to the sea, for the sea is made of melted butter and sugar."

Although we had not converted the priests to the truth, whenever we met with opposition in the school to our teaching on this and similar subjects, we could call up the three Kashmiri teachers to give their evidence. I believe that if one of our boys were asked to-day questions about such matters his replies would be much the same as those of an English boy.

CHAPTER SIX

Early Campaigns

THE year 1902 was nearing its end and my strength was at a low ebb after the long struggle with Mrs. Besant and her powerful state backers. So the doctors ordered me to leave Kashmir for a rest and change for three months. I left with Dr. Arthur Neve who was on his way to Delhi to see the Viceroy, Lord Curzon, about food control, as the poor people were unable to obtain rice owing to profiteering. He succeeded and the Kashmiris had good reason for thanking Dr. Neve for his help.

From Delhi, I went to the delightful home of Colonel George Strahan at Dehra Dun. The colonel was a great landscape painter. When I went into his studio he said: "Please take any painting you like." I chose one of Pahalgam, because his tent was in the foreground where I had visited him about ten years previously when recovering from typhoid. He was the first Britisher who showed any interest in our schools or wished me God speed. The sahibs in those days thought that by educating the Kashmiris we were making a mistake; that an educated thief is more dangerous than an uneducated one. They could, or would not, believe that we were out for character building and not interested in turning out schools of B.A.s and failed B.A.s. Unexpectedly I got into trouble. The Strahans used to go to the Station Church on Sunday morning and to the Presbyterian Church in the evening. I went with them and partook of the Lord's Supper in the Presbyterian Church. For this the Church of England chaplain reported me to Bishop Lefroy of Lahore. Later I met the Bishop and he told me of this report, and "Let me tell you my answer," said the Bishop. "I told him, that he had better leave Biscoe alone," so that trouble was soon over.

The Strahans were much interested in the Leper
Asylum in which was a British leper who lived among the
Indian lepers and did all he could to cheer them up. He,
dear fellow, suffered terribly as his tongue was rotting
away. He said to me: "Although I suffer torture every
time I eat yet I thank God that I am a leper, because it
was through becoming a leper I found my Saviour, Jesus
Christ." I am thankful to say that this brave fellow soon
passed on.

The Strahans took me to Hardwar which is one of the
holiest Hindu places, where thousands of pilgrims go to
wash away their sins. We came down the River Ganges
on buffalo skins, a most delightful experience, dancing
about on the waves of beautiful clean water, so clear that
we could see the rocks and pebbles at the bottom and the
fish disporting themselves.

At Hardwar, on the bank, were many Sadhus, some
lying on beds of spikes, others holding up arms straight
above their heads until they had become fixed in that
position. Others holding fists clenched so that their nails
pierced right into the palms of their hands; enduring these
tortures for the good of their souls, and receiving by the
way gifts from the pious.

At Calcutta, I stayed at the C.M.S. school with Rev.
A. C. Clarke, an old college friend. It was a splendidly run
school, the best I had seen in India. He was turning out
boys like himself, keen sportsmen and gentlemen. He was
one who believed in character building and not cramming
for examinations.

From Calcutta I took ship for Burma in a smart little
coasting steamer. On arrival at Rangoon I took the train
to Mandalay to stay in the Fort with Captain Strahan,
the son of my Dehra Dun friends. Captain Strahan did
all he could to make me comfortable. On his bicycle I
visited the Bhuddist Monastery of the Thousand Pagodas.
The Abbot received me most graciously. He first took me
to a hall at the end of which were long red curtains which
he drew aside and there was displayed a huge figure of the
Bhudda. He then took me to smaller curtains which when
drawn aside disclosed a coloured portrait of Lord Roberts

to whom he salaamed, as he had done before Lord Bhudda. On my asking why he had this picture of Lord Roberts, he took out from his pocket a letter which he handed to me. The letter was written by Lord Roberts in 1886 during the Burmese War for any of the troops who would be visiting the monastery, telling them to show respect for the abbot and the monastery.

I had noticed that there were many carved figures on the roof of the monastery, so I climbed to the roof to look at them, and, to my surprise, saw that the carving at the back, which could not be seen, was as carefully executed as that which could be seen from below. So I asked the abbot why? He answered: "We do not do our work to be seen by men only but for Lord Bhudda."

When I returned to the courtyard there was a crowd of yellow-robed monks to see me off, so I offered any one of them a ride on my cycle. They all put up their hands and shook their heads. So I suddenly picked up the monk nearest me and hoisted him on to the saddle. He was rather nervous and hung on to me with his arms round my neck as I ran along with him. The rest of the monks rolled from side to side with laughter. I returned the cycling monk to his friends and then left the brethren still roaring with laughter.

From Mandalay I returned to Rangoon by steamer down the Irrawaddy. A most delightful experience and full of interest. The steamer was continually stopping at landing stages to disembark and embark passengers, all dressed in pretty colours. They seemed to be a cheery lot.

At Mynjahan I left the steamer to visit my cousin, Bertram Carey, Deputy Commissioner. I put my luggage and self on a bullock cart. The driver and his son, aged about five years, sat on the front of the cart, their legs dangling over the bullock's hindquarters and both smoking large cheroots. We bumped along over the ploughed fields, as it was better going than on the roads on which I found ruts one and a half foot deep.

In Ceylon, where I went next, rickshaws interested me and I was soon aboard one and made the coolie run full out. When he was blown I asked him to stop and change

F

with me, as I wished to give him a run. He refused, at first, saying that I was a raja and he only a coolie, but I insisted that he should be the raja and I the coolie and off I went at a run to the great amusement of the public.

I visited a certain mission school, and as the Principal said he was too busy to show me round, I secured the services of two senior boys. I asked them to show me their dormitories. We arrived in one room with several beds just at the time when the servant was sweeping the floor. In the dust I noticed several cigar ends.

I asked: "Are you boys allowed to smoke in your dormitories?" They put on a look of surprise and said: "Certainly not." So I drew their attention to the cigar ends on the floor. They looked at one another and did not speak, so I still pointed at the cigar ends. "What about it?" I asked. They then admitted they did smoke. I then asked who slept in the cubicle at the top end of the dormitory. They answered: "A master." "Why does he allow you to smoke if it is forbidden?" They answered: "He does not know." I then pointed to a window in the cubicle facing the beds; it was like a booking office window with a wooden shutter. "Surely", said I, "the master can see you boys through this window." "The master always keeps that shutter down," said the boys. "Why?" I asked. "Because he would make himself unpopular if he made use of it," said the boys. "But your master has a nose, hasn't he?" At this they laughed.

With such a master in charge I guessed the boys were top dogs. I went to the outside window and saw what I expected, and then said to the boys: "You do not always stay in your dormitory at night, do you?" Again they looked at one another and remained speechless. So I said I should find no difficulty in climbing this wall and that roof and so passing in and out of the window. Then they allowed that they did make use of that road at night.

Later on I was having lunch with the Principal and asked him if he had much trouble with his boys. Did he ever see them smoking? "No," said he, "my boys do not smoke, they are a very well-behaved lot." This reverend gentleman was an Oxford classical scholar, as were my masters at Bradfield, but unfortunately they had not studied human nature, and hence were utterly useless at the job for which they were paid, viz., building character and turning out Christian gentlemen.

In days gone by the Head of a School had to be an ordained man and a classical scholar. Now at last it has been discovered that what is needed is a MAN, whether ordained or not, and one who sympathizes with and understands youth.

From Ceylon I took ship to Bombay and on to Karachi and thence to Multan. The Rev. Johnson Smythe, Principal of the C.M.S. school there, was laid up with a nervous breakdown on account of his difficulties with his Bengali headmaster. I had experienced exactly the same difficulty some eight years previously so could sincerely sympathize. Both these Bengalis objected to being under youthful British principals. They being B.A.s of the great Calcutta University thought that they ought to be the Heads of the Schools, and tried to make the students disloyal and disobedient to the Britishers.

Johnson Smythe had wished to adapt for football a rough piece of ground close to his school. This entailed some navvy work. He asked his bigger boys to take on this job, but the Bengali headmaster told them they should not do such menial coolie work. This and other similar opposition had made life unbearable and caused his illness. I suggested that when I reached Srinagar I would send him one of my school staff who could, I thought, settle this difficulty.

I sent Shanker Koul, a man keen on any form of social work and loyal to the backbone. He had not started work at Multan for more than a week when not only the boys of the top forms he was teaching but also some of the school staff, were hard at work levelling that rough bit of ground and they carried it through.

It was fortunate that I was fit when I returned to Kashmir for I had several jobs to tackle straightaway. On entering the school compound one morning, I noticed many boys crowded together, who were trying to see something

which was in the centre of the group. They were laughing
and struggling as they strove to force their way into the
centre. As soon as I came up to them, they stopped, and
I saw at once that they were looking at something which
they did not wish me to see. However, I soon discovered
the cause of their interest. It was a book, a manuscript in
Hindi script, illustrated with the filthiest pictures I had
ever seen.

I immediately wrote a note to Dr. Arthur Neve asking
him to let me know how much paper a boy could safely
eat. The reply was that three ounces would not do him
much harm. I then ordered the whole school to assemble
in the hall. I called for a cane and a glass of water. I then
called up the boy who had brought it to the school and
told him that as he had evidently enjoyed this book and
had taken it into his heart and his head, he must also take
it into his stomach. I had already had part of the book
cut out and piled on the desk and now ordered him to eat
it. He replied that he couldn't as he was a Brahman and
to eat paper would defile his whole body. I said that this
was nonsense, he had already taken it of his own free will
into his mind and heart, and his stomach must also share
in the feast. I pointed out that the glass of water would
help it down, moreover, if he did not swallow it at once, I
should be under the painful necessity of shoving it down
his throat with the cane. This was too much for him and
he took up the pieces bit by bit and, with the help of the
glass of water, swallowed the lot.

I then told the boys that they might all bring such books
to the school and eat them. I think I am safe in saying that
from that day to this, full thirty-seven years ago, no boy
has ever brought a similar filthy book to the school.

However, I was not going to permit the matter to stop
there, for if a boy had been punished for bringing such a
book to the school, certainly the devil who wrote and
painted it was worthy of punishment. So I set to work to
discover who made such books and at what shops they
were sold. I soon discovered the shops at which the books
were sold, and also where the pictures were painted. I
immediately visited the Chief Judge, taking a book with

me. This I handed to him and asked what he thought of it.
He said: "This is a very filthy book. Why did you bring
it to me?" I told him it was so that he might tell me if it
was against the law of the land to print such books and
sell them in the public bazaar. He shut the book and looking at me said: "Mr. Biscoe, you must remember that
Hindu law permits a certain amount of impurity." He
himself being a Brahman I asked him if that was not beyond the standard of Hindu legalized impurity. On his
answering "Yes", I congratulated him. I then asked him
what punishments these devils would be likely to receive
if I were able to catch them. He told me that under Victoria Act so-and-so, he could give them two years' imprisonment, coupled with a heavy fine. "Well!" I said,
"That will suit me very well," and wished him good day.

With this information I took the book to the British
Resident. After he had glanced at it he asked me why I
had brought this foul book to him. I said I wanted to
know if he had any objection to my taking the police to
raid the shops which sold this abomination and so end this
beastly traffic. After consideration he answered: "I have
no objection if you promise me that there shall be no
row." I answered: "I do not wish for a row, all I want to
do is to save the city from this sort of thing." As I was
leaving he called me back, saying: "Now, Mr. Biscoe,
mind you there must be no row." I answered: "Certainly
not, sir, not if I can help it," and left.

Next day I sent one of my men with instructions to go
to one of the shops, purchase a book and sit there till the
police came and took it from him. I then got hold of the
Inspector of Police and told him that I wished him to come
with me at once with his men to raid certain bookshops,
stating my authority for doing so. He hesitated at first
and said that he must first consult his law books and I
feared that he intended to warn the shopkeepers. But within twenty minutes we were off to the bazaar. He was on his
horse and I on my cycle and the constables at the double.
When we arrived at the street just outside His Highness's
Palace in which were shops chiefly kept by priests, I saw
my man sitting by a shop reading a book. I walked up to

him, asked him for the book and handed it to the police.
I said: "This is the book. Please raid this shop at once
and collect all copies of this book."

While the police were collecting the volumes and de-
positing them in a heap in the street, I saw the priest book-
seller next door hard at work pitching his books down a
trapdoor. When he had finished disposing of them, he shut
the trapdoor and sat on it. The first shop being empty I
turned my attention to the second shop. The police asked
this man to give up his books. He said he did not keep any
dirty books, for was he not a holy man? I told the police
that he was sitting on the top of a trapdoor through which
he had thrown his property, so the police ordered him to
get up. He replied that he had a stomach ache and could
not move. When the police told him that he would get a
pain somewhere else if he did not move, this holy man
stood up, the trapdoor was opened and his books thrown
into the street. While this was going on, another Brahman
in a third shop had not time to dispose of his books, instead,
so far as he could, he got them under his voluminous
skirts and sat down on the lot. His books, too, were swept
into the street.

By this time a fairly large crowd had assembled to watch
this unusual scene, and I remembered the wishes of the
Resident that there should be no row. I told the Inspector
that we would move off by a boat which I had ordered to
await us on the river hard by: we then dropped down the
river to where these wretched books were being made.

By careful manœuvring to circumvent interested people
from giving warning, we got to a large brick house in the
priests' quarter of the city where the filthy painters were
busy. We were soon running upstairs to the top floor.
The women in the lower rooms began shrieking, but we
paid no heed to them and had soon reached the top story.
In a small room on the right I saw an old priest, with a
grey beard, busily engaged painting one of these dreadful
pictures. As soon as he saw me he began putting about
twenty under his voluminous garments and sitting upon
them. At that moment the police inspector came puffing
and blowing up the stairs. I told him to look after this

priest and his pictures, whilst I tackled a second priest at the same job. By the time I had reached him he also had hidden all his pictures. But on making him get up we saw also his wicked handiwork.

My next move was to see the Head of the Police. When I told him that I wished to make a public example of the priests, he said it was impossible because one of these holy men happened to occupy a most important position. I answered that the law included everybody. When I told him further that the British Resident had given his consent to my taking action he said he would do as I wished.

These priests were not put on trial until I left Srinagar for a holiday. They were not tried by the Chief Judge, but by a brother Brahman Judge who let them all off with a fine of Rs2 each, on the ground that they were ignorant that it was against the law to make and sell such books.

Although I failed to get adequate punishment for these holy rascals, never to my knowledge have these books been on sale again in the bazaars.

That summer we experienced a second flood. Houses built with unseasoned mortar went down like a pack of cards, and there was destruction and distress in all directions, not only at Srinagar but all over the Kashmir Valley. There was no need to be idle; in fact we had quite a busy and exciting time, with some comic opera thrown in to keep our spirits up.

When the flood had subsided, the Kashmir authorities deputed Dr. Arthur Neve and Colonel George Young to estimate the damage done to the villages. The mission school was asked to do the same in the city, with the help of four Indian officials. The officials were not keen on the job so the work fell on us. It was a fairly heavy task and took about a month, but what was harder still was the distribution of the relief money. Everybody wanted the lion's share. We felt that we should be mobbed if we tried to pay the householders at their houses, so we decided to do it in our school compound which, fortunately, is surrounded by a high wall.

Pay day arrived! and the compound was besieged by a mob of suppliants. We only allowed the people to come in one by one and made them sit down in rows, the women in front, the men at the back. All the staff was armed with single sticks as we knew the sort of crew with whom we had to deal. We then explained to them that no one was to stand up unless his or her name was called. The men who disobeyed orders could be managed with a judicious use of the single sticks, but the disciplining of the women was another matter.

I had arranged to pay out the rupees from my office window, and anticipating trouble, I had buckets of water placed on the roof just above the pay window, with a man in charge ready to empty the contents on the disobedient. The buckets were in full view from below and their purpose was fully explained. When all was ready I asked the first woman in the front to come up, but when she stood up, all the others stood up also. They were then all ordered to sit down. Again it was explained that no money would be given unless they obeyed, and no woman was to move until the first woman had returned to her seat.

We began once more, and called the first woman, whose name was Azizi which means "beloved one", to come to the window. This time only Azizi got up and came to the window, but no sooner did the other women see the rupees being given to Azizi than they all ran towards the window. I told them to go away otherwise they would receive a ducking. I told them a second time. No one moved. I told them a third time to go away, and still no one attempted to move, but kept screaming and shouting for the rupees. I ordered the water to be poured on them, and they at once beat a hasty retreat. It was not till they had suffered three separate drenchings that they tumbled to the school's idea of discipline and came up one by one. After the last woman had been paid we called the men, one by one, and gave them their money. They gave us no trouble and thus ended the last act of our flood relief work.

CHAPTER SEVEN

The Plight of Widows

THE time for our second furlough had arrived and none too soon, so far as my health was concerned. On December 21st, 1903, we and our three boys found ourselves in my old home, Holton Park, where we received a great welcome from my brother Stafford and his wife.

Before I left Kashmir my friends made me promise to go to Sir Victor Horsley, the nerve specialist, and gave me £20 to help to defray medical expenses. So to Sir Victor I went. After a short examination he pronounced that I was like a man whose banking account was over-drawn, and that my heart might give out at any moment. My only chance was to go at once to a nursing home and be massaged back to life. I soon found myself comfortably in bed at a nursing home in Bournemouth where I had to lie "doggo" for one month, see no visitors, write no letters and only read what the matron put in my hand. At the end of the month I was feeling myself, and more than myself, for I had put on three stone and was anxious to see my wife who had come to Bournemouth to be near me.

When the morning of release arrived, I asked the nurse for my clothes, but she refused, so I asked to see the matron. She came after a long time but said the doctor had ordered her not to let me go. I then said I must see the doctor to know what all this meant, for I had agreed to be a prisoner for one month only and that month was up. I had visions of trying to escape but I had only pyjamas and no money. In the end I promised to stay for another week if my wife so wished. She did, so I stayed.

At the end of the fifth week of massage, good food and no exercise I was a sight! To add to my girth and to surprise my wife I put a mass of clothes round my lower chest. It was a great success, for she could hardly get near enough to throw her arms round her dear husband's neck. The next job, now that I was fit, was to settle on a school for Harold and Julian.

We finally decided on Glenalmond as an old Cambridge friend, Archie Hyslop, was the Headmaster.

Having settled our boys at school I was free for deputation work for the C.M.S., chiefly to the public schools, as I had done on previous furloughs. I had some interesting and amusing experiences. One headmaster told me that missionaries didn't know how to talk to boys but, during a furlough five years later, when he was head of an even bigger school, he asked me again, so I can't have done so badly.

In February of 1905, my wife and I, with Eric, left England for Kashmir. On our drive of 200 miles from Rawalpindi we were done proud, for I was mistaken for the British Resident, Sir Francis Younghusband, as we had secured his tonga, he having been delayed for a day. So at every Dâk Bungalow we were received with much bowing and courtesy, and ate the food prepared for the King's representative.

In the summer of this year we experienced a third flood. The water did so much damage to our ground floor that we were unable to use that part of the house for many months.

During this flood Miss Newman was at her C.E.Z.M.S. hospital. As the waters rose the walls began to crack and she, getting anxious about her patients, called to her servants, but they had all bolted and she found herself alone. So she carried her patients on her back one by one through the flood to a safer building. Then she carried over her medical instruments and precious drugs. By then she was completely exhausted. A native boat was moored near by so she waded to it and was just climbing on board when the boatman demanded Rs100. Miss Newman told him she hadn't got Rs100. "Then you shall not come on board," said he. There stood Miss Newman, shivering in the flood. Fortunately, help was at hand for a British

THE PLIGHT OF WIDOWS

subaltern was near by in a small boat and seeing Miss Newman standing there asked her why she did not get into the boat. On hearing the reason the subaltern leaped out of his boat into the big native boat and the owner of it was deposited suddenly into the lake. Then he said to Miss Newman: "Lady, this boat is yours, please enter." Yet again, all's well that ends well!

This was the last flood that Srinagar suffered, although we had many false alarms. Why we escaped further floods was that a canal, 150 yards in width, had been made by Major Joly de Lotbinière. It started three miles above the city, ending at the Wular Lake thirty miles below.

Talking of floods, the real cause of the floods was the goat. Years earlier goatherds in India had been allowed to bring their flocks to the pasture high up on the mountains; they came by the ten thousand and destroyed all the undergrowth, young trees and bushes, which formerly held up the melting snow. This protection having disappeared into the stomachs of the goats, the snow on the mountain tops found its way to the rivers in *hours*, instead of days, and the river banks were neither wide nor high enough to take this volume of water; hence the flooding.

About this time I was a guest at His Highness the Maharajah's banquet at the Palace on the King's birthday. I was sitting close to the door leading to the bazaar when I noticed a crowd of people outside conversing with the Palace servants. Two days later I learnt why. The Maharajah's servants had been busy selling His Highness's liquor at bottom price. One man told me that he bought a bucket of champagne for one rupee. It is no wonder that His Highness, after seeing his liquor bill, said to a friend of mine: "Sahibs do not eat much at my banquets, but they *do drink*."

I had been invited by a Hindu gentleman to attend a temperance meeting in Srinagar. There was a large audience to listen to the speakers who talked at great length.

A Hindu friend who afterwards accompanied me part

of my way home, told me how interested he was in the temperance movement and spoke to me of a certain Sadhu whom he said was a very holy and religious man. I asked him in what way he showed his holiness. Did he care for the poor and help widows? "No," he said, "but he can hold his breath for three minutes." So I asked him what use he made of this power. Did he plunge into the water and save drowning people? "Oh no!" he said. "He never does that. He thinks of God." I fear I did not show myself enthusiastic over the holiness of this gentleman.

Another Hindu who was enthusiastic about this temperance meeting asked me if I could help him to start a temperance society. I told him that I thought there was no need for a temperance society in Srinagar as yet, there were no public houses and I had hardly ever seen anyone drunk. Indeed, if we talked about drunkenness, it might draw the attention of the Kashmiris to drinking intoxicating liquors and might do more harm than good. However, he did not agree with me and started his temperance society. He collected from his friends money for tables, chairs, and carpets in order that the meetings could be held in comfort.

At the second temperance meeting a speaker said: "What is the use of our talking about temperance if we do not know what drunkenness is? Would it not be better at our next meeting to bring bottles of brandy and drink until we are drunk, then we shall know how drunkards suffer." So at their next meeting brandy was brought and they drank themselves silly. When they became sober they agreed that drunkenness was more exciting, and pleasanter than temperance, so these temperance meetings were not a success.

How I came to know about this matter was that some of the temperance members came to me for help, saying that the President had taken the whole of the furniture for which they had subscribed to his own home and refused to part with it. Thus ended the first temperance society in the city of Srinagar.

My Punjabi Christian headmaster asked for a year's

leave, which I granted. As I needed a man in his place, I put an advertisement in the *Civil and Military Gazette* as follows: "Wanted a headmaster for the C.M.S. schools in Kashmir; no one with a proud look or high stomach need apply to the Rev. C. E. Tyndale-Biscoe."

By return of post I received a postcard from the Head of the Cambridge Mission in Delhi, saying: "We have all been very sorry to see your advertisement in the *Civil and Military Gazette*, for you have upset the whole of Delhi." That was a bad business! But nevertheless I received seventy applications for the post. But I could accept not one, for I could see by their letters that they had high stomachs and I guessed that proud looks were above these stomachs. So failing to find a suitable man from the colleges in India, I appointed one of our staff, Mr. Shanker Koul, who remained our headmaster for forty years.

No school could have had a more capable leader of boys and a more loyal worker. A very successful teacher in the classroom, but as a leader in all social services for the welfare of his country, he was superb. From being a leader in preventing cruelty to animals he tackled a far greater evil, cruelty to women. Out of the hundreds of instances of tackling cruelties to animals I will mention an amusing one.

I was standing in the school compound and happened to look at the entrance gate which was under an arch, when lo and behold! a pair of donkey's ears appeared, so high up that they could hardly pass under the arch. Then gradually, as this apparition came into fuller view I perceived that a donkey was riding on a man's back, its forelegs sticking out over the man's chest. Shanker Koul then explained that as he came to school he saw a little donkey doing its best to carry a man nearly as big as itself, so he thought it better that the man should carry the donkey. He made the two change places, somewhat after the fashion of my changing places with the rickshaw coolie in Ceylon.

Of all the many evils he attacked, the remarriage of Brahman widows required the greatest pluck and perseverance. It has been a long, long campaign. It began in 1857, when Lieut. Urmston was sent to Kashmir by our Government to induce His Highness the Maharajah Gulab Singh to send help to our army besieging Delhi.

The story in short was this. Urmston was lying ill in bed when the Wazir called to tell him that His Highness the Maharajah had died in the night and that his corpse would be burned at sundown, and with his corpse his two chief wives would be burnt alive. Urmston was horrified, and said: "You surely do not mean that you intend burning these ladies alive?" "Yes, certainly," said the Wazir, "for it is according to our religion, and thus God's order." "But", said Urmston, "don't you remember Queen Victoria's order that Satti was to cease?" "Yes," said the Wazir, "but that order was for India, not for Kashmir. We must follow our religion and God's order." "Very well," said Urmston, "wait a minute," and he called to his bearer to bring to his bed his map of India and a red pencil.

"Now", said he, "watch my hand," and Urmston drew a red line right round the boundaries of Kashmir joining it to British India. "You burn these ladies at your peril, for if you do, you will lose your country."

Now, just for a minute, think of the pluck of Urmston. He had been sent by the Government to win over Kashmir to the side of the British and here he was interfering with their religion! Well, later on in the day he could hear the band playing in front of the procession of mourners; thousands on their way to see the great "tamasha"; two ranis about to be burnt alive with their husband's corpse, everyone wishing to get front seats.

There was Urmston on his bed waiting for his servants to return to tell him what had happened. What must have been his thoughts? The servants at last returned, saying that it was a great "tamasha", thousands of people, the corpse burned very quickly as much ghee had been thrown on the wood (speed in the burning shows that the gods are pleased). "Stop!" said Urmston. "Tell me, were the women burnt with the Maharajah's corpse?" "No, sahib," said they, "no women were burnt." Urmston, through his trust in God, had saved the lives of these two ranis, but further, no wives have been burnt alive since that day through the courage of a young British lieutenant. I am proud to say that I had the honour of knowing that MAN and several members of his family.

To give an idea of what views the elder boys held regarding Satti I relate the following incident. The boys were about twenty years old, and married. I was reminding them of what the British had done for India, such as founding hospitals, fighting famines, cholera, and bubonic plague, &c., and also how they had put a stop to the cruel practice of Satti. When I mentioned the last item, a black-bearded fellow jumped to his feet and the following revealing conversation ensued:

The black-bearded boy asked: "Why did the British interfere with our religion?"

T.-B.   I was not talking about religion, but cruelty.

B.-B.B.   But Satti is our religion.

T.-B.   Do *you* wish your Brahman widows to be burnt alive?

B.-B.B.   Of course we do, it is our religion, it is God's order.

T.-B.   Have you a mother and father?

B.-B.B.   Yes.

T.-B.   When your father dies do you wish to see *your mother* burnt alive?

B.-B.B.   Of course I do!

And then all the youths in the class jumped up and shouted out "Of course we do, it is our religion". I then turned to one of the youths who was especially vociferous, and asked if he had a sister, and was she married? He answered in the affirmative. I said to him: "When your brother-in-law dies do you wish to see your sister burnt alive?" He answered: "Of course I do, it is my religion."

I then asked them: "Suppose it was the other way round and God's order that the Brahman *husbands* should be burnt alive when their wives died. How would you like that?" At this suggestion, the whole class roared out: "That is not religion."

Although I was somewhat flabbergasted at this outburst I was glad to discover where I stood. It made it quite clear how I should have to tackle the inhuman and unmanly views they held towards women. It also made me more than ever determined, with the help of God, to turn these youths from religious fanatics into MEN. All cruel customs in the city of Srinagar practised against the weak, whether on men, women or animals, must be fought and done away with, as my grandfather had succeeded in putting a stop to the cruel sport of bull baiting in England, one hundred years before.

But what happened to the Brahman widows no longer forced to die with their husbands? I used to hear very unpleasant tales about these widows which I trusted were untrue, and was assured by my Brahman friends that they were unfounded. But I happen to possess eyes, as well as ears, and I feared that these tales were true. For on my daily journeys up and down the river by boat to the schools, I was continually passing baby corpses in various stages of decomposition and sometimes with crows having their meals off them, and when one of my old pupils was in charge of lowering the river barrage every month I heard from him how many baby corpses he had to clear out. But it was not until Dr. Kate Knowles joined our school staff in order to visit the sick female relations of our staff and boys that I learnt the terrible truth of the unholy lives the young widows were forced to live. As there was no restriction to early marriages, there were numbers of child widows who were obliged to live in their father-in-law's house, and do as they were told. I came to know of the cruelties practised on these girls, especially by the Brahman priests, who were often the fathers of the drowned babies. The infants were thrown either in the river or to the pariah dogs at night so that the Hindu religion should not be disgraced.

These facts, and others which I do not like to put into print, set me thinking hard. I called together some forty or fifty of my school staff, all Brahmans with the exception of about five Mohammedans and two Christians. I told them that they had thrown dust in my eyes and we had thereby lost fifteen valuable years which might have been used in fighting this great evil.

We were unable to alter the satanic Brahman laws regarding widows but we could save our own widows in future from being forced to live impure lives. So there and then we started a pension fund for the widows of the school staff. Every master had to pay a portion of his monthly wage into this fund and I promised that a like sum would be paid monthly from the school treasury. With this pension the widow would be able to be free of her late husband's family and could live the life she chose. The Dixon Fund, called after Mr. John Dixon of Pitlochry, who started it with a gift of £50, grew year by year until it totalled Rs125,000. To-day it is helping thirty widows. But this effort of the mission school was only a drop in the ocean. What was needed was to get the law altered, but that seemed to us at that time an impossibility, yet we never lost hope.

We were destined to go on pegging away for another twenty years before the first re-marriage of a Brahman widow took place in Kashmir. It was performed at Matten, a place holy to the Brahmans, through the courageous action of Shrider But, the Headmaster, and his staff of the C.M.S. school at Islamabad. But it was not accomplished without opposition, physical force, and a little blood spilling.

On a May morning in 1928 at six-thirty, Shanker Koul, Headmaster of the C.M.S. school, Srinagar, led his school staff and 100 old students, all Brahmans, to a house where two Brahman bridegrooms, who were brave enough to face the music, were ready to march to a house a mile distant, where two young Brahman widows were also prepared to face the ordeal. Shanker Koul had arranged with three Brahman priests to perform the marriage ceremonies. But their courage had failed and they bolted. So one of our school staff, a Brahman priest, a brave fellow, married them. This marriage caused a great uproar in the city. But like all storms, this one blew itself out in time.

A certain ultra holy Sadhu was so shocked at the news of the re-marriage of a Brahman widow having been per-

G

formed that he fasted for forty days and nights to cause
the death of Shanker Koul. But as the gods took no notice
of his fasting and prayer, he concluded that he had made a
mistake. Indeed, he himself actually arranged for the re-
marriage of a widow.

Shortly afterwards Shanker Koul led a deputation of
old school students to His Highness the Maharajah to ask
him to enact a State Law, permitting the re-marriage of
Hindu widows. But their request was refused. Undis-
mayed, two years later, he tried his luck again with the
help of Mr. Wakefield who was Secretary to His Highness, and this time his request was granted.

The re-marriage of Hindu widows became law in
Kashmir, but the Brahman Sabha refused to accept it. The
President, however, of the Yauk Sabha (grandson of a late
much-feared President of the Brahman Sabha who was a
great enemy of the C.M.S. schools) persuaded his party
to put an end to the persecution and cruelties perpetrated
on Hindu widows, and so at long last brought victory! I
never expected in my lifetime to witness this miracle. I
have for fifty years witnessed the results of the cruelties
perpetrated on Hindu widows and also the wonderful acts
of chivalry performed by our school staff and old students,
which, if put on paper, would fill a book and would, I
expect, receive the same torrent of abuse as did Miss
Mayo's book, *Mother India*. No reformers can escape
curses. But what matter! Think of those who fought the
slave trade. They were even threatened with death.

God grant that we may ever have the Spirit of the
Psalmist:

The Lord is my Light and my Salvation;
Whom then shall I fear?
The Lord is the strength of my life;
Of whom then shall I be afraid?

Here are two instances of help given to women in distress by members of our school staff. One Sunday afternoon Pandit Amar Chand was coming from his home in
the city to the Bible Class I held for members of the school
staff at my house. He noticed a Punjabi woman walking

with a small boy and that she was weeping, so he asked what was her trouble and if he could help. She seemed unwilling to tell him, but when he said that he was a teacher in the mission school, she unfolded her story. It was this. She was seated in a tonga with her little boy and her daughter of thirteen, on her way back to the Punjab, when a woman keeper of a house of ill fame, and a policeman, seized her daughter and took her off. She knew no one to whom she could go for help. How could she rescue her daughter? So Amar Chand told her to stay where she was and he would soon bring help.

I was with my class in my garden when Amar Chand arrived much out of breath and told his story. We wasted no time. I despatched the whole class with orders not to walk, but to run, to the wretched house and surround it and await me. Prompt action is necessary in Kashmir lest one be checkmated.

I cycled off to the police station and with some difficulty made a constable accompany me. Outside the house stood my men with the bereaved woman and her little boy. I ordered the constable to go in and fetch the girl out. He refused at first. However, he changed his mind, or rather we changed it for him, and in he went, and soon appeared with the girl, whom we handed to her mother. Mother and child fell into one another's arms and wept. But the mother turned and said to me: "What is the use of your restoring my girl to me? As soon as you go that woman and the policeman will drag her away from me." I turned to my teachers and asked who would take care of the three until I could run this matter into court and have the devils punished. One of the party volunteered and took the little family off to safety.

While all this was going on outside, the painted woman, who was bedecked with jewellery, was at an upstairs window, giving tongue, saying she was going to report us to her many official friends, mentioning some by name and shaking her fist at us.

My thoughts went back to the Old Testament story, when Jehu was being addressed in a similar manner by Jezebel. There did not happen to be any eunuchs there to throw her down, but there was no lack of pariah dogs ready to do what the dogs of Jezreel did.

Well, we left the painted woman to continue her cursing and we all went to our several homes, thankful that we had been successful so far.

Next day I succeeded in setting the law in motion and, to my great surprise, by the end of the week the case was finished and judgment pronounced. Imprisonments for six months for both the woman and the constable, together with a fine.

On another occasion three of our school staff were out in the country, for a walk, when they saw a woman sitting alone under a chenar tree. Surmising that she was in distress they asked if they could help. When the woman realized that these strangers were teachers from the mission school she told them her story.

She was a Brahman widow and had been seduced by a Brahman priest. When it became known that she was pregnant her relations turned her out of her house and the villagers, led by the same priest, being unable to look at so wicked a young woman, drove her out of the village. She tried to get help in other villages but failed until a Mohammedan met her and promised to help her if she consented to become a Mohammedan and marry him. This she could not do and, feeling hopeless, wished to die. The teachers won her confidence, so she put herself in their hands. They fetched a tonga and drove her to the C.E.Z.M.S. hospital where she received a loving welcome.

One of our teachers warned the doctor that, if her relations discovered where she was, they would try to poison her, so it was arranged for the hospital entrance to be guarded. In a few days she gave birth to a child, who soon died. Our school meanwhile had found a young Brahman who would marry this young widow. The last I heard of the couple was that they were very happy with their growing family.

Since the members of our school staff arranged the first marriage in the year 1927, there have been over one hundred re-marriages of Brahman widows.

But I must hark back to where I made this digression,

the year 1906, the year in which the Rev. Frank Lucey joined our staff. He had rowed stroke of his college boat, Worcester, Oxford, besides being a scholar, so he was a great addition to our staff, but, what was far more important, he threw himself heart and soul into all our school activities, and almost at once had an opportunity of demonstrating his keenness to give a helping hand.

At certain times in the summer months, when the snow melts, there is a strong rush of water through a water-gate into the canal close by. In the fairway was a boulder, just under the surface, which often damaged passing boats. So Lucey tried to persuade the boatmen to help him to remove this obstruction, but they refused to help unless paid, although it was chiefly for their sake he took up this matter.

So the school staff took on this work. With crowbars, the boulder was loosened at its base. A strong rope was attached as we had learnt from a previous experience how much strain a hawser would stand. The boatmen assembled to enjoy a laugh at the Brahman teachers doing coolie work, but the boulder was landed with far less trouble than was expected, and many a boat's bottom has been saved from damage ever since.

I now come to an important event, the first swimming of the dreaded Wular Lake, which at its narrowest point was five miles wide. About ten years previously I had taken the twelve-oared cutter with a crew of twelve Brahman teachers and a few passengers to introduce them to the joys of boating.

The Kashmiris are terribly frightened of the Wular Lake on account of storms that now and again blow up. As all the boats are flat-bottomed, not built to face storms, they often capsize and the crews and passengers, being non-swimmers, are drowned. These deaths are supposed to be caused by djinns, or the god of the lake.

We had not left the shore many minutes when a breeze sprang up and the boat began to heel over and toss a little. This put the "wind up" those on board and they started to call out to their gods, Ram and Shiva. Some quite lost their heads and began to weep, thinking of their loved ones at home safe on *terra firma* whom they would never see again. They threw out handfuls of rice and sugar as baksheesh to their gods. I am afraid I was unsympathetic and, like Elijah of old, told them to cry aloud to their gods, for perchance they slept.

In a short while the god of the lake had pity on them, the wind dropped and our boat was soon on an even keel. We took to our oars and were shortly at our destination across the lake.

Arrived there, we found much stir among the people, who told us that the day before there had been a heavy storm and eighteen fishermen had been drowned. On my asking why they had not swum ashore, they said that no one around the lake could save their lives by swimming for the djinns always pulled them under the water, so what was the use of learning to swim.

Our school teachers seemed much upset at this tragedy, so I said to them: "Don't you think that it is up to us to do something about this? Surely the mission school should teach these Wular Lake folk how to avoid such happenings in future. You fellows must swim across this lake, and show them that it is possible to save their lives by swimming." The teachers said this was impossible so I said we would have to make the impossible possible. With this determination in our minds we set to work when we returned to Srinagar to tackle the impossible. We made it a rule that every boy in the schools must have passed the swimming test of 70 yards by the age of thirteen, otherwise his father would have to pay extra fees. Many parents objected to this rule. My answer was: "Take your son away and put him in a school where they like non-swimming gentlemen." We won through and some hundreds of boys passed the swimming test every year.

At last the day arrived when I thought the attempt to swim across the dreaded Wular Lake might be made. So, on a beautiful September morning in the year 1906, we arrived at the lake, having travelled the thirty miles down the river from Srinagar in our doonga. At about seven o'clock in the morning the swimmers dived into the lake for the five-mile swim to the farther shore, three Brahman teachers, one Mohammedan and myself. Dr. Sam Barton accompanied us in a boat in case any of the swimmers should need medical attendance.

The first half-mile of the swim was a trifle dangerous owing to the weeds. After that the water was deep and clear until we reached the shingle beach at a village nestling under a pretty twin-peaked hill. On the top of one of the peaks is a tomb sacred to a Mohammedan saint named Baba Shukr-U-Din, to whom the boatmen are accustomed to give money to secure a safe passage across the dreaded lake. It was a very pleasant swim except for the sun, which gave me a sore back for a day or two. Three of the swimmers found the swim too much for them, and climbed into the boat following us; but Darim Chand and I reached the village beach. The dreaded Wular Lake had been swum. The impossible had been made possible.

As Dr. Barton was anxious to re-cross the lake quickly in order to start on his journey to India that day, we boarded a Wular Lake boat with a crew of eight paddlers.

When we had done about three miles we heard shouts from a boat about half a mile away. On asking the boatmen the cause of this shouting, they said that the police were out catching boatmen to tow an official's houseboat up the river to Srinagar, and that they themselves were going to be taken by the police. I ordered our crew to make their escape. Then followed a great race, but as the police boat had ten paddlers, they gradually overhauled us. Both Barton and I lay flat at the bottom of our boat, so that the police should not see us. When the police drew near, their language was of the Billingsgate type, and they told our crew how they would punish them for paddling away when ordered to stop. The police waxed very eloquent and gesticulated wildly as they were about to grab our boat. Then Barton and I disclosed our presence by standing up smartly. The police at once changed their tune, saying they had come to help us on our journey across this dreaded lake. We, of course, thanked them for their thoughtfulness, and they made off after other prey.

When we reached the opposite shore we saw about 100

men crowded together, under the pretence of being needed to tow the official's houseboat. At most twenty men would be needed. It was the custom for the police to collect ten times the number of men needed for Government work. They would then go amongst this crowd of impressed men to collect their dues for having had the trouble of collecting them. Those who paid the police sufficiently, were released, and those who paid least were marched off to tow the official's boat. That has remained a red-letter day as we conquered the demons of the lake and that slave-raiding police boat.

One evening as I was starting for Sunday service, a police officer called to see me, dressed up in full war paint with the tail of his puggari standing up towards heaven like a fan. He said he had heard that a pretty Punjabi Christian nurse had run away from the mission hospital and not been heard of since, and that the police were anxious to trace her. He then described her appearance, which certainly tallied with the nurse we had lost, especially when he said that she knew English. "Well," said he, "this nurse is in a certain house of ill fame. I have only just discovered this fact and have come to inform you."

I decided to act at once in order to save this girl from another night in such a place. I cut the evening service and sent off to the city for one of my trusty men to accompany me.

All of a sudden it flashed across my mind that this might well be a police trick to blacken my character by making it public that I had been found in such a place. So I mounted my cycle and hurried off to my friend Mr. Mukerji, the Chief Judge. After telling him what had happened, he said: "Mr. Biscoe, don't touch it! I will send my court chaprasi the first thing to-morrow morning to the house and have the girl brought to you." Next morning the girl was landed in my garden, an ugly, bold-faced woman not in the least like the pretty nurse we had lost. It was fortunate that I had had a premonition and gone to Judge Mukerji.

This was not the only trap laid for me by the police. I

do not blame them, for the C.M.S. schools and the police had quite different ideas about the duty of citizens, and the carrying out of these ideas sometimes clashed.

I was once visiting the headquarters of the police in a small native state. On asking how many policemen the state possessed I was told ninety-seven. On my asking why so few police, I received the answer: "Because there was so little crime. Why so little crime in that state? "Because", said the police officer, "there are so few police."

At least three of the Inspectors General of Police in Kashmir have told me that they had to give up their commands because they were forbidden to clean out the Augean stables on account of vested interests. As long as heads of governments prefer bribery and corruption it is impossible to have an honest police force.

An honest police officer in a native state has a most difficult and dangerous life. One British Inspector General of Police in Kashmir said to me: "I have not one honest man in my police force to put in charge of a station." "Begging your pardon," I answered, "you have one, Sub-Inspector Abdul Karim." "Yes, you are right," he answered, "I had forgotten that man. I will at once put him in charge of a station and allow him to choose his own men." Abdul Karim chose old students of the C.M.S. schools. When he took over he found a list of thirty-two robberies undetected. Within a fortnight he not only tracked down twenty-two of these robberies and caught the thieves, but recovered the stolen property; an almost unheard of event.

A few years later Abdul Karim with another sub-inspector, an old student of ours, suffered punishment for three years for refusing to obey the order of their superior officers, which was to tell lies before a Commission of Inquiry.

In 1908 Sir Francis Younghusband called me to the Residency to tell me that he had received three anonymous letters threatening my life. He did not think they were to be taken too seriously, but I had better be careful. One letter said I would be shot, another suggested the dagger would be used, and the third threat I have forgotten. All three letters agreed in this, that if Sir Francis wished to save me, he must expel me from the country at once. Unknown to me, Sir Francis told the Raja of these threatening letters and said he would hold him responsible for my life. The Raja Sahib called for the Inspector General of the police and made him responsible for my protection.

I knew that no Kashmiris would murder me, but I thought it quite possible that my enemies might hire assassins from India to do the killing, as in the case of the murder of Sawal Singh the Private Secretary of the Maharajah. In that case four men were given a thousand rupees each to murder him, as was proved in the trial. The four murderers were hanged but the gentlemen who paid the four thousand rupees for the deed got off scot free.

Remembering how Sawal Singh was caught by those four assassins, I made my plans. I took care never to mention to anyone which of the five schools I would visit on any day, nor how I would travel, whether on horseback, cycle, or by river. I would start off in one direction and then double back. I thought in this way the assassins, not knowing my route, would have to divide forces, so that I should never have to face four would-be murderers at one time.

Then in my house at night I always slept with a loaded revolver under my pillow and, when all the servants had gone to bed, I fastened a string zigzag across the outside stairway to the upper veranda with tin cans at intervals.

But I had to get up early in the morning before the servants and remove all these traps, so that no one should know about the threats. Well, this game went on for six weeks, and the police evidently did not intend to catch my particular enemy. So Sir Francis told the Raja that, as the Kashmir Police were not able to do their job, he would call a British C.I.D. man from India who would settle this matter at once. This move of Sir Francis did the trick. The Raja Sahib called a State Council meeting that afternoon and the name of the man who wrote the threatening letters was divulged and the police were ordered to apprehend him at once.

The council meeting was then dissolved. At nine o'clock that evening a police officer, a friend of mine, came to see me and told me of the council meeting and the orders to the police. But the police had also received other secret orders that the rascal was not to be caught. I thanked the friendly policeman, and when he had departed, I went to the Residency and told Sir Francis, with the result that the rascal who had written the letters was sent out of Kashmir by twelve o'clock the next day, never to return. But the real instigator did not come into the picture. He was too big a gentleman to be punished. When afterwards we met he always asked kindly after my health. As I looked at his smiling face I wondered what his thoughts were as he saw his enemy still alive in Kashmir. Anyway, he added some spice to my life for six weeks, and lost his jackal from Kashmir for ever, which was a cause for thanksgiving to many.

CHAPTER EIGHT

A Valiant Man

KASHMIR attracts thousands of visitors every summer. As most of them have no interest in Christian missions, and some are opposed to them, we made it our business to invite them to visit our institutions and judge for themselves if they were worthy of support or not. After a breakfast at the school itself, we would show them round the classrooms. Every classroom represents a country in the British Empire, with pictures of that country hanging on the walls, so that a boy climbing up the school, class by class, passes through many parts of the Empire.

In the school hall are the honours boards, not as in our public schools in England, proclaiming only scholars and athletes, but for *body*, *mind* and *soul*.

No. 1 Board. For pluck, skill and endurance. Those who have swum five miles across the Wular Lake or the eight miles across the Dal Lake and down the river to the school: or have leaped from the roof of the school, fifty feet up, into the river.

No. 2 Board. The top boy in the school with the most marks for body, mind and soul.

No. 3 Board. Those who have risked their lives for others. The pluckiest deed each year, chosen from the various instances of life saving in the year. In one year thirty lives were saved by members of the C.M.S. schools.

No. 4 Board. The kindest deed to an animal.

No. 5 Board. Those who have given their lives for others and on that board hangs the beautiful picture of Jesus Christ, "The Light of the World", who has shown us the way.

When the visitors have finished seeing the classrooms,

a bugle sounds. It causes the school to be cleared of boys within twenty-five seconds. This is accomplished by poles and wooden chutes from the roofs and upper windows of the school buildings.

Then follows mass drill, gymnastics, boxing, &c., a regular Barnum show. The school drum and fife band, plus bugles, enlivens the proceedings. The show concludes with a call to attention when the Headmaster reads a prayer and prays on behalf of the King Emperor, His Excellency the Viceroy and H.H. the Maharajah, after which the Union Jack and Kashmir flags are hoisted while the band plays the British and Kashmir National Anthems. Then follows sixty seconds of absolute silence and no movement. The band strikes up a march and then a double, and the boys disappear to places of vantage, to see the plucky boys jump or dive into the river off the school roofs. The show is now over and we bid our visitors farewell. In whatever frame of mind our visitors arrive at our school, we trust that from henceforth we have their goodwill.

To give an instance, a certain senior British officer who had no use for missions, and had no love for me personally, was brought to our school by a mutual friend. Knowing that he did not like me or my works, I kept out of his way as he was being shown round. As I was seeing him off the premises, he said: "Mr. Biscoe, I must apologize to you for never having visited your school before. I had no idea you did such excellent work. I should like to help in some way. What can I do?" I answered: "You can help by seeing that our schools have fair play in this native state." "Why, are you not given fair play?" said he. "Certainly not. The reason why boys are sent to school by their parents is that they may obtain employment in Government offices. But unfortunately when we hear of vacancies and send our boys as candidates they are turned away by the Indian officials because they have been educated at our school and not at the Government school." The British officer asked: "I suppose the Director of Education (an Indian) has visited your school?" I answered "No". "Well, then, he *shall* visit it."

The great Director of Education arrived, beautifully dressed in blue coat, brass buttons, a huge turban and carrying a walking-stick with silver handle.

After being shown round the school, he said: "This is a very good school. How can I help you?"

T.-B.   By seeing that we have fair play in this state.

D.-E.   What do you mean by fair play?

T.-B.   That when clerks are needed in the Government offices, the best boys should be selected, whatever their school.

D.-E.   But are not the *best* boys taken?

T.-B.   Most certainly not. The boys educated in the mission school are refused, because they have been educated at this school.

D.-E.   Well, Mr. Biscoe, when boys come for selection to my office I will ask them from what school they come. If they say from the mission school, I will say "Come into my office" and if they say they come from the Government school I will say "Go away!"

T.-B.   That is just what I do not wish you to do, for that is not fair play. The best boy should be selected, for the good of the state, for the good of education and for the good of the office.

D.-E.   No! Mr. Biscoe. I will never do that, I will never do that. I will always take your boys.

And the great man took his departure.

Needless to say, he never took a mission school boy into his office so far as I was aware. Although a Director of Education, he had not learnt "fair play". But the British officer from that day to this backed up our school against all comers. That first visit converted him.

About three hundred Britishers visit our school in the year, and we much value their backing. But we meet some whose thoughts are not our thoughts, and whose ways are not our ways. For example, Mr. XYZ, of an American mission in Central India, arrives and the following conversation takes place:

Mr. XYZ. Well, Dr. Biscoe, I suppose all your boys are Christians?

T.-B.   Certainly not.

Mr. XYZ. But why not?

T.-B.   Because they prefer the religion of their forefathers.

Mr. XYZ. But why don't you *make* them Christians?

T.-B.   That's no easy matter and they would be subject to severe persecution and possible death. Do you make many Christians?

Mr. XYZ. Certainly, from one hundred to three hundred at a time.

T.-B.   How do you do this?

Mr. XYZ. It is quite easy. We go out into the villages taking a musical instrument or a magic lantern. In the evening we collect the villagers together and, after preaching to them and singing and showing pictures till about midnight, when they are *well worked up*, we call out: "Hands up, all those who wish to follow Jesus Christ." Sometimes one hundred, sometimes two hundred and sometimes three hundred hold up their hands. Well, then we divide those who hold up hands from the others and baptize them.

T.-B.   Surely it takes a long time to baptize so many?

Mr. XYZ. Not at all; I just fill a bowl full of water and sprinkle the whole crowd at once in the name of the Father, the Son and the Holy Ghost.

T.-B.   That method is easy enough, but what happens to them afterwards?

Mr. XYZ. Ah, Dr. Biscoe that is the difficulty.

This was the first time I had ever met a missionary who baptized at sight, though I had been told about them, but would not believe it. Since then I have met several missionaries who truly believe they are doing God service by putting water on heads and calling them Christians. These poor illiterate low caste folk think that by pleasing the missionaries they will have their support in bettering their condition, or will find suitable employment for their sons.

I have had to suffer for this foolishness. Those poor wretches who have accepted baptism are cast out by their own people and possibly lose their employment and then come to me to find work for them, saying they are brother Christians. The missionary who is responsible for their wretched plight has gone elsewhere to work for the Lord, as he calls it.

Shortly after I had met this baptizer, a Methodist missionary called upon me of a quite different type. He was a white-bearded old man who had been working all his life in India. He asked if he could be of any help in our schools. I gladly accepted his kind offer as I saw him to be a true follower of OUR MASTER, and wanted our boys to know him. This dear old man used to walk from his houseboat to the school, some three miles, every day, through the heat of the summer months, to take his Bible class. I asked him to come to our weekly missionary meetings and tell us of his experiences as he could doubtless teach us much, but he always refused, saying that he did not wish to hurt us. I assured him the truth can hurt no one, and that we should be ready to give him a hearing. But he held out and refused to tell us.

Shortly before he left Kashmir he asked me to dinner. After the meal, when he and I were alone, he said: "I think I have known you long enough to know that what I have to say will not hurt you. But I warn you it is a very sad story, Mr. Biscoe. I tell you, my life as a missionary has been one long martyrdom. When a young man, I was sent to an American Methodist mission in the north of India, to what is called 'Mass Movement work' which consisted of preaching and baptizing. After twelve months the senior missionary went on furlough. He called me to give me instructions before handing over to me. His instructions were that I must see that the catechists kept up their work of preaching in the villages and that the number of baptisms must be kept up. Well! I tell you, Mr. Biscoe, I had seen the results of these mass baptisms and

A VALIANT KASHMIRI

Samuel Bakkal whose story is told on pp. 108–122. This picture was taken when serving in Palestine in
World War I. On return to Kashmir he helped to feed, in a man-made famine, the very people who
had once wished to kill him.

could not believe that it was the Lord's work for it did not make followers of our Lord.

"So when the missionary returned after a year and had called for the baptismal roll, the trouble began. 'What have you been doing all this year since I left? Why have you not kept up the number of baptisms? How shall we obtain the dollars from America when it is known how the numbers of Christians are not kept up?' I tell you, Mr. Biscoe, from that day my life as a missionary has been wretched. I was reported to the Headquarters in America and was sent off to South India to another mass movement area, where there was the same trouble.

"A year or two later there was a great Missionary Conference which I had to attend. I, of course, need not have spoken, but I thought it was the Lord's will that I should speak. I gave my reasons for being unable to fall into line with mass baptisms having seen the results in the north and south of India. You may imagine my speech at this conference did not make my life easier. So, as I told you before, my life as a missionary in India has been one long martyrdom." This gentle, aged missionary left Kashmir for America, but he did not reach that country. He passed away on board ship and was buried at sea.

Later on I met an old grey-bearded missionary who told me that he held the record for baptisms, as he had on one occasion baptized one thousand in a day. I naturally asked him how that was possible. He said it was quite easy for he lived on one of the great rivers of the Punjab. "I just collected all those who said they wished for baptism and told them to go into the river whilst I stood on the bank to give the order when to disappear under the water, while I pronounced the words."

His wife was standing by his side to corroborate what her husband told me. A British colonel and his wife, friends of this missionary, were also present when I listened to this amazing statement. This old missionary did not live to baptize many more thousands, for he was murdered and, I fear, by one of the thousands he had baptized.

Referring again to the remark of the missionary who

H

visited our school that it was quite easy to make Christians, the following may be of interest.

Soon after my arrival in Kashmir I received calls from Hindu youths wishing to read the Bible with me. Some of them asked if they might come to my house after dark for fear of persecution from their co-religionists. This request I granted as I thought they were genuine seekers after truth. Later on so many came that I had to arrange for them to go to other missionaries. Hence a great deal of our time was taken up with these small groups. Before very long I began to suspect their motives, and, ere long, I was sure that they came for two reasons. One was that they wished to learn English from an Englishman as they asked us to use the English Bible instead of the Urdu Bible. But, what was more important, was that we might become interested in them personally and find lucrative posts for them in Government service, with a few other advantages thrown in.

When they became too persistent in asking for more time to be given to them, and increased their sloppy talk, I thought it about time to draw the line. So I gave out that no one could "go Christian" as they called it, unless they first had a boxing match with my gardener, who was a Mohammedan. These "go Christian" hypocrites were all Hindus.

Of course this unexpected change of conditions staggered them; and the Bible classes ceased; and we had time to get on with more important matters. But some of them continued to come to my house with their "go Christian" stunt and had to box the gardener but I began to feel I could not spare the time for those boxing matches. So I substituted a new notice on the board instead of the boxing test. It read: "Anyone wishing to see the Rev. C. E. Tyndale-Biscoe must pay one rupee per minute of his time but, if the conversation is agreeable to the reverend gentleman, he will return the rupees."

This notice proved my salvation. For I was never again worried by crowds wanting to "go Christian". It cost too much!

Here is a typical request of a would-be convert:

"To Padre Biscoe Sahib Ji,

"You shall be glad to read the following and your dear brethren will get an opportunity of rejoicing. I have heard that you are a Padre Sahib. At the same time I have heard that whosoever joins your religion all his desires are accomplished and that you accept every one to join your religion. You shall have to look at my writing carefully and thereby fulfil my wants. I have read sufficient books about your religion such as Luke Anjil and Mark which say how good your religion is. One wishes to tear one's clothes and join your religion but what can be done, for all the people of your religion are rich. Hence you shall have to help me sufficiently such as when I shall be converted my monthly expenses shall be at least Rs200. Because when one is a christian one ought to have a hat, boots and many suits. Such a thing must not happen to me that to-day I shall be converted and to-morrow I shall not get a pice for my books. I am a wise man and have read to a certain class. I wish to be converted at Lahore not here. Should you accomplish all my wants I will then join your religion."

In Kashmir nearly every village possesses a mosque and a saint's tomb called a Ziarat, to which Mohammedans go to offer prayers. Among the many saints' tombs in Srinagar there is one saint, Nakashbandi, whose power is supposed to be greater than most, and he is especially successful in answering the requests of women who pray for a male child.

A certain woman had been there often to request the saint to give her a boy, and tied the usual coloured rag to a bush or tree near by to remind the saint of her request, but without success. But at last her request was granted, and great were the rejoicings in a particular house in Rainawari, a suburb of Srinagar, for a boy had been born, and when seven days later the child was circumcised he was given the name of Māmā.

When he reached the age of six he was sent to the mosque school near by and put under the care of the Maulvi who was both priest and schoolmaster. On his arrival his legs were duly stamped with an inked dye, which must not be washed off for it was to be a sign to his fond parents that he had not been in the water. He was also shown the bunch of nettles with which he would be chastised should he need chastisement. He had brought with him a slate of wood, a reed pen, a wooden bottle of white liquid chalk and the bottom part of a beer or whisky bottle. Also his father had supplied him with an old family Koran in Arabic characters, so now he was ready to start his schooling.

School began at about 10 a.m. and closed at 4 p.m., with a break for a meal at midday. No sort of recreation is allowed as that would interfere with the education. Each hour succeeds the other in undisturbed monotony with reading, writing and arithmetic, the boys all swinging and shouting as they read and commit the words to memory, not knowing their meaning, or wishing to know them, and this goes on all day unless the teacher falls asleep, for which they thank Allah.

Māmā did not stay out the usual period at that school as he was more spirited than the other pupils, and for this the Maulvi practised on him one of his patent punishments for teaching obedience which was to hang him by his wrists from a beam in the school building. To this both father and he objected, and as the Maulvi was unrepentant, Māmā was removed and sent to the C.M.S. branch school near by. Māmā's father was averse to sending his son to a mission school, for he was a faithful follower of the Prophet, but, after strictly warning his son against the false teaching he might hear, he trusted no great harm might ensue.

Māmā found himself in quite a different atmosphere in this school, as were the schools of Shammai and Hillel in Jerusalem two thousand years ago, for what was allowed in one was disallowed in the other and vice versa. He found that bodily exercise was considered part of the school education, and that far from being punished for going into the water, boys were punished if they did not go in and attempt to learn the art of swimming immediately. Then again, boys were taught to understand what they

read, and religion did not consist in reading only a holy
book, but rather in putting into practice every day a living
religion. Then Māmā discovered that when his mother
went to the mission dispensary or hospital she learnt there
about Jesus Christ and the Sahib's religion, which he
learnt at the school, which his father had told him was very
bad. But he could not understand why it was such a
wicked religion when the people at the mission dispensary
and hospitals gave so much time to helping people in
distress. It might be true, as his father said, that Christians
eat pig and drink wine and do these kind deeds in order
to obtain the favour of God, but anyway they led better
lives than the Maulvis and his Mohammedan relations.

Then there was another matter which impressed him
very much. There had been a severe epidemic of cholera;
hundreds of the citizens were dying and he saw that the
mission school teachers braved great dangers in going to
their help. He also noted that the mission school formed
an engineer corps to set an example to the citizens in
cleaning up their filthy city.

He watched these teachers and boys working away in
the streets, digging, draining, and even carrying the filth
in baskets on their shoulders, all the while being cursed
and jeered at by the very people they were helping. This
daily picture made a great impression on him, as he compared the results of the teachings of the opposite faiths.
With these impressions in his mind he watched narrowly
the lives of his relations and compared them with those
who taught the religion of the living Christ. So when he
joined the High School he threw himself heartily into the
whole life of the school. He worked hard in class, and at
physical exercise he became proficient, gaining a place
very quickly in all the school first teams, football, hockey
and cricket, becoming captain of a crew and an expert
boxer. Into all social work for the betterment of his people
he threw himself heart and soul.

At last in a quite unexpected way the call came to him.
The Rev. F. E. Lucey, the Vice-Principal, was living in a
houseboat on the river some two miles up the river from
the school. One winter night the snow fell heavily and

silently while he and the boatmen were peacefully sleeping. Towards morning the weight of the snow on the roof
became too great for the equilibrium of the boat and she
capsized. Lucey escaped but his property did not. As soon
as the boys heard the news they came running from the
city through the snow and, as is their wont, at once started
to salvage what they could. Māmā, of course, was there,
and amongst the articles he rescued was a framed picture
and, as he was carrying it from the boat to the house,
he looked at it. It was a picture of our Lord nailed to the
Cross with this inscription underneath: "This have I done
for thee, what hast thou done for ME?" These words went
straight to his heart. The spark touched the smouldering
flax and it burst into flame, and this inspired him to become a MAN amongst men—a valiant Kashmiri.

A day or two later I heard a tap at my study door, and
in came Māmā. I saw at once from his face that something
out of the ordinary had happened. That short interview
is indelibly written on my heart. He came to tell me of his
call to the service of Christ, his own Saviour.

I have had many Kashmiri boys and young men tell me
they wanted to "go Christian" as they term it, but this boy
I could see at once was sincere, and that he meant it. When
I reminded him of the great personal risks he ran of severe
persecution, possibly death, he answered firmly, but almost
inaudibly as he hung his head, that he trusted that he was
ready for both.

I felt very bad about letting him go off alone to face the
ordeal that I knew must be awaiting him in his home
among his bigoted Mohammedan relations, but it had to
be. That boy of only sixteen had made up his mind to go
through with it, to live or die for his Saviour who had suffered so much for him. "This have I done for thee, what
hast thou done for ME?" It is only to the generous and
valiant that these words appeal, and appeal not in vain.
Māmā went straight home and told his parents of his
decision to follow Christ. His father was very angry, and
hoped to bring him to order by threats. His mother came
and wept bitterly, imploring him to listen to his father
and not bring the whole family into such terrible disgrace,

and also danger from the Mullahs. As all threats and entreaties failed he was taken to the top room of the house
where a St. Andrew's Cross was made of two beams and
on this he was crucified, his wrists and ankles being bound
firmly to the cross pieces, and there he was left without
food, his persecutors saying as they left him: "As you
so like the Cross you shall have it." When it was considered that he had thought better of his new faith, he was
taken down and promised money and good food, but he
would not give in. The great Mullah was called to argue
with him, but he became so angry with the stubbornness
of the boy that he thrashed him, and again he was taken
to his prison upstairs.

About two weeks after his confession of faith, to our
great astonishment and joy, we saw him back at school and
to our questions he said: "My father had a dream last
night, an angel appeared to him and said: 'Why are you
persecuting your son? Send him back to the mission
school,' so here I am." But the effect of the dream faded
as the wrath of the Mullahs grew and so Māmā was not
seen by us for about three months; we only obtained news
of him through a schoolboy friend of his who, though a
Brahman, honoured and loved him.

During this period Māmā remained a prisoner and
against his will was married to a girl much older than he,
as the Mohammedans hoped through her to win him back
to the faith of the Prophet.

It was not until August that we saw Māmā again when
he managed to escape, and came to us for protection. He
was so changed, through all he had suffered, that we hardly
recognized him. He was lodged in the hospital for safety,
and came daily to school, but as it was a distance of over
two miles we provided a guard of our three best boxers
to accompany him to and from school.

Some Mohammedan friends having warned us that
their co-religionists had determined to seize him, we
doubled the guard, so that he had the protection of six
boxers. But one day the guard was attacked and over-
powered, fortunately near the school, so the whole school
turned out and Māmā was in danger of being dismem-

bered in the fight both parties put up for his person. However, the school won, and he was brought back to the school buildings, where he was safe for the moment. Very quickly the school was besieged by a howling mob of the sons of the prophet who demanded that he be handed over to them, and the howling lasted for three hours. Only those who have heard the roar of an angry mob can realize the scene.

Our staff and boys behaved magnificently, so that the mob feared to rush the premises. Finally, Lucey arranged for Māmā's escape through the water-gate by boat, but even on the river he was not safe for the river was watched, and the enemies came in boats to capture him. Fortunately, our fellows had not learnt aquatics in vain, and started to sink the enemies' boats, and as the Mullah's party had not learnt the art of swimming they thought it wiser to go back to *terra firma* and wait for another land attack.

To cut the story short, Māmā was safely landed at Dr. W. U. Weitbrecht's house and next day he was disguised in European dress and taken out of Srinagar by Dr. Henry Holland and myself in a closed carriage. He was then handed over to Rev. and Mrs. Hares who were on their way to the Punjab, and by them to my brother George at the Baring High School at Batala. After a few days he was baptized in the school chapel by Dr. W. U. Weitbrecht and was known thereafter as Samuel Bakkal. From this school he passed the matriculation examination of the Punjab University and then went to Rev. Willie Holland at the Oxford and Cambridge Hostel at Allahabad, where he remained until he took his B.A. degree. While there he endeared himself to both professors and students. He became an excellent hockey player and went with the college team in their tour round India. Here also his boxing came in useful for there was another Christian in the hostel whom the Hindus enjoyed tormenting. Sam took up his cause and that settled the matter once for all. There is nothing like the naked fist to settle bullies.

After taking his degree he went to the Central Training College at Lahore where he took his Bachelor of

Teaching. While at Lahore he introduced the students to the joys of social service.

One night there was a big fire in the city. When Sam arrived he found a house blazing and no one was willing to go on to the roof so he got hold of the fire engine hose, was soon on the roof and by this means he saved the neighbouring house from destruction. This house happened to be that of a pleader and editor of a native paper, in which articles defaming the mission school at Srinagar and its Principal continually appeared. Sam pumped tons of cold water on this gentleman's property, instead of coals of fire on his head, but I am sorry to say it did not cure the Brahman editor of his song of hate.

An account of this fire and the bravery of a certain student who saved the house of the editor of this well-known paper appeared in the Lahore papers but our hero's name was not given, as Sam had refused to give it.

After taking his B.T. degree he returned to Kashmir hoping to join the school staff, but immediately the Mohammedans were at him again, and he had to be rescued once more and sent out of harm's way.

Then the Great War broke out, and he joined up as Secretary of Y.M.C.A. at Lahore and went with the Indian troops to France. Later on he was sent to Palestine, and was the first Y.M.C.A. secretary to enter Jerusalem with Lord Allenby. For his excellent work he was mentioned in dispatches. He became known for his remarkable powers of organization, his wonderful energy and bravery to which many have testified. He was beloved and respected by officers and men both European and Indian. Later we find him with the troops in Mesopotamia and then back in India in time for the Afghan war, when he took three of our school staff, Shanker, our Headmaster, Bagwan Dass and Suraj Raina to work with him in the Y.M.C.A. among the Indian troops. After the war he returned to Kashmir and joined the school staff, and was at last allowed to work unmolested.

From here he was chosen by the Maharajah of Mysore, who was on a visit to Kashmir, to go to his state to start a school on the lines of the C.M.S. school in Kashmir. Here he made many friends among the Mysore cavalry whom he had helped in trying times in the Jordan Valley. He ran the Maharajah's school with his accustomed energy and started the Mysore Boy Scouts which became famous in India.

He then returned to Kashmir at a time of great trouble, for the profiteers were holding up the food of the country. He was soon in the fray, for he was chosen as Executive Officer to sell grain from the state granaries to the people, and thus became a second Joseph. You would see Sam standing among his rice boats selling this precious food, and his brethren, who formerly tried to kill him, now bowing themselves to the earth before him. Then came his marriage with Victoria Thornaby, a real helpmate to him, to whom two girls and a boy were born.

Sam's life at this time was a very hard one. He had to fight day in and day out with unscrupulous Kashmiris who were always trying to sell him either watered or adulterated grain which they tried to persuade him to pass by offering him large bribes, sometimes running into thousands of rupees. To circumvent these rascals, and they were legion, he would sometimes be out all night in order to upset their plots.

This continual fighting with these scroundrels in his endeavour to do his duty, took the strength out of him, so that when he was attacked by pneumonia he was quickly carried off, his wife lying desperately ill with the same complaint beside him. But she, thank God, was spared to mother the three little children. So passed from us a very gallant man whom we had hoped would become a leader of his people from gross darkness to the marvellous light which he had found, and held through the fires of persecution. But it was not to be.

His body was followed to the grave by a throng of nearly two thousand men, and one recalled that angry howling mob round the school once demanding that same boy to be delivered up to them.

One day the mob shout "Alleluia!" and the next "Crucify him!" The valiant man cares for neither for he has seen the Christ.

CHAPTER NINE

College Talks

AT the end of October 1910 my wife and I, with Eric and Frances, started on our furlough to England.

At Lahore I attended the Diocesan Conference and there heard the following story. Padre Wright of the Cambridge Mission to Delhi, and a brave man, was preaching at the Station Church on Easter Sunday to a crowded church. Among the congregation was Lord Roberts, C.-in-C. of India, and his staff. Wright said: "Before I begin my sermon I feel compelled to say how grieved I was to hear that the British officers in Delhi cantonments went pig-sticking on Good Friday instead of attending the church services. And you, sir," looking down on Lord Roberts sitting in the front pew, "joined in that sport on that day!"

After the service Wright was in the vestry. There was a gentle tap at the door, and in walked Lord Roberts holding out his hand to Wright and, shaking his hand, said: "I have come to apologize for not observing Good Friday, but I am sorry to say I clean forgot that it was Good Friday, otherwise I would certainly have been in church." I delight in that story, for it shows the greatness of that splendid soldier and Christian, Lord Roberts, and also the courage of Padre Wright.

At that Diocesan Conference the two best speeches were made by Presbyterians, Dr. Ewing, Principal of the Forman College, and the Chief Judge, Fred Robertson. Both were knighted later, and both were true knights.

From Lahore I went on ahead of my family as I had been invited to stay with Mr. XYZ, the missionary who visited our schools, the baptizer of from one hundred to three hundred a night. I wanted to know more of his

mission and found him a most charming host. He had
evidently taken a great fancy to our C.M.S. schools and
our methods in Kashmir for he had arranged that I should
tell the people of Jhansi what we meant by Christian
education. The hall was full. The Commissioner, Mr.
Silvered, an active and brave man, was in the chair and
several British officers and their wives were in the front
row. It was one of the cheeriest gatherings I have had the
pleasure of addressing. I fancy Col. Charles Young, an
old Bradfield school-fellow of mine, had helped to fill the
hall.

We had a pleasant voyage to Marseilles, arriving on
December 4th. On the quay we were met by Captain
Lamport of the Missions to Seamen who was a great help
to us as he spoke French. We first met in 1888, outside St.
Mary's Church in Whitechapel on a Sunday evening
when I was inviting passers-by to come into the church for
a short service. Among those who came was a young man
who told me, after the service, that he had come, oddly
enough, from Bradfield, and was trying to find work. He
had been walking the streets for days to find a job and was
on his beam ends.

Well, we found him work and soon he showed his
thanks by becoming a teacher in my Sunday School, and
then a keen church worker until he was taken on by Preb.
Carlisle into the Church Army, from thence he joined the
Mission to Seamen where he has been doing splendid
work.

In Paris we had to change trains to one several plat-
forms away. Everyone else had porters, but our luggage
was left on the platform. I managed to find a trolley on to
which I loaded our luggage, and was off at the run, when
porters shouted at me to stop and a race followed. They
soon caught me up, but after much talk and hullaballoo on
their part, we got aboard our train, plus our luggage.

We landed at Folkestone and stayed with my wife's
sisters, Sophie and Helen Burges, who ran a flourishing
Girls' School not far from Shorncliffe, where my brother
Julian was commanding the 11th Hussars. I then went to
Trent College to visit our sons Harold and Julian, where

I found the boys hard at work as coolies levelling their sports ground.

The C.M.S. put me on to deputation work, and during my journeys I preached fifty times in churches and addressed or preached at about fifty colleges and schools. Amongst them, my old school, Bradfield, where I was welcomed by my old and honoured Headmaster, D. H. B. Gray, who, as I have already stated, turned a hell into heaven; Eton, Haileybury, Harrow, Malvern, Marlborough, Shrewsbury, where Dr. A. C. Alington gave me a hearty welcome and bought two hundred of our school logs to distribute among his boys, and Loretto where the boys came in straight from the cricket field and squatted on the floor or anywhere, whilst I sat on a table and yarned to them. A most unorthodox missionary meeting.

At Felsted I met Fred Jacob, Headmaster of the Junior School where our friendship began. That friendship was to bear fruit in great profit to Kashmir some years later.

At Sandhurst I preached at their parade service and had decided to interest them by telling them how Lord Roberts, when C.-in-C. of India, had been such a blessing to Kashmir. But I was unable to make use of what I had prepared, for there in the first pew under the pulpit sat Lord Roberts with his A.D.C., Willie Furse, later to be Sir William Furse, Lt.-General, K.C.B., an old Oxfordshire friend of my boyhood.

Among the many helpful deeds of Lord Roberts during his visit to Kashmir were the following: At that time India was menaced by a possible invasion by Russia, via Kashmir. So Lord Roberts wished to inspect the Kashmir army to see if it was fit to defend its northern frontier. Amongst the changes he made was to put in command Col. Neville Chamberlain, his A.D.C. in the last Afghan war, a most gallant soldier and delightful personality. Col. Chamberlain told me that when he took over command, this army of 24,000 had not been paid for three years. I naturally asked how this was possible. "Quite easy," he answered. "These soldiers are sent out into the villages to loot, like an invading army, and when they were sent to the frontier posts such as Gilgit, where the inhabitants are brave men, the officers would sell some of their own men into slavery and so obtain the wherewithal to buy food." Chamberlain very soon put an end to these barbarous practices by seeing that the money sanctioned for the army was paid, instead of going into the pockets of the officials.

The garrisons on the Gilgit frontier, over two hundred miles from Srinagar, had to be fed from the Vale of Kashmir, which entailed the collection of about 10,000 coolies every summer, as the loads could not be carried in winter owing to high passes often being under twenty feet of snow. These coolies were forced to go, and many never returned; some died and many were sold as slaves to the Chinese over the border. The march to Gilgit was known as "the journey of death". Lord Roberts put a stop to this by having a road constructed so that the loads could be carried by ponies, mules and camels. Now contractors vie with one another in their eagerness to carry the food from Srinagar to Gilgit. Legitimate trade has replaced slavery.

Lord Roberts discovered that there were no hospitals for women, as women were not allowed by their men folk to go to the state and C.M.S. hospitals already in existence. Although the money to build a women's hospital was forthcoming, the Maharajah had refused land on which to build it. Lord Roberts, however, induced him to do so—a real blessing.

I addressed over sixty missionary meetings in private houses and halls while home on furlough. At Queens Hall, London, Sir Mackworth Young was in the chair. We had not met since he was Governor of the Punjab. I was always pleased when the chairman was one who knew India and could vouch for what I said.

I had travelled in the same bus to the hall with Sir Mackworth. The last time I had met him he had a grand carriage drawn by six magnificently caparisoned camels, with gorgeously attired postillions, and servants galore to wait on him. As Sir Mackworth descended from this public bus, he would not even allow me to carry his bag, but preferred to be his own coolie.

In February we left for Kashmir, bringing Ruth Lovelock to look after Frances, and she became a lifelong friend of the family.

Soon after our arrival back in Srinagar, I discovered the brutal treatment of Nabira, the man who was sentenced to two years' imprisonment and afterwards came over to our side. I went to the Chief Judge in anger. He was very apologetic and said that there must have been a miscarriage of justice. I said "Certainly", and asked how it was that I, a layman, had discovered this fact and not the dispensers of justice. He asked me what I wanted. I said: "I demand that he should be put on trial, and if guilty properly punished, but if innocent he should be released at once." The Chief Judge promised that the trial would take place at once and I left.

Next day Nabira was brought to court. The Judge was a Hindu who had been to Oxford. I had sent three of my school teachers to watch the trial. As soon as the Oxford LL.B. sat down on his judgment throne his secretary pointed out to him the three C.M.S. school teachers, and he asked: "Who are you?" "School teachers," said they. "Who sent you here?" "Padre Biscoe," said they. Then said the Judge: "Leave my court at once," and he ordered the prisoner back to his prison.

My teachers reported to me how they had been turned out of the law court. So once again I went off in wrath to the Chief Judge. He, poor fellow, had to admit that justice had again gone west and promised to try the case himself next day, which he did, and Nabira was released; but no one was punished for this miscarriage of justice.

CHAPTER TEN

Character Building

I FELT sure that the introduction of games would give the boys that sense of fair play and sportsmanship which they so much needed. The first obstacle to be overcome was the objection of the Brahman youths to touching leather. As the cricket ball has a leather cover, it had to be handled in such a manner that their hands did not come in contact with the unholy leather.

Fortunately, the boys in those days wore "pherons", a long garment like a nightgown, with sleeves five feet in length, so that by keeping their hands up their sleeves they had the cloth of their garment between their hand and the untouchable cricket ball. When they had to stop or catch a ball they spread out their garment over their knees, or between their legs and thus stopped or caught the ball. So a game of cricket as played by the C.M.S. school boys was a well-conducted comic opera from start to finish.

It took quite two years to persuade these Brahman teachers and boys that the gods would not be angry if they permitted the leather ball to touch their skins.

The next sport to which we tried to introduce them was sliding on the ice. My first winter happened to be a severe one. The canal near our school was frozen, so I suggested that they should come with me and learn the art of sliding. They all wore wooden clogs as even *leather* boots were anathema to them in those days. They objected to my proposal, saying that their fathers told them that ice was very slippery and that they would probably fall and hurt themselves.

However, I at last persuaded them to come with me to watch me slide, and see how quickly one became warm by this exercise in cold weather. But I advised them to leave their fire pots on the ground, and not carry them under their nightgowns, as was then the practice of every teacher and boy when the weather was cold. Most of them followed my advice, but one or two refused to take it and they soon learnt that my advice was well founded. Before the day was over, the boys had discovered that a fall on the ice was not very dangerous, though at times a little painful. It was not long before they became keen and agreed that it was good fun. So that fight was soon won. But two boys had yet to learn that ice and firepots were not brothers. They were squatting comfortably on the ice with their fire pots well covered by their nightgowns and enjoying the warmth rising up their bodies and out at their necks, when suddenly they and their firepots had a very cold involuntary bath.

When I brought my bride to Kashmir in November 1891 I brought also a leather football. When I held it up before the assembled school they asked, what is that?

T.-B. It is a football.
Boys   What is the use of it?
T.-B. For playing a game.
Boys   Shall we receive any money if we play that game?
T.-B. No!
Boys   Then we will not play that game.
Boys   What is it made of?
T.-B. Leather.
Boys   Take it away! Take it away!
T.-B. Why should I take it away?
Boys   Because it is jutha (unholy) we may not touch it, it is leather.
T.-B. I do not wish you to handle it. I want you to kick it (it was a soccer ball) and *to-day* you are going to learn how to kick it, boys.
Boys   We will not play that jutha game.

So instead of the usual English lesson with the top class, where many of the boys had whiskers and beards and some were married and had children, I then described

I

the game and, with the help of the blackboard, drew a map of a football ground, showing the position of the players, &c.

I then called the teachers, who were all Brahmans, and ordered them to go ahead to picket certain streets to prevent the boys running away before they reached the public common. When all was ready I gave the orders to proceed to this common and shooed them on like sheep or cattle to market. It was a great sight never to be forgotten. All these so-called boys shuffling along the street wearing their wooden clogs, carrying their firepots under their flowing pherons on their way to play football. Some were wearing huge gold earrings, some had nose rings and all of them wore their caste marks.

I soon had the goal posts up and the teams in their proper places as I had shown on the blackboard.

There was a crowd of townsfolk which was growing every minute, all eager to see what new mischief this foolish young sahib was up to now. When everyone was in his proper place, I put the football in the centre of the ground and ordered the centre forward, a boy with a nice black beard, to kick off.

The black-bearded Brahman looked at me, then at the crowd of his fellow co-religionists standing around, and then hung his head, remaining motionless. I again gave the order, "Kick!" but still nothing happened. So I said: "I will give you five minutes to think, and then something will happen which you will not like." What was going to happen I had not the slightest idea, but fortunately I had armed my teachers with single sticks, in order to drive the boys to the common. So I lined up the teachers at the goals and told them that when they heard me shout out "kick", should the order not be obeyed immediately, they were at once to rush from the goals at the teams waving their single sticks, and shouting blue murder for all they were worth.

As the five minutes was reduced to the last ten seconds, I called out: "10 seconds left, 9, 8, 7, 6, 5, 4, 3, 2, 1. Kick! ! !" and down came the teachers shouting and waving their single sticks. Off went that ball and in five seconds all was confusion, for the boys forgot their places on the field, or that they were holy Brahmans, and a rough and tumble began. As they tried to kick the ball, but generally missed it, their clogs flew into the air and their pugaris were knocked off while their nightgowns flapped in one another's faces; a real grand mix-up of clothes and humanity.

Then all of a sudden there were sounds of agony and horror and the game stopped. A boy was brought to me sobbing, with his horror-stricken friends around him, for this Brahman boy had had the unholy leather kicked bang into his face. What was he, or they, to do? A truly terrible predicament, what could the gods be thinking about it all? I told them to take him to the canal close by and wash him. Away went the crowd with the defiled boy and for the moment there was peace. Back came the washed boy and the rest of the players, all of whom to my surprise at once resumed the game and continued until I called time. Then all the sightseers and teams went off to their houses to give their various accounts of this first game of football played by Brahmans in Kashmir.

But, and a big *but*, when the black-bearded boy reached his home, the news of his wickedness had reached his parents before his arrival. He was not allowed to enter his home and so defile their house. For three months he was not permitted to enter his own home, but some relation, less bigoted, took pity on him and gave him a home.

Some forty-five years after this episode a certain bishop in England heard of this first football match in Kashmir, how a missionary had *forced* his Brahman boys to play football in spite of their religious prejudices, and he wrote a letter of protest. I visited that same black-bearded boy who was now on his death bed and told him of the English bishop's pity for him at having been forced to play football. He thereupon wrote a letter for me to send to his lordship saying how he thanked God for having been taught to play football and other games which had proved such a help to him in so many ways in his life and in his efforts to run straight amid the bribery and corruption in the Government offices.

On one occasion when he first joined the Accountant General's office a clerk tried to make him put his name to a false account. He asked this clerk to come outside the office and in a quiet corner he taught that clerk with his fists not to try his tricks on him again.

Well, to get back to football. Our troubles did not end after that first game as the Brahman priests had decided that it was a naughty game. For a long twelve months there could be no football unless I was present to play or referee. Often when I was present the football had a habit of becoming deflated, which made me imagine that I had bought a very old stock of bladders, until it dawned upon me that a pin can deflate a bladder. So I gave out that the boys would pay the price of every deflated bladder. From that day, that particular trouble ceased.

After a period of ten years or so the state school thought that, after all, football was a game for high caste gentlemen to play and later other schools followed. The Hindu or Mohammedan schools bought footballs and before long inter-school matches were played, and then the trouble began, for although they had learnt how to kick a ball, they had not been taught sportsmanship and soon I was to be made wise to the gentle art of cheating in any and every sport.

At first witchcraft was used, in which art the Kashmiris thoroughly believed and practised; when we were playing against one of the other schools in the yearly tournament our opponents would bring a Brahman priest to exorcise our goal so that the mission school goalkeeper would be unable to prevent the enemy's ball passing between his goal posts.

As our Brahman boys still believed in the power of magic they often succumbed to this nonsense and lost the match as they well deserved.

One day we were playing the state school when someone drew my attention to the fact that the state school were playing thirteen men to our eleven. I asked one of the masters of the state school if he wished to play thirteen a side. "No," said he. Then I asked why he had thirteen boys on his side. He denied this fact. So I asked him to count his boys, when he was obliged to admit that my addition sum was correct, and he ordered the extra two to go off the field. The game had not proceeded long before there were again thirteen playing in the state school team. So again I had to ask him if it was his desire to have thirteen a side, and if not would he order the extra two players to leave the ground, which he did. So we finished the game with eleven players on each side to our satisfaction.

At a cricket match, after the toss, one had to keep close watch on the flagposts marking the boundary, for if the state school were to bat first the flagposts would be moved to make the ground smaller, so that a boundary hit would be easier, and when our team were to bat the ground would suddenly be enlarged. But where we were often let down was in the composition of the teams in all sports, as outsiders would have suddenly become members of that particular school.

To give an instance. I read the following in the daily paper one morning when an accident had happened on the road from India to Kashmir: "Among the passengers was Mr. X, a student of such-and-such a school, who was on his way to join the eleven of the Kashmir State School in the annual inter-school tournament, so it is feared that his services will not be available."

In the inter-school boat races, it was difficult to prevent one of the masters of the other school from putting river-boatmen into his crew and when we were able to point to these boatmen in the boat, it was very difficult, if not impossible, to persuade the Inspector of Schools to take action.

Compared with the cheating art practised in all the athletic sports other arts were child's play, and if I started to describe them I should weary you, so I will mention only one. We had come to the last item in the inter-school tournament, the tug-of-war. The mission school and state school were in the final. His Highness, the Maharajah, and all his court were present. The British Resident and officials plus a great crowd of visitors, British, Indian and Kashmiris, were seated under shamianas eager to witness the last contest in this yearly tournament. A high official was in command and gave the order "Pull" and then stood by the state school team, waving his arms and shouting at the boys to pull "zor se" (with strength).

I was surprised to notice that neither team moved either one way or the other, although they were straining all they knew. Then one of my staff pointed out to me that the end of the state school rope was anchored round a raised flower-bed. I at once pointed this out to the shouting official. He answered "No matter!" and went on shouting to the state school team to pull harder. I then spoke to him peremptorily, ordering him to release the anchorage, which he did, but almost immediately the end of the rope was anchored again. This time I went up to the official in anger, and ready for action, and forced him to release the rope. No sooner had the rope been released than the state school team were pulled over the line. Then when the teams changed sides they were pulled over again as there was no anchorage at that end of the ground.

Yes! The C.M.S. schools won the tournament that year, but what of that? Winning a tournament is nothing. After all these years of labour I had to see my failure to turn out sportsmen—honest athletes, leading to honest manhood. Where stands Kashmir?

Are we to give up the battle? Never! Victory is ahead.

It was not only in the athletic field that one needed a double portion of faith and pluck. When I returned from furlough at this time I found my colleague Frank Lucey in the midst of superintending the Punjab University examinations. He had been at it for some days, a very tiring business if one wished to have a clean examination, so I took over the superintendence of more than 500 examinees. I asked him if there were any of his learned assistants whom I should have to watch. He gave me the names of two Brahman gentlemen about whom he had his suspicions, for it was these gentlemen appointed officially, rather than the students, who needed a watchful eye on them.

I had been superintendent of several of these university examinations, so had picked up a little useful knowledge.

I also remembered what I had learnt at my public school, when a boy. Just another case of the truth "that God meant it for good". It was my practice when in charge, to put the sons of the officials and rich men close to my table, for their parents could afford to pay the supervisors at a higher rate for helping their boys in their difficulties. It was also my practice to checkmate these kind helpers of the rich, by not allowing them to hand the examination papers to the examinees. I would instead bring members of my own school staff to do this little job. They would then go off to their own day's work.

Well, I found that Frank Lucey had not followed me in this, hence he was uneasy about two of his paid helpers. I therefore ordered two of my trusty teachers to be present outside the examination hall with their cycles as I might have need of them. In a few minutes the two gentlemen whose names had been given to me by Frank Lucey asked permission to leave the examination hall. One told me that he had a painful arm, and the doctor had told him to see him at the state hospital at that hour. The other was suffering, poor fellow, from a very bad stomach ache. I sympathized with him, telling him that I had suffered much from the same trouble in my youth from eating too much.

As soon as these two helpers left the hall I ordered my two cyclists to follow them and see where they went, for I was convinced they had examination papers in their pockets. I impressed upon my two cyclists that they must not allow themselves to be seen following them.

In less than an hour these two paid helpers were back, having both been cured in a miraculously short time. On their good fortune I congratulated them, but to their sorrow I told them that I did not need them in the hall, as they would be of greater service if they would remain outside the examination hall. These two men were profuse in their desires to help me inside the hall, and I was equally anxious about their health as the examination room was very stuffy and the fresh air outside would complete their recovery.

When these two had left for their outside duties, my two cyclists arrived with the following information. The gentleman who had had an appointment with the doctor at the state hospital evidently forgot about it, and instead visited a Government office where sat certain barristers waiting for the examination papers, as they had the sons of certain rich clients waiting in the examination hall for the answers to the questions of to-day's papers. The examination papers were left with the barristers to write the answers, which would be called for later.

From this office our paid helper cycled to another government office where the officials wished for the success of a rich friend's son, he was ready to answer the questions for him. After a while our kind helper pocketed the answer papers from the Government office and from the barristers and arrived at the examination hall, but alas! he had no opportunity of delivering them to the expectant examinees. The second kind helper with the stomach ache had not gone home but to a houseboat on the canal near the college where sat a teacher of the state school who had been placed there by the Government officials to answer the questions for the son of a prominent citizen.

After the examinations were over I wrote to the authorities an account of my contretemps with these two helpers. But from that day to this I have received no answer. I knew that my letters reached Lahore, because some months afterwards one of the learned gentlemen whom I had reported told me that he had heard that I had reported him and he threatened to run me into the courts in Lahore for my shameful conduct. But he apparently thought better of his threat, for nothing came of it. But I was to see more than I liked of the law courts in Kashmir later on.

Let me turn away from strife and comic operas to our daily labour, which is character building.

I will ask you to look carefully at the boys' character sheet which was not drawn up in a hurry; each item having been added as one felt the need for it.

In order that the filling of the character form may be truthful one must know the character of one's staff,

Boy's Character Form Sheet

Each boy has a page in the register to himself, and three times in the year his character is overhauled and written down thus:

Name .... Son of .... Entered Central School .... Class .... 194 . Entered .... Branch School

Roll No. .... Ocpn. of { Guardian / Father } Left .... " .... " .... Class .... 194 . , ... 194 . Left .... 194 .

Date of Birth .... Date of Marriage .... Father's Salary

Section		Item	Full marks
		Date	
		Class	
		Age	
		Average Age of Class	
		Position in Class	
		Ears and Throat	
		Eyesight	
		Teeth	
		Height	
		Weight	
		Chest Measurement	
		General Health	
		Tutor	
MIND		English	150
		Urdu or Hindi	150
		Persian or Sanskrit	150
		Science and Drawing	300
		Mathematics	150
		History	150
		Geography / Physiology or Hygiene	150
		Calligraphy	100
		General Knowledge	150
		Total	1,600
BODY		Gymnastics	400
		Boating	200
		Swimming	200
		Headers	100
		Games: cricket, football, etc.	200
		Manual Labour	100
		Total	1,200
SOUL		Scripture	200
	CONDUCT TOWARDS	Masters { Obedience, Respect-fulness, Truthful-ness and Honesty	400
		Boys { Pluck, Unselfishness and Good Temper	300
		Esprit de Corps	School	300
		Duty to Neighbours	City	300
		Colour of Heart*	
		Total	1,500
	MANNERS	Deportment	200
		Absence of Dirty Tricks	100
		Self-control	100
		Total	400
	DISCIPLINE	Body { Cleanliness and Tidiness / Clothes }	200
		Attendance	100
		Punctuality	100
		Total	400
		Grand Total	5,100
		Signature of Principal	
		Remarks	

* We have eighteen shades between white and black. More boys, thank God! become lighter in colour each year, if not each term.

The result to the true boy is a recommendation, to the other condemnation. When a boy considers that he has not been treated fairly by his teachers, the whole class is asked to decide the question. I have met one or two boys who have considered themselves too highly marked. I never put down my signature until the boy assents to the truth of the marking.

It is fortunate in the C.M.S. school, that most of the staff of sixty are old students. They not only understand thoroughly the working of the school, but they also know from experience the temper of their captain (myself). More than this, both the captain and the crew are friends of from ten to fifteen years' standing, hence working together becomes not merely a duty but a pleasure. With so many boys passing through the school every year, we have a wide choice when there is a vacancy on the staff to be filled.

Feeling the importance of friendliness, it is my custom, before engaging a teacher, to ask privately those with whom the new man will work whether they are friends and can pull happily together; and upon their answer hangs the fate of the applicant. It is not possible to make friends to order.

Another reason why a captain in Kashmir can easily gain the goodwill of his crew, is this. In the East the teacher is in the place of honour next to the parent. Hence it comes to pass, if you take old students on your staff, you have men tied to you by a bond at once ancient and strong, for both religion and custom demand this reverence of pupil for teacher. Where custom and religion are joined together, woe betide the man who has the temerity to break the bond. We know this fact from much experience.

Sometimes it becomes necessary to punish one of the staff. This is, of course, the prerogative of the chief; but in this matter also I prefer to take my men into my confidence, for punishment or dismissal, if necessary, comes with far greater weight if it proceeds from several people rather than from an individual. We have two courts, one to settle minor offences, and the other for graver ones, with the chief as the final arbiter.

I have cause to be most thankful for this arrangement, for by the aid of these courts I have been saved hours of most worrying and difficult work, in the sifting of evidence. It is only natural that in some cases the offender should plead not guilty and wish to fight his case. I, as a foreigner and no lawyer, am not up to all their peculiar manners, customs and devices, and am likely to fail in getting at the truth. But the court-martial is composed of Kashmiris who know their own race, and in every case so far (and the cases have not been few) they have settled the matter smartly and sharply, and the guilty have come to me for mercy. Not only does this court-martial save me work and bother, but it acts as a deterrent, for the Kashmiri sinner knows it is very much of an off-chance that he will escape when confronted by three honest men of his own country who are doing this unpleasant duty, not for rupees, but for the honour of their school.

Some years ago it was no uncommon sight to see one of the staff standing before me with hands clasped in the attitude of prayer, with his head on one side, and possibly the toes of one foot scratching the other bare leg, asking for a favour. The sight was a sickening one! A so-called man, standing like a slave before a slave-driver. Those days are gone!

The slave chains were not struck off with one blow: it took years. Various happenings brought this about, constant intercourse out of school; going trips together on the mountains or on the lakes, where we shared fatigue, and more than once passed nights without sleep; many upsets in river and lakes; and once and again in danger in fires; and squalls on the lakes when sailing, for it has been a tradition with us—a very foolish one, no doubt—not to take in a reef, but to trust to the shifting ballast of a dozen or so of the crew to the windward gunwale. These are the times when we get to understand one another.

It is the custom in this country, when men of different standing go out together, that they never walk side by side, but one just a pace or so behind the other. It is a most amusing sight to see a lot of clerks leaving office together. The head Babu stalks in front, then comes the second clerk a few inches behind him, and then the third, and so on, each one wishing to get up to the front, but not daring to do so. That is how my staff used to try to treat me. I should, by rights, walk in front with my lower chest well to the fore, head erect, and at a respectable pace (two miles an hour), throwing my words behind me to my faithful followers tailing off in the rear. But now they understand my peculiarities, and walk by my side, in front, or anywhere.

What perhaps helped as much as anything else to break down serfdom were those God-given opportunities when a master was ill or in sorrow, or in stress of some kind. For instance, I discovered, quite accidentally, that more than half of my staff were in debt, mostly to blood-sucking moneylenders, who charge 36 or 40 per cent interest *per mensem*, and are not at all anxious to be paid off. A fund was started, and we took on all their debts, so that they might be in debt to the school; for how can a man be free when he is tied hand and foot to a blood-sucker? We charged them 10 per cent, 5 per cent to go to the person who advanced the coin, and 5 per cent to the School Benevolent Fund. The result is that nearly all the original members are out of debt, and we used the fund for helping others in monetary difficulties.

In apportioning marks to pupils we give fewer marks to mind than to the body, because Kashmiri boys prefer their books to physical exercise, as the former literally brings in rupees in the end, and the latter does not. Although the marking "for body" looks no easy matter, it is not really so difficult, for each master is only responsible for the boys in his class, i.e. about twenty-five, and if he is always in the field or water with them on compulsory days (which he has to be) he naturally knows those who are keenest on games. Marks in sports are not necessarily given to the best cricketer or swimmer, but to the boy who tries hardest.

Take a concrete instance: Govind is a strong, well-made boy, with a fair amount of flesh on his bones; his father happens to have a fair share of this world's goods, so can give him plenty of ghee (clarified butter), which makes fat. He, without any great difficulty, swims across the Dal Lake (three and a half miles), for which feat 150 marks are awarded.

Neila is a weak, thin, timid little boy; he is underfed, and with great difficulty passes the test (75 yards); passing marks are 50. But on character both boys get 100 marks. Why? Because nature and circumstances have smiled on

Govind and frowned on Neila. Why should we follow nature and circumstances like sheep? We don't. We try to rectify the inequality.

To give you an idea how faithfully the staff watch their charges and do their work of "foster-father" (which is by no means a sinecure), I will pass on to you the conversation which took place between me and one of my staff who was bringing before me the members of his own class, one by one, to pass them for their character sheet for the term just ended.

Case 1. A tall and very serious-looking youth has just appeared before me, and on his departure I ask why he has been given such high marks for "citizenship" as he did not give one the impression of being very energetic.

The F.F. answers: "His looks belie him; he has a very kind disposition, he is in the habit of going off by himself and hiring a boat on the quiet and taking sick neighbours out on the lake for fresh air and change.

Case 2. An athletic strong fellow, a member of the school cricket team, with hard and insolent-looking eyes.

I say to the F.F.: "I do not like the look of those eyes. I see that they are not so unpleasant as they used to be; but why is it that this look dies so hard?" F.F. answers: "It is not altogether this boy's fault; it is this way, Sahib (waxing vehement), his father, brothers and cousins are all in the Forestry Department, and they have plenty of opportunities to loot the villagers. They do not neglect their opportunities; he is much better than they, but it is hard for him not to follow their lead."

Case 3. A boy with a hunted-hare look now stands in front of me. "What is the cause of this?" I ask. Answer: "He has not a happy home, for he has lost both his parents, and his stepmother, with whom he lives, has not a very agreeable temper. Hence the hunted look."

Case 4. A boy with cheeky, deceitful eyes. On asking the reason, I am told to look at the trade of his father. I look and note that his father is a moneylender.

In sports we have put on pace, boys have not to be driven to their games as formerly, which is a great relief;

also many parents have been won over to the view that exercise of the body is good for the health. Will wonders never cease? The other day a parent brought his son to us to be beaten, for he had discovered that he had been absenting himself from the games. That father is worthy of a place in the Kashmiri Museum, say the title of Rai Bahadur, or something great. In September last thirteen went from school to the dreaded Wular Lake in order to swim across, seven out of the thirteen accomplished the task, a distance of five miles. The first reached the opposite bank in three hours and a quarter. Last year we got the first Kashmiri across, so we are going ahead. The feat of crossing the lake is not due to the distance but to the great dread that all Kashmiris have of the terrible monsters that are supposed to inhabit it, and also of the storms, which really are dangerous.

Again, boys are not rewarded by prizes for sports, as we feel that true sport in the West is being killed by "pot-hunting". We pit one school against another, giving marks to the school and not to the boys, and the school that gains the greatest number of marks in regattas and sports wins the challenge cup, or rather the wooden paddle. In this way we hope to take the selfishness out of games, and create a true desire for honour for the school and the community, as opposed to the individual.

For example: in our last regatta over 250 boys took part, and put their whole energy and keenness into the two and a half hours' programme, although there were no prizes dangling before them; only honour for their school. We are working for the future—the race of life—and must therefore fit all the boys for it.

Marking for soul is the most difficult of all, for it includes so much, and man's judgment is so liable to err. One of my Hindu teachers said to me the other day: "I feel so keenly the difficulty in being just in my marking, that I always pray to God to help me before I commence."

We start off with Scripture, as religion is the foundation of conduct, manners and discipline. The life of Christ is put before the boys for them to follow. It is not simply the talking business, but they are encouraged to follow His example by making use of their knowledge and muscle in helping their neighbours.

In marking conduct, the first two items are easy, as the masters know those who are obedient, respectful and truthful, and those who are not. The conduct of boys towards boys is put entirely into the hands of the boys themselves. So far this has worked splendidly as in practice we find that all the boys are more or less of the same opinion about the virtues and vices of their companions.

Manners come into the "soul" category.

We start with deportment. It means a great deal. It covers all kinds of insolence and conceit, which we find in the untrained Brahman youth. He cannot help their being part of his make-up; they are hereditary; he drinks them in daily, as he learns more and more of his superiority over mortals who are not the darlings of the gods. Only those who have seen that look in the eye can understand. It is a mixture of insolence, cunning, contempt, deceit and conceit; if any one trait is stronger than the others, I should say it is insolence.

Well, this look has to go out of the eye, if any of the 200 marks are to be gained. And it is wonderful how quickly it does go; how and why, I don't quite know; but I think it is when they begin to learn to like and trust those whom they have been taught to despise. As these hateful barriers of caste prejudice are broken down, truth and light come into their souls and show themselves in the eyes. It is one of the most interesting parts of our work to watch the eyes changing, for it means so much; it means growth and strength. Our men go to work on what the eye implies with keenness, for they themselves had this disease once and know its cure.

In order to help the conceited boys we placed on the walls opposite each other two large looking-glasses so that a boy standing between them can see his face and the back of his head at the same time. The conceited gentleman has to stand between these two mirrors until the disease is cured. I do not remember a case in which these two mirrors have failed to effect a cure.

It was in these very glasses that I first discovered that my head was bald at the back and I felt humbled.

School life in Srinagar is by no means dull, as we look upon this city of 130,000 as our field of sport, attacking social evils, and trying in various ways to play the citizen. Many of the boys, I think I might say most of them, take a delight in lending a hand in any job where they can be of use, as they have tasted the jolly feeling of giving pleasure and help to their neighbours; for instance, this week as I write I heard of a small boy who found an overloaded coolie resting in the bazaar; he at once took some of his load of earthen pots and carried them for him. Then again two men, each with a little child in his arms, came to tell me how one of the boys had rescued these two mites from a burning house, as the men of the house were away, and no one would go in to get them out.

The other day a Brahman boy saw a sweeper woman being ill-treated by a man, and, in her efforts to escape, she fell down; he at once went to her aid and picked her up. Those who know what caste means will appreciate this act. Our boys are not always successful in righting wrong, for, on one occasion, two boys tried to remove two Mohammedans who were riding the same donkey, the Mohammedans fell upon them and smote them hip and thigh.

The boys have taken about two hundred sick people on the lake for fresh air during the summer months. Taking out the sick is not so easy as it sounds, for the invalids often object to being moved as they are not accustomed to have so much attention bestowed on them, especially by boys; they at first think that there must be some ulterior motive behind their attentions, consequently much persuasion is sometimes necessary on the first visit of a boat's crew.

The hunting ground which yields the greatest amount of sport is the mission hospital, through the kindness of the doctors and nurses, who allow the convalescents to be carried off for a change of air; but it entails a tramp or paddle of two or three miles from their homes to the hospital, then the trip on the lake, and again the tramp home, so that their work of love takes them several hours. It is a most pleasing sight to see several Brahman boys helping a blind or lame Mohammedan down the hospital hill, and placing him carefully into the boat. The boys sometimes treat their passengers to tea, and often on a summer evening you see a boatload of sick coming homewards, joining in the chorus of the boys' songs as they paddle citywards. Our aim in all our sport is to impress upon the boys that athletics are only a means to an end, and that end is not to win prizes, pots, or honours for themselves, but to make muscle and increase strength for the sake of their weaker neighbours, and, what is more, many of the boys are grasping these ideals to some purpose.

In the present cold weather all the boys are learning to saw and chop up firewood, so that they can go to the aid of people who are too poor to pay for wood-cutters, and to those houses where there are only women. When one thinks of the days when they looked aghast when I suggested such work to them, and informed me that they were gentlemen and not coolies, and to-day, when they beam all over when a job is suggested to them, I just thank God and take courage.

We have been pounding away for years on the lines that true religion is not a mere talking business but is a life, and a lively one too if one desires it. A certain European in Kashmir who employs many hands, said to a friend of mine the other day: "I used to be against the mission school; but I have had to change my mind, for I have so many mission school boys working for me, and they are so different from the other men. These fellows will put their hands willingly to anything I tell them, even when it is not in their line of business."

K

CHAPTER ELEVEN

The Living Welcome

STUART FRASER, C.S.I., a strong and kind man who had already done good work in various parts of India, came as our British Resident. When tutor to the heir of Mysore, he made a great point of telling his pupil about the villages and introducing him to the farmers, so that he might have sympathy with all classes and castes in his country, and see for himself how the officials often bullied and oppressed the poor. The result was that when this young prince became the ruler of his State of Mysore, it became known as the best-governed native state in India.

In May 1912, at one of the weekly Residency Garden Parties, Stuart Fraser pinned the Kaisir-I-Hind Gold Medal on my coat. He had invited all the members of our school staff to be present. His Highness the Maharajah was there and also an old school friend of mine, now a Commissioner in the Punjab. I mention him because when we had last met at Amritsar some twenty years earlier, he said: "Biscoe, whatever made you come as a missionary to India? Missionaries can do no good in India. Take my advice, pack up your boxes and return to your own land where you may be able to do some good."

A few days later at the commencement of school when I had finished my usual five minutes' address to the assembled school in the hall, two Brahman boys aged about sixteen stood up before the whole school, saying that they wished to be Christians. After school one of the Brahman teachers went to their homes to acquaint their parents and immediately the music began. They were handed over to the priests who at once arranged for their persecution. They brought a town crier with his drum and tied a label

146

to each boy's back, describing his crime, and then marched them round the city for all Brahmans to insult. Later they were taken to their homes again for ill treatment.

During this time I was warned that some people intended to drop stones on my head as I passed in my launch under a certain bridge on my way down the river to school. So I arranged to ride my pony to school next day and to be crossing over the bridge just as my launch was passing under the bridge and so give them a surprise. Kashmiris, as I have said before, possess that saving grace of humour, so could appreciate this joke.

Several Brahman members of the school staff were really sorry for these two boys, as they admired their pluck, and when the summer holidays came they took them away to a village seven miles from Srinagar to comfort and strengthen them.

One night one of my old students, a Brahman, but one who sympathized with these youths, came to my bungalow secretly to warn me. (He was the same boy who was expelled from his home for three months for playing football.) He happened to call on a rich Brahman and found him occupied with other rich Brahmans. He was asked to wait until their business was finished. He fortunately overheard their talk. They had met to discuss what should be done to save their religion from disgrace through Brahmans becoming Christians and the decision was to poison one of these boys.

I did some hard thinking that night. In the morning I wrote to this rich Brahman saying I wished to speak to him on an important matter. As soon as he arrived, I took him to the garden and told him that certain persons in Srinagar were plotting to kill a Brahman student of mine because he wished to become a Christian, and that if he were murdered I should come down upon him. I said this very slowly and distinctly to him, twice over, and then sent him off. I hoped I had frightened him but I was still thinking hard when to my surprise who should arrive but Badri Nath, Private Secretary to the Maharajah and son of the Prime Minister, his face wreathed in smiles and shaking my hand warmly he said: "I am off to-morrow

with His Highness to Gulmarg (the hill station twenty-
eight miles distant) and have come to ask you if I can be
of any service to you before I go." I told him of the murder plot. "Don't you worry about that," said he. "I'll
settle that scoundrel, but whatever you do, do not write
to me for I know all my letters are opened before I receive
them, but three days hence meet me at gunfire (the big
gun at the fort is fired at midday to give the correct time
to the city and the country around) at the top of the hill
and I will tell you what I have done." He then stepped
into the Maharajah's grand carriage and was off. I, with a
lighter heart, went on with my work.

Three days later I set off early to meet him and on
reaching the spot I noticed a white turban, then a horse's
head and then the rider. It was Badri Nath on one of His
Highness's walers. He dismounted with a leap and
grasped my hand firmly, saying: "All is well. When I left
your garden that evening I went to the Palace to see His
Highness, and on coming down those winding stairs
whom should I meet but that devil who was coming up to
see His Highness. Well, I got him into a corner. I need
not tell you what I said to him or what I did, but you can
rest assured he will not harm that boy."

Well, Badri Nath's words proved true. That rich
Brahman dropped out of the picture.

Later on a Bengali Hindu official, a follower of Mrs.
Annie Besant, succeeded in persuading one of the boys
to give up the fight, which unfortunately he finally did.
The other boy, dressed up as a woman, escaped to Lahore
to the mission house, but his relations followed him. So he
was sent to a town in the Bombay Presidency. Later, he
again returned to Lahore, where he fell ill and was sent to
the Government hospital. Hindus then sent the news to
Kashmir and soon Brahmans arrived who took him back
to Kashmir and lodged him in a temple. The next day
there was a great gathering, and our school teachers, who
had befriended this boy, were called before the assembly
to be cursed and kicked.

The following speech was made by the President of the
Brahman Dharma Sabha.

"My dear Brethren, I have to relate to you a sad story.

"A certain Brahman youth has been led astray by the missionaries through his desire to wear Christian clothes, such as the trilby hat and the Albert collar and allowed himself to be taken to India where he was baptized.

"But he has been brought back to Srinagar where he will be cleaned, but as he was led astray in his youth, we do not propose to force him to go through the whole performance of cleansing, but only enforce him to remain a prisoner in the Rugnath temple for twelve days to feed on the five products of the cow (i.e. milk, butter, ghee, dung and urine) so that he may be once again purified and thus received back into our Dharama."

His Highness gave him a post in the Medical Department, and he was married to a Brahman girl and thus ended his desire to become a Christian.

So ends a very different story from that of Samuel Bakkal. It is given to only a few to have the courage to be ready to lose their life.

"Let him that is without sin throw the first stone at him."

On October 7th, 1913, I was standing on the upstairs veranda close to the door of one of the classrooms watching a teacher at work with his pupils when suddenly there was an earthquake. The teacher, forgetting that he was in charge of the boys, made a bolt for the door. The boys at once followed him and, in a few seconds, the boys in the other classrooms followed suit and made for the same staircase, with the result that it became so tightly packed that the boys behind could not make their escape.

Fortunately, the shaking was soon over and no harm was done, for which we were thankful. But this picture of a helpless mass of boys wedged tightly on the staircase set me thinking. I remembered my visit to the London Fire Brigade during my curacy in London. Captain Shaw was in charge and he kindly showed me round the buildings. Men in the top story were lying on their beds. Men in the second story were doing clerical work. Others were engaged in various jobs. Suddenly the alarm was sounded and immediately everybody in the whole building became alive. Men shinned down poles straight on to the fire engines and within a few seconds they were speeding along the streets. There seemed to be no reason why a school should not be dealt with similarly, so I ordered the carpenter to fix long poles to the school roof and windows.

Since the fixing of those poles, some 200 to 300 boys leave their classrooms when the alarm bell sounds each day at noon and are assembled within twenty-five seconds on the school playground. If they are not, they have to return to their classrooms and shin down again in double quick time. The school has been emptied of boys within fifteen seconds on several occasions.

His Excellency the Viceroy of India, with Lady Hardinge and his suite, were expected to arrive in Srinagar on October 11th, 1912. So we arranged to give him a living welcome at one of our schools situated on the river in the centre of the city.

P.W.D. officers very kindly lent me a wire hawser which had to be brought on a bullock-cart from Baramulla, thirty-six miles away. We anchored one end in the school compound and brought it over the roof of the school building, then across the river and fixed it to a tall tree on the opposite bank. On this hawser we hung the letters WELCOME, made of bamboos on which sixteen boys were to take their places, the boys being dressed in the colours of the Union Jack. This "living welcome" was to hang thirty feet above the water.

When all was arranged I received a letter from the Education Minister saying that, as I would be endangering the lives of the boys, he could not allow me to do this. So I visited the British Resident to ask his advice about obeying this order, he answered: "Certainly carry on, Biscoe." I thereupon wrote to the Minister of Education and told him that I was responsible for the lives of my boys.

As all the sixteen boys were good swimmers I did not see where the danger came in, so long as they did not fall on the top of the boats which would pass under this "living welcome", and I myself could see to that. Thus it came to pass as His Excellency and his staff, His Highness the Maharajah and his staff and the British Resident came up the river in His Highness's barge propelled by sixty-eight paddlers, with a steam tug towing as well, they saw written in the sky above the river as they neared the school the word "welcome" in colours of red, white, and blue.

Lord Hardinge told me afterwards that when he first saw the "welcome" he thought that the letters were made of bunting, but, just before the state barge reached it, I blew a whistle and immediately the "letters" plunged into the river and swam ashore.

Lord Hardinge doffed his cocked hat and cheered the boys.

A few days later His Excellency, with Lady Hardinge, honoured us by a visit to our school and presented a silver medal to be given to the boy who performed the pluckiest deed of the year. Lord Hardinge showed a keen interest in our school from that day, and he and Lady Hardinge left behind a very happy memory of their visit.

About this time the first Punjab volunteers had their field day. I, being a member of that corps, took part in the action fought near the Dal Lake. A few of us were ordered to discover the whereabouts of the enemy. When I reached the banks of the lake I saw an old boatwoman paddling a small boat, so I called her to come ashore and persuaded her to let me put on her outer garments and headgear. I then took her place in the boat and paddled myself down the lake towards the place where I expected to meet the enemy. I soon came across them. I then paddled back to the shore and gave my report to the Commanding Officer.

I expected to be commended for doing my job so quickly but I received censure instead, for he considered that I was not playing the game. I was rather surprised!

From Lahore I went to Bannu to see the place where Dr. T. L. Pennell had lived his brave and wonderful life,

On leaving the train I went straight to see his grave in
Bannu Cemetery. I had no difficulty in finding it for there
was a pathway across the grass made by the feet of his
many worshippers. I say "worshippers" for many of his
followers looked up to him as their prophet.

There were already some men standing round his grave
and one man, a stranger, who had followed me reverently,
was also at the grave. He asked a Pathan standing near:
"Whose grave is this?" The Pathan gaped with surprise
at such a question. Again the man asked the same question. The Pathan answered: "You do not know whose
grave this is? Why, it is the grave of the great Doctor
Pennell. He was our doctor. I saw him just when he was
starting one time for England, he was weeping." "Why
was he weeping?" asked the stranger. "Because he was
leaving *his* country." Those of us who know something of
the life of that courageous missionary will understand the
remarks of that Pathan. Lord Roberts, the C.-in-C. of
India, said of him that his presence on the frontier was,
for purposes of defence, worth three British regiments.

General MacDonnell had very kindly asked me to stay
with him in the castle. The next day being Sunday he
asked me to preach in the little station church and he sent
round a notice saying that the Bishop of Kashmir would
preach.

When I was leaving Bannu, General MacDonnell told
me that if I had no revolver he could not permit me to
travel by tonga the seventy miles to Kohat. Shortly before
two officers driving in a tonga along that road had just
crossed the river when they saw a tall man standing on the
bank holding out a beggar's bowl. The driver pulled up
to put some pice into the bowl when, suddenly, the beggar
took a gun hidden in his garment and shot both officers
dead.

Fortunately for me, Major Trench was travelling that
day to Kohat and both he and his servants were armed,
so the General permitted me to go under their protection.
When we reached the river a very tall beggar holding out
a bowl stood there on the bank. Major Trench ordered
the driver to put the ponies to the gallop, telling him that

A 'LIVING' WELCOME

C.M.S. School boys suspended across the river Jhelum in honour of the Viceroy's visit. When his barge had passed, a whistle blew and they dropped all at one time into the river.

his life would be forfeit if he stopped the tonga. The driver obeyed so the beggar had not time to use the rifle he may well have had.

When I returned to Lahore I met Mr. Mott, the great American missionary. That evening he was addressing the university students in the Y.M.C.A. hall, which was entirely filled. After he had finished his address he said there would be an after-meeting for those who would like to speak to him privately about their soul's welfare.

About forty remained behind and he was talking to them individually for about an hour. Next day Mr. Mott at breakfast told us that the meeting had been a disappointment to him. Most of those who came for a private talk were not interested in their soul, but whether he could find employment for them. They had heard that he was staying at Government House and therefore must be a friend of the Governor of the Punjab. We all have to live and learn and missionaries are no exception to the rule.

CHAPTER TWELVE

Fuzzy Wuzzy

ONE of my first jobs on returning from India was to undertake the building of a boathouse. Mrs. Montague, who visited Kashmir a few years previously, had taken an interest in our schools and wished to raise a memorial to her brother, George Cunningham Doughty. So she gave me fifty pounds in order to carry out her wishes. As her brother had been a keen oarsman I thought a boathouse would be an appropriate memorial.

Hitherto we had been obliged to keep our boats in the open, exposed to the sun in summer and to the frosts in winter, as I had not succeeded in persuading the Kashmir Government to grant me a piece of land on which to build.

Fortunately, one of our wealthy old students came forward and offered me an excellent site on the Dal Lake. I then went to the Commissioner to ask him if there would be any objection to my erecting a boathouse on that bit of land which Pt. Sham Sunder Lal Dhar had most kindly granted for the purpose. The Commissioner, Mr. S. W. Talbot, said that he saw none, but I ought to consult the Governor of Kashmir, a Mohammedan from the Punjab, about it. I said to Mr. Talbot that I feared he would raise objections, but if that was his wish, I would do so, and went at once to see the Governor. On my asking him he said that he could not give me an answer until he had asked His Highness the Maharajah.

A month or two later, when His Highness came to Srinagar, the Prime Minister Dewan Amar Nath showed me a telegram which had been sent to the Maharajah from the Governor. The telegram read: "May Mr. Biscoe build a boathouse on Shankaracharya Hill?" Now Shankara-

charya Hill is one thousand feet in height and is sacred to
the Hindus and very sacred to His Highness. He climbed
it barefooted every year to visit the god in the temple on
the summit.

The Prime Minister said: "I have not shown this telegram to His Highness for he would certainly have refused
to grant your request. I have kept it in my pocket to show
to you." Dewan Amar Nath had been friendly to me ever
since I had prepared his son for Cambridge.

I was much amused by the Governor's telegram for a
picture arose in my mind of our crews climbing the mountain to bring down their boats and then, when the races
were over, dragging their boats up the one thousand feet
back to their boathouse. The piece of land given to the
school for the boathouse was, of course, on the bank of the
lake, and there it stands.

Shortly after this episode I was asked to arrange for a
royal regatta, in honour of the Raj Kumar Hari Singh's
birthday. One of my first jobs was to clear the course from
weeds and I had to employ between twenty to thirty boats
with their crews of fishermen. To my surprise, when I
reached the fishing village close by, I was told that the
Governor had taken them all off for state work, thus hoping to cause me trouble, but fortunately I had many willing
helpers who were successful in completing the job.

The regatta was a great success for the mission school,
our crews winning 4 first, 3 second, and 4 third prizes.
After the regatta Hari Singh congratulated me on the
success of the mission school, saying that we deserved to
win. Such recognition in those days was quite remarkable.

A certain Colonel of Cavalry stationed at Peshawar
asked me whether I would take in hand an Abyssinian
boy who was so utterly out of control that no one seemed
able to tame him. I replied in the affirmative. Who was
this Abyssinian boy named Samuel, whom we re-named
Fuzzy Wuzzy?

When Lord Napier took his army to Abyssinia to teach
King Theodore a lesson on account of his barbarities to
Britishers in his country, an Indian cavalry regiment took

part in that little war. After the capture of Magdala and
when our troops were returning, a certain sawar picked
up a baby boy, whom he brought to India. When this
boy grew up he became bearer to a British officer. Later
on he married, and master Fuzzy Wuzzy was the result
of this marriage.

When I first saw Fuzzy Wuzzy he was fifteen years
old and was put into the C.M.S. hostel. He made himself
at home at once and became very popular with the boys,
as he was continually giving them sweets and cigarettes.
But after a week the boys were not so pleased with Fuzzy
Wuzzy, for he had helped himself from the money he
found in their boxes and, if there was no money, he extracted articles which he could easily sell in the bazaar.
The number of articles which he had stolen was twenty-
six. So I called Fuzzy Wuzzy and asked him to tell me all
the things he had stolen. He was much surprised that I
should imagine that he was a thief and looked hurt at my
suggestion. However, I told him not to be a fool and that
it would be better for him if he owned up to every single
article that he had stolen. He then admitted that he had
stolen six articles but would not own to any more.

Now I had learned at Bradfield that in dealing with
thieves you must make them own up to the last farthing,
otherwise you have not conquered. I said to Fuzzy
Wuzzy: "If you don't own up in full I will order the
housemaster to see that you have nothing to eat." For
three days Fuzzy Wuzzy had no meals in the hostel and
I thought he must be feeling hungry, but not so. The
young rascal had made friends with some woman who
worked at the State Women's Hospital some three miles
away and had managed to secure all he needed for his
stomach. Fuzzy Wuzzy was a bit distressed when I discovered that his stomach was not empty and he became so
amenable that he owned up to having stolen twenty-five
articles and to that he stuck fast, saying that twenty-five
articles was the correct number.

It was not until two weeks later and after considerable
persuasion, mental and physical, that he thought better
of it and said he wished to speak to me. "What is it,

Fuzzy Wuzzy, that you want to tell me?" He said: "I have remembered at last that the twenty-sixth article I had stolen was a pair of boots." "That is true," said I. "But why didn't you tell me that before?" He answered: "I had sold them to a Punjabi and I could not get them back."

One of the next episodes with Fuzzy Wuzzy was on a Sunday. After the morning service was over I was counting the money in the offertory bag which amounted to Rs7/3, plus a piece of brick. The brick interested me. So I went to the pew where Fuzzy Wuzzy had been sitting. It happened to be close to the brick wall and I discovered at once the exact spot from which the piece of brick had been detached. I gave it to the hostel manager and told him to put it in Fuzzy Wuzzy's dish of curry for his evening meal. The evening came and so did the curry and all the boys were enjoying their meal. Fuzzy Wuzzy was entertaining his friends with the trick he had played on Padre Biscoe and how angry it must have made the sahib. As he was telling his story he suddenly stopped eating, for his teeth had bitten something very hard. His companions, who were watching him, saw that he extracted from his mouth a piece of brick. They exclaimed: "Why, that must be the piece of brick you put in the offertory bag, an angel must have put it there."

The final episode occurred at nine o'clock one evening. We had just finished our dinner when the servants ran into the dining-room, in great excitement, saying that our hostel was on fire, which was only too true for flames were mounting sky-high out of the roof in a glorious flare. My first remark on seeing what had happened, was "Thank God", and I meant it, for I always hoped that the hostel would be burnt down some day soon, because, when building it, I had put in two fir-wood beams, instead of deodar, to support the floor above the hall, with the result that they were bent by the weight and I was always ashamed when this fault was noticed.

Before many minutes crowds of people came to the fire, some to help and others to enjoy the sight. The police were among the first to arrive, which did not add to my comfort for a certain thin policeman who went into the hostel and to the room where Sydney Gray, our short-service man from Cambridge lodged, came out fat. This interested me, so I ordered him to take off his blanket. Then I saw the reason of his sudden corpulence. It was caused by his having wrapped the whole of Gray's evening dress suit round his body.

Then came a battery of artillery from the barracks, bringing fire buckets instead of guns. Numbers of our European friends also came from the Munshi Bagh, a mile and a half distant, to do fireman's work. The hostel, however, burned so quickly that very little was saved.

Fortunately, the insurance just covered our loss. But where was Fuzzy Wuzzy? After having started the fire, he ran straight into the housemaster's house, hid under his bed and spent the night there. I still had hopes of conquering Fuzzy Wuzzy but the law would not allow me. He had to go to prison, for which I was very sorry because there was no suitable prison for boys.

However, when we visited him in prison he said he was very happy there and the prison was much better than the C.M.S. hostel as they fed him better and he had plenty of friends. I was not happy at leaving him in prison, so I wrote to the Salvation Army in India asking if they would be sporting enough to try their luck with him. They most nobly agreed.

Kashmir police took him down to the borders of Kashmir, where the police took him to India and entrusted him to the Salvation Army. Some three years afterwards I learnt that they had been unable to tame him and had sent him back to his parents in Peshawar.

The Colonel who handed him over to me at the beginning had retired and gone home to England, so that I have not since heard news of Fuzzy Wuzzy. I always live in hope that some day I shall hear that someone has been successful, where I failed, in turning Fuzzy Wuzzy the Abyssinian into a useful man.

CHAPTER THIRTEEN

The Heroism of Shanker Koul

IN the spring of 1914 I had the pleasure of having my brother, Commander Edward Tyndale-Biscoe, and his wife with me at our annual school camp at the Wular Lake. I had anchored our twelve-oared cutter about two hundred yards out in the lake and had lined up our boys for a race from the shore round the cutter and home, when the lambardar (headman) of the village came up to me and asked if the men of his village might race with our boys. I said I should be delighted, but as I had no idea that they could swim, I asked him since when had they learned the art of swimming, and he answered: "Ever since your schoolboys swam across the lake, all the boat people here have learnt to swim." My thoughts went back to that day when we first sailed across the Wular and heard the news of eighteen Wular people having been drowned the day before, and my determination to bring to pass what everyone said was impossible. Our efforts were not in vain.

Later in the year cholera broke out again in the city and took its toll of hundreds of lives. Amongst those who were seized was the headmaster of the Government School who had been a teacher in the Christian Boarding School at Batala under the principalship of my brother George. This man had only lately arrived in Kashmir, and I had warned him of the danger that he and his family were in, if they lived in the city. But as he lived near our Central School I trusted that he would be safe, for there we kept medicine handy, masters being in attendance every night with lanterns and bicycles ready to dash off in any direction where medicine was needed. He said: "I am sure I shall not be attacked by cholera." Unfortunately, when he was attacked he, like many others, tried to make himself believe that he had only diarrhoea and would not send for the help which was at hand. As soon as I heard that he had been attacked by cholera I rushed down with medicine to his house and found him insensible, in the third stage of cholera and, although we brought a doctor, it was too late and he passed away.

Samuel Bakkal and two Brahman masters came down to his house to put his body in the coffin. As Samuel Bakkal and I were about to lift him into the coffin our two Brahman masters asked if they might help us. I purposely had not asked them to help because I knew that it was defilement for Brahmans to touch a dead body. So I was very pleased at their request and we all four put the corpse in the coffin.

It was always a great joy to me to see my men doing acts of kindness in this terrible epidemic of cholera, for it is through stress and danger that men are born.

During this epidemic a curious thing happened. Near where I was standing one day was an old man whom I saluted. Thinking that I was a stranger he began pointing out to me the various places of interest in the city which lay like a map before us. Pointing to the right on the river bank he said: "That is Biscoe Sahib's school," and then to the left he pointed to the mission hospital of which he spoke in terms of gratitude, saying: "When I was a boy a very holy man lived in a cave under the hospital hill. He was very old but he said he would not die until a white man arrived from the West who would teach me (the narrator) the way to God. Then, in the year 1880 Doctor Arthur Neve arrived to work in the hospital with Doctor Downes. When he saw Doctor Arthur Neve he had said to himself: 'This is the man I have been waiting for, who will teach the Kashmiris what is good,' and then he breathed his last." These last words of this holy man certainly became true.

The time had unfortunately arrived for our much respected Resident, Stuart Fraser, to leave Kashmir with his family. I was present that morning at the Residency when a great crowd of Indian and Europeans, friends, came to see them leave in their car. Just as the car was about to

DOUBLE UP THERE! MORNING BREAK

As a fire precaution and as a lesson in smartness, 500 boys leave their classes on three different floors and fall in on the parade ground within thirty seconds of the signal.

start from the front door steps, Violet Fraser, aged seventeen years, jumped out and ran up to the front door, where
all their servants were standing, and shook hands with
each of them, from senior servant down to the sweeper.
The dear girl, in her haste, had forgotten the servants for
the moment. I would not have missed that episode for anything. We all felt very sorry to see that delightful family
depart, as we can never forget their constant kindnesses.
But we were fortunate in being able to welcome an old
friend, H. Henry Venn Cobb, who some years previously
had been our Assistant Resident. A true MAN, he was both
kind and strong and, like Stuart Fraser, backed up our
schools and hospital, and any institution working for the
uplift of India.

In November 1914 I left Kashmir for England. En
route I went to Peshawar to see my friends, Dr. Starr and
Sister Lilian Wade, who later were married. Their married
life was to be cut short as I shall describe later. At Lahore
I received a very warm welcome from the Bishop, George
Lefroy, who was a great champion of our schools and was,
in this respect, the exact opposite of the former bishop.
George Lefroy afterwards became Metropolitan of India.

I arrived in England in time to see our two elder boys
join up. Harold, who was at Jesus College, Cambridge,
joined the R. Naval Air Force. Julian, who was at Trent
College, joined an R.A. battery.

During my furlough in England I had slept in eighty
houses, preached in fifty-eight churches and school
chapels, and spoken at one hundred and one meetings.

Eric had just gone to Haileybury College, and a little
later our two elder boys were in the fighting line. Our little
daughter, Frances, was with her mother at our house at
Surbiton. We decided that my wife should remain at home
to be ready to receive our boys when they came home on
leave.

I left London on February 1st, 1916, for Kashmir via
Marseilles. While in Paris I witnessed an interesting
ceremony of military awards being given to certain sailors.
A general gave out fifty medals and fifty kisses.

L

I joined the P. & O. vessel, *Nagoya*, at Marseilles. When our ship was about to leave it was stopped, and the passengers wondered what the reason could be. Later, after we had left Malta, we were told that a German submarine had been waiting for us outside and that the cargo vessel which had left the port at the time our ship was expected to leave, had been torpedoed and sunk; also that the German submarine had been sunk shortly afterwards by one of our destroyers.

When I reached Srinagar I found plenty of work waiting for me, as the Rev. Frank Lucey had been called away to military duty and sent to the Indian State of Poona as recruiting officer. Also my short service man, Sydney Gray, had joined up, and soon found himself in Egypt with his regiment guarding the canal.

Besides my work of looking after the six schools, I had to take charge of St. Luke's Church and the Indian Christians. In addition to this I found myself responsible for All Saints' Church services and the European community as there was no chaplain, but here I was fortunate in having my old friend, Cecil Hadow, who, with the help of the Assistant Resident, H. D. G. Law, C.I.E., took over from me the morning service and was ready to help me in every way.

At the Annual School Prize Day the Resident, Jack Manners-Smith, V.C., and his lady, kindly did the honours. The first time that I met Manners-Smith was when he was a lieutenant. He, with other officers, asked me to hold a service for them in the English Church before starting for the Hunza Nagar campaign. Both Manners-Smith and Lieutenant Aylmer won the V.C. shortly afterwards.

After the prize giving and display was over and I was on my way up the river to start the ten school boats in their race for the head of the river, a telegram was put in my hand which I dared not open for I feared it might be bad news of my sons from the battlefront, so I put it in my pocket. With trembling hands I opened it after the race was over.

It read thus: "Julian Tyndale-Biscoe awarded the M.C. for gallantry."

You can understand with what different feelings I put that piece of paper back again into my pocket.

Islamabad is a town with about 4,000 inhabitants. The Rev. H. J. Knowles had founded a school there before I arrived in Kashmir. In that school there was a different class of boy from those we had in Srinagar, as there were more villagers than townsfolk; hence they were healthier and had more physical energy. But at this time we had no playing-field.

Fortunately, a new Revenue Minister arrived in Kashmir named Mr. Maqbool Hussain, who was anxious to help me to secure ground for football and hockey. Hitherto the Kashmir officials had done their best to prevent our having any playing-fields.

The origin of Mr. Maqbool Hussain's helpfulness was remarkable. Our friendship arose in this way. With Capt. A. V. Myles's assistance I was once in charge of the matriculation examination for the Punjab university. Myles came up to tell me, whilst it was proceeding, that an undergraduate persisted in talking to one of the examinees and when asked to leave the hall, had become insolent. I went down from the dais and ordered him out, but he did not obey me, so I told him that I only spoke three times, that now I was speaking to him for the second time. As he failed to obey at my third request I caught him by the back of the neck, ran him out of the hall, then down the college corridor and at the front door I helped him down the stone stairs with my toe to his pants. I was putting into practice one of our school maxims, "As thunder follows lightning so punishment follows disobedience".

Within an hour a red-coated chaprasi handed me a note from the Revenue Minister, Mr. Maqbool Hussain. It read: "Dear Mr. Biscoe, my nephew has just returned from college and tells me that you assaulted him and kicked him down the college stairs. I could not believe it possible, but still I should like some explanation from you."

I returned the following answer: "Dear Mr. Maqbool Hussain. What you have written is perfectly true. I did kick your nephew down the stairs and I shall do so to anyone who tries to interfere with the examinees in the hall when I am in charge, and I hope that if you ever catch any of my boys being insolent to you, you will take the same action. I remain, &c."

Soon the chaprasi was back with the following note: "Will you and Captain A. V. Myles do me the honour of dining with me to-morrow at 7.30 p.m.?" I accepted his kind invitation and had a very pleasant evening, and our friendship began.

To continue my remarks about the absence of playing-fields I must go back to the days when Islamabad School was first started. Mr. Knowles had secured a house for his school on the edge of a maidan and on it our boys played games. Then the Minister of Education built a state school in the middle of it, putting a fence round it which came to the entrance door of our school, so at one fell swoop our playgrounds were taken from us. I should not have minded so much if the state schoolboys had been encouraged to play games, but they were not.

I reported this matter to our friend the Resident, Stuart Fraser. He went to Islamabad and asked the Wazir if it was true that the maidan had been fenced round, so that the mission schoolboys had no playground. The Wazir admitted it was true, but that he had ordered the fence close to the mission school to be removed. Fraser asked the Wazir to come with him to the ground. He made all sorts of excuses, but eventually they visited the spot. When Fraser saw that the fence had not been removed, he asked the Wazir why he had told him a lie. His answer was: "Please forgive me, Sahib, it is the first lie I have ever told you and I will order the fence to be removed to-morrow." Fraser said he would not wait until to-morrow, but requested the Wazir to call coolies and remove the fence immediately. The fence was removed, but even then the piece of land was not large enough for football or hockey, that is why Mr. Maqbool Hussain was anxious to find us a larger space.

The boys at Islamabad became very proficient in athletic sports and gymnastics and won the gymnastic trophy for many years, but, what was more important than games, was their keenness for social service.

A boy called Shrider Buth came to the school and, in course of time, became headmaster. He possessed an outstanding character for courage, kindness and determination and his great joy in life was that of uplifting the Kashmiris.

Whilst he was a master in the school a lady missionary, Miss Annie Coverdale, started a school for girls. She and Shrider Buth did everything they could for each other's schools. If anyone congratulated Shrider Buth on his success with his school and in social service, he always said it is all due to Miss Coverdale's example and help.

Miss Coverdale lived with Dr. Minny Gomery and Miss Katie Newnham at the C.M.S. mission hospital at Islamabad. They had devoted their lives to the women of this town and district for years. It was most strenuous work and we all marvelled at their strength and courage.

Miss Coverdale eventually retired to England but was unfortunately one of the many victims in an air raid. She and her sister's cottage at Bexhill received a direct hit from a bomb. In the hereafter many will call her blessed!

November 2nd, 1916, was our Silver Wedding day and I gave a garden party for all those who had kindly sent us presents. Our friends belonged to various classes of society. When I asked a British officer of the Kashmir State to fix up a lawn tennis foursome, he looked superciliously round the garden at my visitors and said: "I do not know anybody here." So I said: "Do not bother, I will arrange a set." It is distressing that in India, where there are so many different castes, each one imagining that his own is superior to all the others, Britishers should be such fools as to try to copy this evil custom by bringing class distinctions into sport. In sport, as in worship in church, we surely should forget "who's who".

At this time the city of Srinagar was excited over its municipal election. Our Headmaster, Mr. Shanker Koul, was asked to stand and was naturally backed up by all who wished to have an honest municipal officer. When our masters and old boys presented themselves at the election booths they found it impossible to vote as the municipal secretary was there with hooligans to prevent them voting, so we had to send some lusty fellows to see fair play, and Mr. Shanker Koul was duly elected.

Now I would like you to know something of the life and character of Mr. Shanker Koul our Headmaster, who was now an honourable member of the municipality of Srinagar.

He came to the mission school in 1892 together with two boys from the state school. Their first half-morning's work was finished when the bell rang for them to go into the playground for the twenty minutes' exercise, drill, boxing and gymnastics.

When I ordered my class to shut their books and to go to the playground, these three new boys said that they had come to school to learn and not to play. So I told them that this school was not a lunatic asylum and that, if they did not wish to have their bodies trained, they had better return at once to the state school. I then forced them downstairs to the playground and put them in line with the squad fronting the parallel bars and, when their turn came to perform, they refused to mount the parallel bars. So I took out my watch and told them that I would give them five minutes to think the matter over and then something would happen. Something did happen. Shanker Koul was on the parallel bars but his arms were too weak to hold himself there, so two boys were called to support him on each side.

When this first exercise was finished we dealt with the other two newcomers in the same way. All three boys accepted this treatment with good grace, and, later on, all three became gymnastic instructors and thankful that they had come to the school.

To speak of Shanker Koul's life at the C.M.S. schools and the enormous amount of useful work and brave deeds that he has performed would fill volumes. He was the leader of the boys at fires in the city, at epidemics of cholera, and when the Jhelum river overflowed its banks, causing destruction and distress all around. He was in the van too in preventing cruelty to animals, and in rescuing women and girls from impure devils. He also did useful work in standing up to the state officials when they tried to harm our schools and was always ready to join battle with anyone who decried the school.

To give an instance. An exceptionally holy Sadhu visited Kashmir and began preaching against the mission school as he had been incited by our enemies.

Shanker found the Sadhu sitting at a holy place on a leopard skin. Among the accusations against the mission school he happened to mention was that Jesus Christ had taught His disciples that they must fight against anyone who was not a Christian, so Shanker asked him if he had read the Bible. He answered in the negative. He said he could not read English but could read Hindu, so Shanker Koul brought him a Hindu Bible and asked him to show him this passage. Finally the holy man allowed that he had been misinformed, so Shanker Koul asked him if he would come to see the school and judge for himself. He replied he would like to do so, but it was impossible for him to leave his leopard skin for a month, as this happened to be the time when insects were crawling about and he might tread upon them, which would be a great sin. So Shanker Koul suggested that he and the teachers should carry him to a boat and paddle him down to our school, but he refused. His refusal was due to his fear that those who carried him should tread upon the insects and thus commit many sins.

Shanker Koul waited till the insects had stopped crawling about, and got him down to the school. He explained to him all that we did and did not do, with the result that the Sadhu said he would in future let everybody know the truth concerning the school, and Shanker and he parted as friends.

By the autumn of 1917 I was ordered by the doctors to leave Kashmir for rest and change, so I went to Madras to stay with that G.O.M. of the C.M.S., Canon Sell, who had been working in India for fifty-two years and was still hale and hearty, and hard at work as usual. Then to the Bishop of Madras, Henry Whitehead, where I had a very pleasant time. I visited various educational institutions in Madras. The one which pleased me most was the S.P.G. boys' school run by Rev. H. J. Edmonds, for he interested his boys in matters more important than the everlasting examinations for the university.

From Madras, Dorothy and I travelled to Bangalore to stay with the British Resident, my old friend H. V. Cobb. The night before we arrived, Mr. Cobb had given a dinner party to no less than seventy missionaries in honour of one of them who had lately received the Kaisar-I-Hind Gold Medal for Public Service in India.

From Bangalore I went to Hyderabad, Deccan, to stay at the Residency with another old friend, Stuart Fraser. He showed me an education report by Sir Henry Sharp, Director of Education in India, and said how glad he was it contained such high praise of our C.M.S. schools in Kashmir. Fraser asked if I had received the report. I said that I had, but the part which referred to our schools had been eliminated and therefore this was the first time that I had heard of Sir Henry Sharp's appreciation.

At a banquet given in those days in the palace by the Nizam one of the courses was a pie put before each guest. When they cut the pie-crust a bird flew out, so that within a few seconds the great dining-hall became an aviary, which is believed to bring good luck. Of course this reminded the British guests of the song of their childhood, "Sing a song of sixpence".

Fraser also told me that when King George V came to the throne, the Maharajah of Kashmir told him that he wished to please the King by setting free a number of prisoners and asked Stuart Fraser if he thought that would make the King happy. He replied that he was sure it would, if they were the right class of prisoners to be set free. Later, the Maharajah procured a list of those to be released and saw that no one who had killed a cow was to be set free. So Fraser said to His Highness: "If you really wish to please the King Emperor you will reduce the terribly severe *life* sentences which you give to all those who kill cows." So His Highness reduced the punishment to seven years.

This Hindu law for the preservation of cows is the cause of endless cruelty. No wounded or sick animal is allowed to be put out of its pain, and the cow that ceases to give milk is left to starve. Farmers cannot afford to feed useless cows.

From Hyderabad I went to Bhopal to stay with my old friends Dr. and Mrs. Lankester. One morning Dr. Lankester took me to the palace of Her Highness the Begum of Bhopal. We were shown into an upper room where there was a big sheet stretched right across the room, to divide Her Highness from her male visitors. As a matter of fact I could plainly see Her Highness's profile, for her head was between my eye and the window behind her. She said she had heard of me and my school and that I was very fond of aquatics, and asked me to choose a good spot for a swimming bath by the town lake as she wanted her people to be good swimmers. She was a pleasant old lady, and easy to talk to, except that I was unable to see the expression on her face through this white sheet.

When I returned to Srinagar I found plenty of work waiting for me of various kinds, some pleasant and some the reverse.

A very distressing case had been brought to my notice of a young Britisher who had succumbed to temptation, put in his way deliberately by the owner of the houseboat in which he lived, with the result that he contracted a dreadful disease and when I was called to minister to him I found him paralyzed. The only part of his body which could function was his head. He said: "I have called you, Padre, to see me in this dreadful state, so that other young men may take warning from me and be saved from this terrible death." He was wonderfully brave and, in his distress, he was not thinking of himself but of how to save others from suffering a similar fate. Within an hour or two he passed away.

There are hundreds of houseboats on the river and lakes

of Kashmir. Some of the Mohammedan owners use them as floating houses of ill-fame. They have been death traps to many young British officers.

I went to the Head of the Visitors' Bureau to ask him if he could not post a black list of those particular boats, so that innocent men might not find themselves trapped by these devils. In order to influence this officer I had visited the two British agencies and secured their co-operation and they willingly started a black list.

The following incident will show how young Britishers are tempted. On my brother Julian's first visit to Kashmir in 1893 he and a brother officer arrived at Baramulla and were looking for a boat to take them the forty-five miles upstream to Srinagar. A Mohammedan boat agent came to them telling them he had just the boat to suit them, and as they stepped on to it, the agent pointed out two Kashmiri girls in the boat, saying that he had procured these two very pretty girls for them. Fortunately, the agent was standing on the prow of the boat, so that when my brother's fist caught him squarely, the agent disappeared into the waters of the River Jhelum.

I guess that ducking taught the rascal to be more careful in his introductions. Later I had the good fortune to catch the rich manager of this particular agency in a spot from where there was no escape. I fancy that our heart to heart talk was not altogether in vain.

This summer the schools did more swimming than usual. In our annual swim across the Dal Lake, a distance of nearly four miles, 134 boys started and 86 finished. Two or three continued to swim on down the river.

I was following one of the swimmers who was doing his seventh mile, when I was told that we were passing his father's shop, so I sent a messenger to tell him of his son's pluck and to suggest that he should come in my boat and cheer his son on. The father was soon in my boat, but to my surprise he took little or no notice of his son. He kept his eyes fixed on me instead, and kept telling me what a fine fellow I was and what a benefactor I had been to Kashmir. I told him that I had not called him to talk but to encourage his son in this long swim. But no! His son was nothing to him and I was everything.

When we landed after the swim and were busy in warming the swimmers with hot drinks, his father, seeing that I was pleased with his son, asked me to find him a good job in one of the state offices. That was the sum total of his interest in his son's feat.

This is only one specimen of the feelings of the Kashmiri parents towards their sons in the athletic line. As there is no money in it, they ask what is the good of wasting time over sports.

Our new British Resident, Colonel Jack Manners-Smith, was keen on all athletic sports and when I told him of my difficulty in inducing the state schools to join us in swimming, he offered to give a challenge cup to the school which produced the best swimming team of twelve, so it was arranged that all the schools should compete. Unfortunately, no other school was able to produce more than three competitors, so three became, perforce, a team.

We rowed the competitors in our twelve-oared cutter to the starting place. A Hindu master of the state school asked to be allowed to accompany us in the boat. Being a gentleman, he was of course a non-swimmer. When the cutter was in position at the starting point, the crew stood along the thwart to balance the swimmers who had mounted the gunwale on the opposite side. When all was ready, the competitors leapt from the boat at the word "go" and the crew, having failed to move smartly into the centre of the boat, the cutter capsized, and all its occupants were thrown into the water and were enjoying their bath, except the Hindu master. Our men were laughing so much that they found it difficult to save this gentleman. The reason of their laughter was that this teacher, although a Hindu, was calling out for Allah to save him. In his terror he evidently forgot to what religion he belonged. The winners were the C.M.S. team. All the others gave up except three boys who had been taught at our school.

Our next swim was across the Wular Lake, a record year, for twenty-seven accomplished the five-mile swim. It was a curious fact that, although swimming was not considered a sport for gentlemen, anyone drowning in the river or lake was quite ready to accept help from the C.M.S. school swimmers.

On that day after the annual swim across the lake I received the following letter of appreciation from an onlooker, an extra religious gentleman.

"Sir, I write to thank you for all the trouble you have taken for so many years to encourage your boys to swim and save lives. I happened to be on the bank of the lake close to the spot where the boys were arriving, when one boy sank from exhaustion, and one of your boys went to the rescue and saved him."

When I later met this friendly gentleman, I asked him why he himself did not plunge in and save the boy. He answered: "Sir, I was saying my prayers at that time, so was unable to rescue him."

I was called upon about this time to try to prevent a man of twenty-five marrying a little girl eleven years old.

This girl was in Miss Fitze's C.M.S. girls' school and Violet Fitze was in great distress over this marriage, so I went off to interview the man, a shopkeeper. I tried to appeal to him as man to man and if possible to touch some spark of kindness, but I utterly failed. He was adamant and evidently thought it great cheek on my part to interfere with his private affairs.

One reason why I was so anxious to stop this marriage was that a week or two previously, a little girl eleven years old had been brought to the mission hospital to be delivered of her child. Notwithstanding all the care and love bestowed on that little patient, her life could not be saved.

You can understand that we sometimes became very angry when we met such cases of cruelty. We hope some day that a law will be passed to make it criminal to marry girls of tender age. But passing a law is no good unless the general public have been brought up to honour chivalry.

CHAPTER FOURTEEN

Profiteering & Child Murder

AFTER the Great War the galladars, i.e. sellers of grain, fuel contractors, butchers and bakers, backed up by certain high officials of the state, combined to prevent food and fuel from entering the city and they thereby succeeded in raising the price of necessities.

Narindra Nath Koul, who was then Governor, had been disappointed at having been ploughed in the I.C.S. examination in London and hence became disgruntled against the British. He hated the mission school and all its works.

As the city people were half starved, Shanker Koul and I visited him to offer the help of the school staff and boys to fight the famine. The Governor received us very coldly, but our answers to his questions changed his manner, and he accepted our offered help. The questions and answers were as follows:

T.-B. I have come to offer you the services of my school staff.

Gov. What can they do?

T.-B. Anything you order.

Gov. I suppose they will want a lot of money.

T.-B. They will not work for money, they are patriots.

Gov. Are they honest men?

T.-B. They are honest with me, you must prove them.

Gov. Honest men! I have not a single honest man in my department.

T.-B. I know that is true, and therefore I am offering you my men.

Gov. If I take your men I will put on two of my men to each one of yours, to watch them.

T.-B. I am glad to hear it. Put on as many of your men to watch my men as you think fit.

I went to our friend and adviser, Mr. Cecil Hadow, telling him of the Governor's altered attitude and he came with me to the Governor and the latter accepted Hadow's offer of twenty-five men from his carpet factory, who were Mohammedans, as well as fifty of our school teachers who were Hindus.

The Governor sent members of our staff together with two of his Government servants (to *watch* our men, lest they accepted bribes!) for thirty miles up and down the river to bring loaded boats containing rice, grain, "shali" (a form of rice) and firewood into the city.

Many boats arrived. When the salesmen in the city realized that food was in the city they closed all the food shops. The Governor then opened state shops and put our men in charge. These shops were besieged and the male bipeds prevented the women from obtaining food. Our men then provided themselves with single-sticks, and by using them freely they kept a path open for the women to approach the shops. The women then began fighting one another for the shali.

What were our men to do? They were given orders to serve first all women with babies. The salesmen reported next day that every woman had a baby and were still fighting one another, so they were ordered to supply those women with twins first, and then those with one baby only.

Next day the salesmen reported that every woman had two babies, so, not wishing to encourage triplets, the shali was placed in boats, which were moored to the bank of the river. A plank connected each boat with the bank and our boys were placed at the plank, armed with single-sticks, to prevent bipeds pushing on board before the women. This worked well for two days, until the bipeds, being angry, shoved the women into the river and one or two were drowned. The boats were then anchored out in the river and shali sold only to those who arrived in the authorized tender, and so at last all went well.

The Governor summoned to his court all the city fathers, head butchers, bakers, galladars and fuel contractors, and fixed a "nerik", i.e. the price of food. Against this order all the butchers, bakers, &c., protested loudly, but the city cheered and praised the Governor. The Governor then ordered our men to apprehend all those who were breaking the "nerik" law.

The scoundrels objected strongly, and as our men went round the city they shouted: "There go the friends-of-hell let loose upon our city by Padre Biscoe." But the Tehsildar (magistrate), who happened to be an old mission school boy, seized the culprits and called for barbers and donkeys. These lawbreakers had their faces shaved, on one side only, and placed on donkeys with their faces towards the tails and marched through the city with the town-crier shouting in front of the procession: "These are the men who are cheating the people."

Mr. Hadow and the Governor called the city fathers together, and a co-operative society was started, which took over all food and saw to its proper distribution. We closed our schools for three months, so that our staff could act as clerks for this co-operative society.

The butchers and bakers rushed off by car to Jammu, two hundred miles from Srinagar, to tell the Maharajah that the Governor, aided by Hadow and Biscoe, was persecuting the city. They also persuaded the Maulvis to preach in their mosques against the Governor, so that when His Highness arrived in Srinagar and proceeded in his state barge up the river, the whole Mohammedan population were to crowd the three miles of river bank to curse the Governor. They were to take with them long punting-poles on the top of which empty gunny bags would be tied, and as His Highness passed they would cry: "Starving, starving," at the same time pointing to the empty sacks and patting themselves to show that their stomachs were as empty as the sacks, and shouting: "The Governor is the cause."

On the morning of His Highness's entry into Srinagar I received an urgent letter from the Governor saying that the Maharajah was coming to Srinagar with the intention of turning him out of his post, and that the Maulvis had incited the populace to shout against him and ask for his dismissal. He ended by asking my help in preventing this river demonstration.

A somewhat tall order! for what could the school staff and boys do to counter this huge demonstration? However, I had a brainwave. I gave orders at once for the school boats to be brought from the Dal Lake boathouse, to the school, and explained my plans to the staff. They were to take the school fleet to meet His Highness where he would enter his barge with all his state officials, both British and Indian, and to take position behind the barge to be in readiness to rush to either side of the river where they could act as a screen between the Maharajah and the Governor's enemies on the banks. As we were discussing this matter, a police notice was handed me to the effect that no boats were to come within two hundred yards of His Highness's barge. That a police boat screen would be in position to prevent all boats approaching His Highness. This snag required quick action, so I ordered the boat captains to obey my orders and ignore the police order.

It was 3.30 p.m. The guns at Hari Parbat fort fired twenty-one salutes and the state barge moved upstream with its sixty-eight boatmen and a steam-tug pulling in front. The police boats took up their position in the rear, then our fleet formed up, the twelve-oared cutter with the school band in the bows, led the ten school shikaras, two abreast, containing thirteen to fifteen boys each as crew.

I was in command in my launch with field glasses and megaphone. After the procession had proceeded half a mile, I spotted a large party of empty sack-wavers on the left bank of the river, so I shouted out through my megaphone: "Fleet to the left bank of the river, sharp." Immediately the fleet put on speed, through the police screen they went and right up to the right side of the barge. When in position, I shouted: "Salute His Highness the Maharajah of Jammu and Kashmir." The crews immediately stood with 150 oars and paddles at the salute, and the band struck up "For he's a jolly good fellow". The result was that H.H. saw no poles or bags and heard nothing but "He's a jolly good fellow". When this danger point was passed, I ordered "Fleet to the rear", which they obeyed promptly. About another half-mile on the right bank of the river, I saw a similar pole and sack crowd, so I

PART OF THE SCHOOL FLEET AT THE SALUTE IN FRONT OF THE SCHOOL

It took many years to persuade the first members of the school to paddle a boat, and then only by permitting them to cover their heads with blankets so that they and their families would not be disgraced. Later, weekly regattas became a popular feature, and the boys often spent their free afternoons taking out patients from the hospital for airings on the lake.

ordered "Fleet to the right bank of the river". Up went the
fleet, and when in position I shouted: "Salute His Highness the Maharajah of Jammu and Kashmir." The crews
rose to attention with oars and paddles aloft and the band
struck up "The Cock of the North". The pole and sack
wavers cursed our boys and ordered them out of the way,
but in vain, as there was a gulf of deep water between.
Again the Maharajah heard and saw nothing but the loyal
mission school boys saluting him. Thus we went three
miles up the river to his palace; and the Governor was
saved.

The trouble in Srinagar continued as the food shortage
had not ended. Lord Chelmsford, the Viceroy, visited
Kashmir to see what he could do. As he came up the river
with His Highness in the state barge the officials had
prepared excellent eyewash.

Along both banks of the river for the three miles were
barges full of rice and others loaded with fuel, with notices
in *English* in letters large enough for him to see from his
barge, "Shali for sale", "Price cheap", "Firewood for
sale", "Price cheap", so that he might see for himself that
the city was not short of food but bursting with it. But
what he did not see was that, as soon as his barge had
passed, all these boats were taken out of the city and hidden in nullahs.

As the next day was Sunday I had to preach before the
Viceroy and his suite and was able to let him know something of the sorrows of the citizens of Srinagar. Certain
members of the congregation expressed their views on my
bad taste for having spoken the truth on that occasion.

The following evening, at a dinner party at the Residency, the Viceroy sent for me to sit by him and I had the
opportunity of telling him the truth regarding the sufferings of the people. How the Kashmir state officials had
tried to hoodwink him by bringing scores of barges full of
grain all along his route through the city.

Three days later, when I was holding my staff class in
my garden, an old student rushed up to me breathless and
said: "Please hide me. Two other old students and I have
been seized by the police for having sent a telegram to the

M

Viceroy, but I have escaped, hide me, Sahib." I asked: "What did you wire?" and he answered: "The city is starving." Before I could act a policeman entered, dragging the two old students with him, so I was unable to prevent his being seized. I told the policeman, of course, what I thought of this injustice and then mounted my cycle and made my way to the house of the Indian Chief Judge, a Hindu. I offered to go to prison myself, saying that I deserved it far more than my three old students who had just been taken to prison. Whereas they had only told the truth to the Viceroy by wire, I had told him in his ear what these boys had wired, and a good deal more. Therefore he *must* send me to gaol, for mine was the greater crime. The upshot of it was that he promised to free the three boys the first thing next morning. The three were brought in chains to my house next day by a policeman. As soon as they were set free they ran to me and grasped my ankles in their joy.

But the fight was by no means over, although Mr. Hadow had been giving an immense amount of time and energy to the running of the co-operative shali stores, for several of the senior state officials were on the side of the profiteers, who were pulling strings. So Lord Reading, who had succeeded Lord Chelmsford as Viceroy, came to Kashmir to try and clear up the situation. He started his inquiry by calling Mr. Hadow and me to see him at the Residency. With him as legal adviser was Sir Grimwood-Mears (Chief Judge of Allahabad).

After thanking us for coming, he said: "I have called you two gentlemen, as I know that you will tell me the real cause of this profiteering." We told him that it was due to certain highly placed officials. He answered: "I guessed as much. What is needed here is a law."

Having asked Sir Grimwood to draft a law to make profiteering an offence, punishable by a heavy fine and imprisonment with hard labour, the Viceroy dismissed us with thanks for our help, and expressed the hope that we would join the council of state officials which was to meet that evening. He made a strong speech at this meeting, asking the officials to consider how they would feel if they themselves had empty stomachs. He reminded them there could never be peace and contentment among starving people, and that it was he as Viceroy who had to see that India was a peaceful and happy country. In plain English, that humbug must cease.

The Viceroy spoke again at the banquet at the palace. The gist of his speech was as follows:

"Ladies and Gentlemen, you will, I know, have very great pleasure in drinking the health of our kind host, His Highness, when you hear that there is to be an end of the troubles of the people of this city due to the shortage of food, for His Highness has made a law which will stop people hereafter from making profit out of the sufferings of his subjects."

Narindra Nath Koul, the Governor of Kashmir, whom his enemies the profiteers hoped to discomfort, was raised to the rank of Revenue Minister, but he enjoyed his new powers only for a short period. He fell ill and passed from us, to our very great sorrow. Thousands of his admirers followed his body to the burning ghat bare-footed.

Shortly before he died he told one of our party that he had become a true believer in the Christian faith on account of what he had *seen* in the lives of those who had been fighting with him to save the city in its time of need. He commended his children to my care, but his Brahman relations would not allow his last wish to be carried out.

Later, the state took over the food control from the Co-operative Society, built up-to-date granaries and to our relief, put Captain Wreford in charge. We knew that as long as he was in control there would be no devilry or monkey tricks.

H.H. Hari Singh, nephew of the Maharajah and the heir apparent, gave solid help in the fight to overcome the profiteers. He called to his house all the chief men of the city, also Hadow and myself, to question each one of us, in private, how we would tackle this difficulty.

The following are three instances of his action when he personally came across cases of injustice. At Gulmarg, the hill station, he met a boy crying. On inquiring the cause he discovered that he was in charge of a riding pony for hire, off which a man had just dismounted and paid him a rupee. This rupee had been snatched from him by another man who was making off. Hari Singh immediately chased him, gave him a beating, and returned the rupee to the boy.

H.H. Hari Singh and Mr. Alexander Stow, Commissioner, were big game shooting. After the day's work His Highness ordered the beaters to be given their pay. Mr. Stow discovered shortly afterwards that the beaters had not received any pay. The money had disappeared into the pocket of the officer in charge of His Highness's purse.

Shortly afterwards Alexander Stow was again on a bear shoot with His Highness and told him of the non-payment of the beaters after the previous shoot. When this day's shoot was over he had all the seventy beaters lined up, as he wished to see them paid himself, so that there should be no swindling this time. He ordered his money-bag man to pay the beaters in front of him, but this gentleman said that he had unfortunately no small change and was unable to procure change as they were not near a town.

So His Highness ordered him to go in his car at once to the town, ten miles distant, and procure change and said he would wait until his return and pay the beaters himself.

In the meantime a telegram arrived from the Maharajah asking H.H. Hari Singh to return to Srinagar at once. So His Highness asked Stow to remain behind and see the men paid. The change arrived, and Stow had the pleasure of being able to report that all the beaters had received their full payment this time.

H.H. Hari Singh invited Mr. W. P. Appleford, Chief Engineer, to accompany him on a drive for duck on one of the jhils. As they were in the car en route His Highness noticed that several of the tongas were overloaded and the ponies were suffering in consequence, so he said to Appleford: "You go on to the jhil, while I put a stop to this cruelty."

During the summer months we had several interesting visitors at our school, among them the Rt. Rev. E. Palmer, Bishop of Bombay and the Rt. Rev. Eyre Chatterton,

Bishop of Nagpore. The latter cheered us up by taking part in one of our weekly regattas and sitting in our twelve-oared cutter. We also had our old friend, Norman Tubbs, who afterwards became Bishop of Tinnevelly and later Bishop of Rangoon.

A new disease attacked Srinagar this summer which disturbed many of the inhabitants and especially the Pandits.

The President of the Dharam Sabha invited Doctor Kathleen Vaughan, who was at that time the doctor in charge of the Kashmir State Jubilee Hospital, to lecture at their chief temple and give them advice how to tackle the new disease.

Doctor Vaughan asked me to accompany her to the temple. We found the temple compound crowded with Brahmans, all anxious to hear Dr. Vaughan. Dr. Vaughan was also very anxious to talk to the Brahmans because, while she had been working in this hospital, she had found much to distress her, especially the sufferings of the women at the hands of their husbands and members of their families. She was also horrified at the number of girl babies she had found dead in their mothers' beds, especially when she discovered that they had been deliberately killed. After she had told them how to tackle the new disease, Doctor Vaughan went on: "There is a disease in this state, which has evidently been going on for untold years, which is far more deadly than the new disease in which you all seem to be so interested." She then told them bluntly of the girl babies murdered week by week, in the state hospital, and demonstrated how these girl babies were usually killed; this was by putting the first finger of each hand down the baby's throat and then giving the fingers a jerk.

It was most interesting to me to watch the effect of these words on the audience. They hung down their heads, some of them stuffed their blankets in their mouths or else bit the sleeves of their pherons (like a nightgown), praying inwardly that the lady doctor would cease telling them what they knew only too well.

Doctor Vaughan went on for nearly two hours and I fancy few audiences ever received a straighter talk. When the meeting was over the President of the Dharam Sabha came down the flight of stairs to the river with us to see us safely into our boat. As we pushed off he expressed the wish that we should come again. I greatly admired the self-control of this Brahman gentleman, for he must have wished that our boat would upset and we be properly drowned once for all.

What effect Doctor Vaughan's words had, one cannot say. I expect it made some of them more careful how they put away their baby girls in future, but to change the customs of a country can only be done by a change of heart.

Shortly after this lecture a very sad case was brought to my notice. It was the cruelty of a husband towards his wife. This case, following on the disclosures of child murder by Dr. Vaughan, decided me to visit my old friend the Chief Judge of Kashmir, a Brahman of a well-known family, to ask him if he could not call together some of the right-minded citizens and consult with them how they might tackle these crying evils.

I sent a message to ask when I could visit him. He replied that he would rather visit me at my house. The Chief Judge was a venerable old man with white hair and was much respected, so I opened my heart to him, telling him how distressed I was to have to witness the result of so much cruelty towards women and children. To my surprise he turned upon me in anger, asking me why I interfered with such matters and made the statement that women in England were in a far worse condition than they were in India. I asked him if he had ever visited England. He said "No". So I asked him how he could make such a statement without any experience. He answered that the young Indians who go to England for education told him on their return that English women were treated worse than the women here. "Anyway," he said, "as you are a foreigner, it is no business of yours to interfere with the customs of this country and I don't want to talk on this matter."

You can, I think, understand my feelings when I saw

this venerable Chief Judge out of my house and into his
car. I had always looked upon him as a lover of his people
and one who wished to uplift them. But evidently I had
unwittingly touched him on a tender spot. Kashmiri
Brahmans could do no wrong; were not Brahmans born
out of Brahma's mouth?

About this time Dr. Heber, Dr. Wilson and I arrived
at the Wular Lake about sunrise with a party of boys who
wished to swim across the Wular. It is our custom to see
that all the swimmers are rubbed down with mustard oil
before they take to the water. They are then lined up and
their hearts tested. Boats that have been engaged to follow
them are collected at one spot. Then the order is given to
plunge in. The Wular boats keep a few yards behind the
swimmers in order to see them safely across.

I took Dr. Heber in my motor launch and we kept on
encircling round the swimming party, and were continually
on the spot to give orders to the swimmers or to the boats
which were following them. The swimmers had nearly
finished their swim and the last three were about a quarter
of a mile from the farther shore when I noticed that one of
the swimmers held up his arm, so I asked him if he needed
help. He answered "No" and went on swimming. Again
I noticed his arm going up and called again asking if he
wanted help. Again he said "No", that he was all right.
Shortly after his arm went up for the third time, so I ran
my motor boat up to him and when I was within two yards
of him, he disappeared out of sight. Just over the spot
some bubbles were rising, so I immediately dived down in
the direction of the bubbles, but could see nothing and feel
nothing. When I came up I held on to the boat to re-
gain my breath and Dr. Heber dived, seeking for the
boy but could not find him. So I went down a second
time and searched without success. When I came up
to get my breath Dr. Heber went down again, still un-
successfully. Then for the third time I went down, Dr.
Heber followed me again, but was also unsuccessful in
finding the boy. By this time the other boats had joined us
and members of the school staff also tried to find the boy.

We kept on searching for two hours until a storm blew up and we were obliged to make for the shore.

We sent for fishermen and set them to work with their nets, when the storm had passed over, but it was not until the following morning that they found the body and brought it to us.

When I got back to Srinagar I visited the boy's father. Fortunately, he was an old student of mine and took his sorrow most bravely, saying that he was certain that I had taken as much care of his son as I would have done of my own. That it was God's will and there was nothing more to be said.

However, more was said, not by the father or the relations of the boy but by the enemies of our school who saw that it was a great opportunity for getting me into trouble. Some of the Brahman priests around His Highness the Maharajah persuaded him to order his Prime Minister and the head of the police to visit the boy's father and order him to run me into the law courts for murder or manslaughter. When I heard this I was very sorry for the father, I knew it would put him in a very awkward position, for he would not like to displease the state authorities. In fact it would be very dangerous for him to do so, and of course he did not wish to get me into trouble. After doing some hard thinking I called all my masters together and told them that I had learned that I was to be sued for murder and that I was delighted to hear of it for I had long wished for the opportunity to stand up in the law courts, to ask why His Highness, the Maharajah of Jammu and Kashmir, permitted his subjects to murder so many of their babies every month, by throwing them into the river or to the pariah dogs.

When this speech of mine was noised abroad in the bazaars of the city, as I well knew it would be, the officials of the state thought it would be wiser to let this matter of the Wular catastrophe drop. Consequently, the members of our school staff were able to visit the bereaved family to sympathize with them without fear of the law courts.

On October 30th, 1918, I had the sad duty of having

to commit the body of Jack Patterson to the grave. He was an old college friend of mine at Cambridge in the eighties and had taken over the chaplaincy of Srinagar to the great joy of us all, but his work here was cut short. He was tackling a small fault in his motor-car when he cut his finger with the tool he was using. Blood poisoning set in and within ten days he had passed on. When I visited him in his last hours he asked me to inscribe on his tombstone the following words:

"For I know whom I have believed and am persuaded that He is able to keep that which I have committed unto Him against that day." (2 Tim., 1-12)

The reason why he had wished this text to be put on his tombstone was that those words written by Timothy were the cause of his conversion.

As our friend Jack Patterson was so much respected by the Europeans in Srinagar I sent a notice round the station that Sunday evening service would not take place in the church but at the cemetery over their beloved chaplain's grave, and instead of a sermon I gave them a short description of our departed friend's life, some of which I will repeat.

He was at Corpus Christi College, Cambridge, which was popularly known as the Angel and Devil College, for it was divided into two opposite sets, fairly equal in numbers, the pious and the rowdy. Jack Patterson, being an athlete and specially good at Rugby, was soon driven to the rowdy set and joined their drinking parties. One night, just as he was getting into bed, his eyes fell upon his Bible packed away in an upper bookshelf and then he remembered that he had promised his mother always to read his Bible before going to bed at night. He took the Bible down and as he laid it on the table, it opened at the second Epistle of Timothy and verse 12 caught not only his eye but his heart.

He thereupon fell on his knees and remained on his knees all night, praying God to forgive him for his past folly and asking for strength to stand up like a man and live a Christian life, fearing none. Next day he went at once to his old companions and told them what had happened and how he had determined to give up the follies of his past life at Cambridge and, with the help of God, to live a different life. His friends at first thought he was fooling but soon discovered that he had changed right about face.

After taking his degree and being ordained, he offered himself to the C.M.S. and was sent to India. Being a sportsman as well as a preacher, he would go tiger-shooting, when opportunity permitted, and was so successful in this sport that when Prince George (later King George V) and Princess Mary were on their tour in India and visited Agra, the latter asked to be introduced to a missionary who shot tigers, so Jack Patterson had the honour of an interview.

About this time I had the pleasure of receiving to my house the Rev. and Mrs. J. S. Dugdale who had been sent to Kashmir to help us at our schools. Mr. Dugdale had a great capacity for making friends and he soon had a following of the best.

Also at this time we were honoured by the arrival of Mrs. Starr from Peshawar, formerly Lilian Wade, the daughter of the Rev. R. Wade, one of the first missionaries to Kashmir, who did such splendid work in the great famine.

The reason for her leaving her hospital at Peshawar was tragic. Doctor and Mrs. Starr had gone to bed as usual, when at midnight they were awakened by a rapping at the door. Mrs. Starr jumped out of bed and opened the door. There stood a man with a lantern, asking if Doctor Starr would come at once to the hospital as a patient was desperately ill. Doctor Starr at once answered the call but, as soon as he got out of his bungalow, a sharp dagger was thrust into his stomach three times and his fox terrier, Murphy, that attacked his assailant, received two jabs from the dagger in his head.

Mrs. Starr, hearing her husband's groans, rushed out of the house and tried to catch the assailants, but her husband begged her to remain with him. Doctor Starr, of course, received every attention that medical aid could give, but passed on before sunrise next day. So Mrs.

Starr, who had known me from her childhood, asked to come to my house.

No reason could be given for this dastardly deed except that the murderer was anxious to get to heaven and therefore killed a Kafir, who in this case happened to be one who spent all his life in saving the lives of Mohammedans on the North-West Frontier.

At this time there came to Kashmir from Edinburgh University an Indian doctor to work for the municipality of Srinagar. He was very keen on his job, but unfortunately his superior medical officer, a Hindu, took a great dislike to him. I suppose the reason was that the young doctor was too keen on doing his duty, so he set about trying to find some action of his which might displease the Maharajah.

In this young doctor's dispensary he found a tin of meat extract which this Edinburgh doctor used for growing germs. Of course the Chief Medical Officer knew this, but nevertheless he reported the young doctor to His Highness as an eater of beef. This was one of the greatest crimes that could be committed in Kashmir, so His Highness ordered him to leave Kashmir. Whereupon this young Health Officer came weeping to me to seek my help, for he was much unnerved. I told him to stop crying and to laugh for this was comic opera. He answered: "You, sir, can laugh but I cannot."

However, I cheered him up by telling him that I would go off to see Colonel J. H. Hugo, D.S.O., the Residency Surgeon, and get his help. I went straight to Colonel Hugo, who was always ready to right wrongs and told him of this absurd plot. He at once took action, with the result that the young Health Officer stayed for many years to help Srinagar people to live cleaner lives.

In April 1919 I went on furlough to England. After taking a holiday with my family I was put, as usual, on C.M.S. deputation work. At Worcester the Dean very kindly allowed me to preach on behalf of the Kashmir schools and to take the offertory. I preached my sermon but lost the offertory; the chaplain of the Cathedral gave out a notice that the offertory would be devoted to the S.P.G.

CHAPTER FIFTEEN

The Holy Cow

THE time came for us to return to India but, as we were told that it would be impossible to obtain passages for some time, we went to Switzerland, first to Château d'Oex, and from there to Tusenge where we stayed till March.

While in Switzerland I wrote a book on Kashmir. Seeley Service & Co. had been asking me to write one for the last ten years or more. Later they published it under the title *Kashmir in Sunlight and Shade*.

Soon after returning to Kashmir we had the pleasure of meeting Sir Stuart Fraser, who had come to Kashmir on holiday, and with him the Maharajah of Mysore. Sir Stuart was very anxious for His Highness to see our school, so I had the pleasure of showing him round.

As he was leaving he begged me to come to Mysore and start a school there on the same lines. I thanked him for the honour, but said it would not be possible for me to leave Kashmir, so he asked if I could send one of my staff. I promised to do this and, as already mentioned, I sent Samuel Bakkal, who proved a great success and received much help from the kind ruler of Mysore.

About this time Colonel Duni Chand, chief medical officer in Kashmir, asked me if I would like to see the prison. So one morning he called for me, and took me in his dog-cart to the prison where at that time were 117 prisoners, 97 of whom were Mohammedans, being punished for killing cows. Fortunately, they were imprisoned for seven years only, not twenty-one years as I have already mentioned used to be the term.

Colonel Duni Chand took me into a ward where some twenty-five men were sitting on their charpais. As we

passed, one of the prisoners put his hands in the attitude
of prayer and called out: "Biscoe Sahib, Biscoe Sahib,
have mercy upon me and get me out of this prison."
Colonel Duni Chand asked me if I knew the man. I
answered: "I certainly do and what is more I can tell you
why he is here." I then told him the following:

"I was by the lake at Nil Nagh where my family and I
spend our summer holidays. My servants came to me in
some agitation saying that they were passing a (maize)
field when they heard a woman crying for help. They were
just in time to save a village woman from being assaulted
by a man. The man was much upset at being caught and
implored my servants not to report him to me, and at the
same time gave each servant a rupee, hoping that this
would keep their mouths shut. My servants handed the
rupees to me.

"I ordered them to go immediately after that devil, and
bring him to me at the lake side. In half an hour he was
handed over to me. He utterly denied the charge made and
said it was quite true that he had seized the woman, but it
was because she was stealing the Indian corn. I told him
that I did not want to hear lies, but if he wished to escape
punishment he must tell me the truth at once, if not, I
would throw him into the lake.

As he refused to tell me the truth, I ordered him into a
boat and took him out to one of the partly submerged tree
trunks which stand up about four feet out of the water. I
deposited him on one, leaving him to come to his right
mind. Later on in the day I called across the water to ask
if he had anything to communicate to me, but he did not
answer. About an hour afterwards I shouted to him asking
him if he had anything to communicate, but evidently he
had not, so I left him. It was now dark, so I thought I
would give him another chance, and when I called out to
him again across the water, I heard a faint voice saying:
'Sahib, Sahib, have mercy upon me, I repent," so I
paddled out to him, brought him ashore and let him go.

"Early next morning my servants told me that the devil
had mounted a pony at daybreak and had ridden eight
miles distant to a town, and had persuaded the police to

catch the husband of the woman whom he said he had
caught stealing the Indian corn. So I ordered my pony and
started at once at full speed for the police station, told the
police the other side of the story and warned them that
they would have to deal with me if they seized the husband
of the woman.

"This little matter happened shortly before I was
leaving Kashmir for England, so I told the story to a certain British official and asked him to see that the police did
not prosecute the husband of the woman."

"Now, Colonel Duni Chand," I said, "I have returned
from England and here, before us, is the unfortunate
husband I was so anxious to protect from the police."

Next morning as I was standing at my front door a man
in chains was brought up to me by two policemen and
when he was about two yards distant, the policeman unlocked the handcuffs. The released prisoner rushed towards me, fell on his knees, gripped my ankles, put his
forehead on my feet and thanked me that he was a free
man once more.

The devil who caused all this trouble never got any
punishment, except what I gave him in the lake, but he
did not live long to carry on his wickedness, for he was
called away to that land where we shall all receive our
deserts.

The attitude of the Kashmiri is well shown by two incidents. In one a Hindu official shot a man who had insulted his wife. The Maharajah ordered him to leave the
country. He, however, told His Highness the shot man
had killed a cow. "In that case," said the Maharajah,
"he may stay." In the other case a motorist had killed one
of the mission boys, but the Judge let the motorist off
with no punishment but, when leaving the courts in his
car, he unintentionally knocked over a cow, and the crowd
tried to murder him for having such a serious accident.

I was once at a Residency garden party where there are
generally some 250 guests, both Europeans and Indians,
when my attention was drawn to a certain Mohammedan

smoking a cigarette and talking to some young British officers. I at once recognized him as one who had no right to be there, for he was engaged in the white slave traffic.

His practice was to "marry" good-looking girls. The Mullas who performed the ceremony of course charged higher fees when performing these bogus marriages. He then took these girls down to India, on pretence of giving them a good time, and there shut them up in houses of ill-fame in some large town.

I was quite certain that the British Resident was unaware of the presence of this scoundrel at his party, so I decided that it would be better if that devil's presence were removed. I looked round to see if I could spot an official who would tackle the matter promptly and my eyes fell upon Colonel Hugo, who was a MAN, not a manikin. I pointed out to him this self-invited guest and gave him the reason for my wishing to see him removed.

Colonel Hugo said that he would see to that matter at once. About twenty minutes later I felt a tap on my left shoulder. On looking round I saw the Governor of Kashmir. He put his mouth to my ear and whispered: "It is all right, Mr. Biscoe, that man whom you pointed out to Colonel Hugo is already in custody."

Later on this particular traffic was attacked in a more satisfactory manner. Dr. Kathleen Vaughan, who was head of the Kashmir State Women's Hospital, happened to be in Geneva, where she met a medical member of the League of Nations and told him of the sufferings of the women in Kashmir. He reported this to the League and they asked the British Government why such cruelty was permitted in British India.

They in turn approached the Indian Government asking them the same question. They took it up with the Maharajah of Kashmir, asking why he permitted such cruelty in his country. His Highness ordered his police to make full inquiries and one of our old students in the police, Abdul Karim, an exceptionally brave man, was ordered to visit the chief towns in India to search for Kashmir women in houses of ill-fame, against their will. After his return I had the honour of helping him to publish a pamphlet giving an account of his adventures in tracking down these poor Kashmir girls.

This summer Lord Lloyd, the Governor of Bombay, came to Kashmir on holiday and did us the honour of visiting our school and gave us great encouragement. Later, when he returned to Bombay, he wrote asking if I would accept the command of the training ship for the Indian Navy. I knew that I had not the qualifications for such an important post, so I refused his kind offer. I fancy that one of his reasons for asking me was that our school discipline was like that of the Navy in one respect, for teachers and boys moved at the double. Some years later his brother-in-law bought my old home, Holton Park, in Oxfordshire, where Lord Lloyd often went to stay. So that once more I received letters from the home of my childhood.

Mr. Sam Steane, the Assistant Conservator of Forests, invited me to dinner. After the ladies had left for the drawing-room, he sought my advice on a difficult matter. He had discovered that a certain D.F.O. was about to perpetrate a theft of timber to the value of several thousand rupees. He was undecided whether to report the matter or not. I asked: "Why should you not report this super-thief?" His answer was: "I fear if I report him I shall be turned out of Kashmir, because this man has very influential friends in the state who have the ear of the Maharajah." My answer to the question was: "Do your duty and trust in God." He said: "I thank you, Padre, I will follow your advice."

The following week he again invited me to dinner and, after the ladies had left the room, he handed me a paper and asked me to read it. It was from His Highness the Maharajah ordering him to leave Kashmir within ten days. He then said: "Padre, this is the result of trusting God." I answered him: "Trust in God a little longer." He allowed me to take the paper away with me and I took it to our mutual friend, Alexander Stow, the Commissioner.

When he had read His Highness's order, he said: "We must save Steane. Give me the paper." He then stepped into his motor-car and drove off to Gulmarg, the hill station of Kashmir, twenty-eight miles distant, and went to the palace of the heir-apparent, Prince Hari Singh. After Prince Hari Singh had read the order, he asked Alexander Stow to let him have the paper. He then visited his uncle the Maharajah with the result that Sam Steane continued in Kashmir doing a man's job in every way, fighting against bribery and corruption.

N

CHAPTER SIXTEEN

A Gross Case of Cruelty

I HAD been down in the Punjab and on my return I was soon at war.

When cycling from school I overtook a passing tonga and noticed that the pony was in distress. I looked at it carefully when, to my horror, I saw that its front hoofs were turned upwards and that it was trotting on its fetlocks. I cycled ahead, jumped off my bicycle and laid it on the road in front of the tonga, so that I could be sure of the driver stopping.

It happened to be a private tonga and the owner of it wanted to know what business it was of mine to hold him up. I answered that it was a gross case of cruelty and ordered all four of the occupants to get out, to unharness the pony and told the driver to bring the pony to my garden. I then sent for the officer for prevention of cruelty to animals and handed over the pony to him.

Next day I saw the poor animal being driven again in in the same tonga by the same people, so I had the pony unharnessed and once more brought to my garden and held it in custody until the veterinary officer could see it. He agreed with me that it was a case of cruelty and that the animal's deformity was incurable. He said that it ought to be shot, but as the owner was a rich man he did not dare do so.

However, after having the poor animal photographed, so that I could prove that I was justified in taking prompt action in preventing this cruelty continuing, I had the pony shot.

I have never discovered why the owner of the horse did not take action in the law courts against me, for he was certainly angry with me for interfering in his private affairs.

The matriculation examination for the Punjab University had been in session for a week and, as usual, the University had put me in charge. One candidate, a Brahman youth, was brought up to me by one of my assistants with the books he had brought to refer to for his examination paper. So I turned him out of the hall. He wept, but his tears did not melt my heart. Then his relations came to me in tears, saying he was innocent. When they discovered my heart would not melt they threatened to report me to the Punjab University, and went straight off to the telegraph office.

That afternoon a telegram arrived from the controller of the University examinations asking me to explain my conduct in expelling the Brahman candidate. My answer to the telegram was this: "If you don't trust me, send another supervisor to take my place." That was the end of the matter between me and the University, but not so between the expelled candidate and the supervisor who had caught him cribbing. This candidate, whom we will call Sri Ram, was determined to get his own back, so he lay in wait for him with a heavy stick to brain the supervisor where he had to pass after dark. Twice he was unsuccessful, but on the third night he crept up behind him and knocked him insensible with a heavy blow, but the supervisor's friends were near by and he made a good recovery at the mission hospital.

I did my best in the law courts to get Sri Ram properly punished but, after fifteen months' delay, the Brahman Judge sent him to prison for only half an hour and fined him.

I was never again asked by the Punjab University to superintend their university examinations in Kashmir.

Our annual swim this year across the Dal Lake was a red letter day for us. At the place on the lake side from where our boys were starting on their swim was a small encampment. Out of one of the tents came a British officer who asked me what I was doing, and when I told him that the boys were going to swim across the lake, he became very interested and asked if he might join them. I told him that of course we should be honoured if he would take part.

He went into the tent and was soon out again in bathing kit and swam off with the boys. I asked another officer who he was. He replied: "General Sir William Birdwood, the Commander-in-Chief." I had not recognized him, as it was over thirty years since I had met this delightful soldier. I am glad to say that it was not the last, as you will read further on. The general did not realize what valuable help he was giving us for he was not aware of the attitude of the Kashmiris towards swimming and sport.

At this particular time there were over a hundred boys attempting the long swim and not one of their parents had bothered to come to see them, whereas here was the C.-in-C. of India joining the Kashmir boys in this swimming contest.

On October 14th Lord Reading, the Viceroy, with his suite arrived in Kashmir. With their Excellencies was Miss Megan, the daughter of Mr. Lloyd George. They were met by the Maharajah in the state barge about half a mile below the city.

We, at our school on the river bank, decided to give the Viceroy a "living welcome". I had a white sheet spread along the veranda overlooking the river. In this sheet, which was seven feet high and fifteen yards long, slits were cut, through which seventy boys put their heads making the letters "WELCOME". So His Excellency was able to read the words made by seventy grinning Kashmiri faces. We also gave the Viceregal party a gymnastic display on our hostel ground, and later we introduced them to the school regatta on the river, the last item of which was, as usual, the sinking of the whole fleet at the whistle. His Excellency was evidently pleased at what we had shown him and said: "I should like to present a gift to the school; what would you like?" I answered, after a little thought, that I would like a pavilion. I told him that the pavilion would not only be useful for visitors watching our displays, but also for students who were suffering from T.B. to come away from their unhealthy homes in the city and spend their nights in the fresh air on our playing-field which is surrounded by trees.

This handsome pavilion, the gift of Lord Reading, has proved of great value to our school.

CHAPTER SEVENTEEN

Quality, Not Quantity

IN 1925 the time had arrived for my wife, our son Eric, and me to leave Kashmir for England on furlough.

On the way to Bombay we visited Moga School, a very up-to-date educational institution where practical education is given. Boys are taught by doing.

On our journey from that school to the railway station we had rather an exciting experience. We were being driven in a Ford car, and the road took us across a railway crossing close to a cutting at a curve in the track. It was foggy at the time. As our car was crossing the line it suddenly stopped and at that moment we saw the train through the fog coming round the corner. Our driver made hectic endeavours to start his engine but it remained sulky. Eric and I wondered whether we should jump from the car or stick by the driver, but, to our great relief, as the train was almost upon us, our engine was merciful and we crossed the rails just in time. I am never likely to forget those few anxious seconds, but again "all is well that ends well".

Our next stopping place was at Allahabad as we had been invited to stay with Sam Higginbottom and his wife at their very modern Agricultural Institution. They were a truly remarkable couple for they not only ran a huge educational farm, but also schools for boys and girls, and a leper colony. The lepers live in their own cottages and each cottage has a garden. The lepers who have lost their hands and feet are, of course, unable to work their gardens, so their neighbours who possess both, do this for them.

We were very much struck by the happy atmosphere of this colony, due unquestionably to the common sense and Christian methods of Sam Higginbottom and his wife.

The night before leaving Bombay in the P. & O. *S.S. California*, I dined with an old Bradfield College friend, Colonel Gordon Tucker and his wife. He was Head of the Medical College which had just gone on strike, demanding the dismissal of a certain professor.

He asked my advice which I gave without hesitation, viz., to take a firm stand and not to give in to the strikers. I had been sickened by reading in the papers accounts of so many strikes in schools and colleges in India; in nearly every case the heads of the institutions had given in to the strikers, hence the students had learnt that they held the trump card when they refused to attend their lectures: an utterly hopeless state of affairs. Why can't the Principals of Colleges behave as MEN and lock the college gates, and say they will not open them until the students cease playing the fool?

To give an instance of what a little courage can accomplish. A friend of mine was head of a college in India. The students went on strike and refused to attend lectures. When the Principal approached the college gate, he saw the professors standing around outside. The reason soon declared itself, for the entrance was carpeted by the students lying on their backs. My friend, who was smoking a cigar, pretended not to see the recumbent bodies and calmly walked over them into the college. Result! The college lectures commenced at ten o'clock that day as usual.

Next morning, just as our ship was leaving, a note was handed to me from Colonel Tucker to say that he had won through. By taking a firm stand the strike was off, for which I was most thankful.

Soon after my arrival in London I was invited to the Oxford and Cambridge Club by an old friend who said he wished to tell me how pleased he was, in reading our school reports, to see how keen we were on fighting for women and those in distress, and that in his will he had put aside five thousand pounds for the staff's Provident Fund. He said that I should not see those five thousand pounds myself because he was sure that I should die before him, but that I should have the pleasure of knowing that the money was coming to my staff.

Not very long after, I read in *The Times* that my friend had passed on, and that he had left not only five thousand pounds but the whole of his fortune to the schools. It amounted to thirty-five thousand pounds, together with an island off the north of Scotland. Later, I discovered that he must have gone wrong in the head for he had left nothing to his widow, so of course I arranged that all the legacy should go to his widow, and that was the end of our expectations.

While in London I had a visit from Robert Denton Thompson. He came on crutches because he had lost his leg in the Great War during which he had served as a private soldier.

He had heard of our schools from his boyhood and came to ask me if I thought he could be of any service to us. He told me frankly that he had lost his faith during the war and believed in nothing. Therefore he would not be surprised if I turned him down.

I could see at once that I was facing a MAN and a sincere one at that. So I asked him what his object in life was; to live for himself or for his neighbour? He said that it was his desire to be of use to his fellow-men. So I told him I should be delighted to have his help in Kashmir, for I was certain that he would soon find his faith by service. This matter being settled, he sailed for Kashmir before my furlough was over, and I had the pleasure of meeting him there later on.

Eric had taken his degree at Cambridge, having been at my old college, Jesus, where his brothers had been before him. He was anxious to get some job so had accepted a mastership at Wanganui College in New Zealand and was soon off to that country via the Panama Canal. While on board ship, he gave a lecture on our Kashmir schools, and raked in a goodly sum for them.

I spent most of my time, when not on deputation work, with my sailor brother and his wife at Exmouth in their very comfortable house on a cliff close to the sea. During my furlough, however, I was not exactly idle for I preached in 21 churches, addressed 89 audiences, from private drawing-rooms to town halls, and talked to students in 62 schools and colleges. Again I met many old friends, made new ones, met numbers of interesting people and had many amusing experiences. One of the first was at Manchester. I had been asked to preach in the Cathedral by an old friend of mine, Dean Hewlett Johnson. But when the Canon in residence came to hear of it, he approached the Bishop, who at that time was William Temple, and said to him: "Do you know that the Dean has asked Mr. Tyndale-Biscoe to preach in our Cathedral?" "Why should he not?" asked the Bishop. "Because", said the Canon, "I hear that Mr. Tyndale-Biscoe makes the congregation laugh when he is preaching." "A jolly good thing if he does," said the Bishop.

The Cathedral on that Sunday evening was as full as it could be, with many outside who were unable to get seats. I am sure they had not come to hear me, but because the late Dean, Canon Gough McCormick, was a most beloved man and through him the Cathedral had become a popular place for Sunday worship. Now Canon McCormick's sister had been working in our Kashmir hospital for many years and, like her brother, was much liked. So in the course of my talk from the pulpit I spoke about their beloved Dean's sister, with the result that many became so interested that they started clapping, quite forgetting that they were in a Cathedral. I thought of the Canon in residence who was in his seat in the stalls behind me, probably thinking that the clapping of hands in his Cathedral was an even greater sin than laughing.

Next day there was a great meeting in the Town Hall which, like the Cathedral, was packed with people and the Lord Bishop was in the chair. As I was telling them an amusing story I noticed several of the audience were not quite certain whether they ought to laugh aloud or not. But when they saw the chairman letting himself go, they did the same and I don't think anyone was the worse for giving rein to their feelings. I had already had cause to be grateful to Bishop William Temple for the way he had backed me up.

The Lord Mayor of Manchester very kindly invited me and my wife to lunch at the Mansion House. The butler who waited upon us was evidently a great character, for he told us stories connected with the dining-room while he was serving us. He related the following story of the Shah of Persia's visit: The Shah was being driven to the station with the General commanding at his side, when a dray came past on which several navvies were sitting and, as they passed, they all cocked snooks at him. The Shah, noticing their extraordinary behaviour, asked the General the meaning. The General answered: "Your Highness, that salute is only given to very great persons." Later, when his train was leaving the platform and the General, with the guard of honour, was giving him their last salute, the Shah leaned out of the window and putting up both his hands as the navvies had done, cocked that most honourable salute.

Doctor Alington very kindly asked me to visit Eton and address the "First Hundred". When Dr. Alington and I came on to the platform, I noticed that one of the young gentlemen at the back of the hall left his seat and hid himself behind a pillar. I knew of course that he had gone there to play the fool, and I made up my mind to make that young gentleman leave his hiding place before I commenced speaking. However, Doctor Alington's eyes were as sharp as mine, possibly sharper, for he said: "Before I ask Mr. Tyndal-Biscoe to address you, would that boy behind the pillar kindly stand out." So the eyes of the ninety-nine out of the One Hundred were upon him, and the tables were quickly turned.

It was delightful to me to see how Doctor Alington handled his First Hundred. I had had the pleasure of meeting him before when he invited me to Shrewsbury where he and his lady had given me a very pleasant week-end.

I was sent to Ireland where I had a charming time amongst those cheery Irish folk. One of my first engagements in Dublin was to address the Synod of Bishops and Clergy in Trinity College Hall.

I arrived late as the Secretary had forgotten to tell me the time of the meeting. As I entered the door of the hall I heard my name being shouted. "Is Mr. Tyndale-Biscoe here?" I was able to answer: "Yes! Here he is." As I walked up to the platform, I saw my dear old friend Godfrey Day whom I had the pleasure of looking after when he had typhoid in Kashmir several years before.

He was now Bishop of Ossory. When I saw him last he was thin, but now he was rotund and bursting with health. I was so delighted to meet him that I forgot where I was, and I embraced him round the waist to see if my hands would meet. This action of mine called forth a terrific roar of laughter, some little time elapsed before we could settle down to business. One gentleman even paid me the compliment of saying that I must be an Irishman.

That Synod meeting was, I think, the happiest audience I ever had to face. After the meeting I went with my friend the Bishop for a walk and he told me that it was his intention to raise a hundred pounds a year from his diocese to be devoted to our Kashmir schools. This resolve he carried out nobly.

I preached also in Canterbury Cathedral to a gathering of 1,700 children. Before the service there was a big luncheon party arranged in the Town Hall and I found myself the chief guest and was placed by the side of the Dean of Canterbury, George Bell, a charming personality like his father.

About a month later I was invited to preach a second time in this Cathedral during the Canterbury cricket week, when the Cathedral had a congregation of about three thousand.

It is always my custom, when about to preach in a large church, to ask about the acoustics of the building. If one has to preach it is important that the congregation should know what one is talking about, if, of course, it is worth hearing. Canterbury Cathedral, like most churches, is cruciform in shape, and hence it is not possible for the preacher to be heard in all parts of the building until he knows in which direction to throw his voice. The Dean said that the only way to be heard was to talk over the Bishop's head, i.e. at the top of the Bishop's stall.

As I climbed up the pulpit steps, I thought of the words of the late Archbishop of Canterbury, Temple; "You are only fit to teach the blacks," and yet I had the cheek to hold forth in his Cathedral. After this ordeal was over I was feeling very unhappy. I feared that I must have disappointed those kind friends who had asked me to preach on that special occasion, but two weeks afterwards an old canon stopped me in the street and said he wanted to tell me something.

Last week, he said, he was going round Canterbury Cathedral with a party and when they reached the pulpit one of them asked the verger if they ever had good preachers in the Cathedral. "No!" said he. "They are not up to much, but the preacher here at the end of the Canterbury week was a 'oner', he woke us all up." So I was cheered to know that one man at least had approved of my talk that day and he did not happen to be a "black" man.

There was also one other in the Cathedral that Sunday who approved of my discourse and that was C. S. Hand, headmaster of a school in South Africa. In the year 1876 he was head prefect of Bradfield College and in those days of hell made me forget my troubles, though I only remember him speaking to me once, as he was at the top of the school and I was at the bottom, but I knew him to be a gentleman and the sight of him gave me courage. I did not know that he had been listening to me, but he wrote me a most kind letter of appreciation.

For the third time during my furlough in England I was invited by the headmaster, Rev. Alwyn William, to preach to the boys at Winchester. Staying in the headmaster's house for the week-end were Sir Austen Chamberlain, his wife and daughter, who had come to see their son at the school. At that time Sir Austen's life had been threatened and he had always to be shadowed by a police officer. I thought the detective an exceptionally clever fellow, for although he was continually within range he managed to keep out of sight most skilfully.

The headmaster was taking his house party through the various college garden doors, which were unlocked as we passed from one garden to another, but locked directly we had passed through. When we had arrived in the garden surrounded by high walls we discovered that the police officer had been left on the wrong side of the garden door. We were laughing about it when, all of a sudden, we found he was with us. We had not the slightest idea how he had spirited himself to us, nor did we ask him as he belonged to the secret department of the police.

I had a very happy week-end at Winchester as I have had on former occasions. I always feel that this school lives up to its motto: "Manners makyth man".

I was asked by my old friend the Rev. Colonel W. E. Wingfield to his parish at Bungay in Suffolk. I was to speak at a garden meeting arranged by a mutual friend some ten miles away. Just before starting Wingfield appeared in the costume of a Pathan, telling me that he intended to give them a surprise, as he would pass himself off as my convert. Wingfield had a darkish skin and had lived many years in India and on the North-West Frontier, so that he was able to act his part with great success. The only one in that garden meeting who knew that he was not my convert, was the Rev. Temple Browne, our host, the Rector of the parish in which the meeting was to be held, I fancy he did not feel quite at his ease about this personification.

Wingfield brought with him his guitar and as he knew several Hindustani *bajans*, he gathered the children around him during the interval for tea and within a few minutes they were all joining together in the chorus. That missionary meeting I was told was a great success, until the truth leaked out.

General Sir Baden Powell heard that I was in England and kindly asked me to lunch with him in London and drove me in his car to Gillwell Park, where there were some forty-six scoutmasters under training. There I had the pleasure of meeting Major J. S. Wilson who has been the life and soul of Gillwell for many years.

On our return journey from London Baden Powell said: "As you will be leaving for India shortly, I want you to take this message. It is quite short. It is this: I want quality not quantity." Later on you will hear that I was able to deliver the message. A most important message it was for India, for there the Government of the Provinces give a certain amount of money to help the movement of scouting. Therefore scouting in India, to a great degree, has the smile of the Government upon it. Hence a number of self-seekers take part in this most excellent movement for their own advantage rather than for the good of the youth of India. They think they can please their superior officers by the numbers of scouts they enrol. For the same reason certain missionaries wish to please their Mission Boards by sending in long lists of their converts. The people at home imagine that these "converts" are people striving to follow the life of Jesus Christ. All honest men prefer quality to quantity, whether they be scout or Christians.

CHAPTER EIGHTEEN

Trouble with Shylock

SIR WILLIAM PARKER kindly invited me to Fareham in order to talk to his Hampshire Brotherhood of which he was the President. The meeting in the Wesleyan Chapel on Sunday afternoon had been widely advertised, so there was a crowd of the Brethren gathered together.

At the end of the meeting a down-and-out looking fellow came to speak to me. I found to my surprise that he was an old friend of mine whom I knew at Bradfield when I was a curate there in 1887. He was a farmer, and he and his wife had been very kind to me when I lodged with them in their farmhouse for nine months. His wife had died and he had taken to drink, with the result that he had lost his farm and had become a garden labourer to someone at Fareham. He, poor fellow, broke down and wept. As he held on to me, he said that he had seen my name on a notice-board and had tracked me down to this chapel. I was glad that he found me out, for I was able to hand him over to the Brotherhood, knowing that he would be in the hands of men who are out to help their fellows.

I was invited to Sherborne School and in my address from the pulpit, I told them how a man with one leg had gone out to Kashmir to help in our schools. After the service, one of the masters, Trelawny Ross, said how interested he was in the matter of my one-legged friend having gone to Kashmir to help in the schools, and gave me seventy pounds to buy him a motor-bicycle. I am sure that if Mr. Trelawny Ross could have visited Kashmir and seen the splendid work that Denton Thompson was doing, he would have realized that his most generous gift had not been wasted.

When in March 1926 I reached Kashmir I found Denton Thompson had thrown himself fully into the work of the schools and was doing more work than the ordinary man with two legs. A day or so after my arrival at Srinagar he had driven a motor-car with two of the staff to a place eighteen miles distant in order to pick up a Brahman corpse which he brought to Srinagar for cremation. The corpse belonged to the family of one of the school staff.

A few days later he had taken forty boys to a place twenty-one miles distant for a geological expedition, which meant much climbing among the rocks on the mountain side.

He was a wonderful mountaineer. He would leave his crutches below, then, by making extra use of his arms, he would scramble upwards. He would also plunge into the icy-cold mountain torrents, being a strong swimmer, in spite of having only one leg. The staff and the boys honoured and loved him. So, giving himself full out for others, he found his faith and himself.

The Rev. Colonel W. E. Wingfield often visited us in Kashmir when he was with his battery in India. He took a great interest in our schools and helped us in many ways. He was horrified at the filth in the city of Srinagar and suggested a way of helping members of our school staff to move out of the city into a healthier spot in the suburbs. Within a few months he had collected a few hundred rupees with which to construct the first house outside the city which he hoped would be the beginning of a little colony in a pleasant place by the riverside.

About this time one of my junior teachers came to me in distress. His father had died lately and was in debt to a banker, a friend of the family. The banker was demanding 500 rupees from him at once, and theatened to snatch his garden and house should he fail to pay. The garden was about three acres in extent on the banks of the Doud Ganga river, quite a choice spot, so I asked the junior master if he would allow me to put up a bungalow for any member of the school staff who would be prepared to bring his family from the city to occupy it.

As I had 250 rupees in hand I handed them over to my

WINNERS OF THE INTER-SCHOOLS TOURNAMENT

Gone are the days when bearded students, wrapped in filthy blankets, had to be driven from their class rooms to play games.

teacher and told him to take it to his father's friend the banker and ask him to bear with him until he could pay the whole of the debt. The banker would not accept it and demanded the 500 rupees at once, threatening to seize his house and garden. I wished to prevent that, so I managed to collect another 250 and handed it to my man. He took them to his father's friend but the latter refused it, saying that he did not want the money, he wanted the house and garden.

I then visited the banker myself hoping to persuade him to be reasonable, but no, he was determined to have his pound of flesh. I then visited the chief judge to ask his advice. He told me to send my teacher to his court at twelve o'clock the next day, he would see that the banker was present to receive the money.

Next day in the law courts stood my teacher with the money, but there was no banker there to receive it, the reason being that the two chaprasis sent by the judge to order the banker to be present had pocketed the bribe given to them to go away, and had not delivered the court order. I visited the Chief Judge again and he said: "Send your man to the court with the rupees to-morrow and I will send my own chaprasi to the banker ordering him to be present."

The next day the same thing happened as before, no banker came for the judge's chaprasi had taken the bribe.

Once more I went to the judge, who apologized for having given me so much trouble, and told me to send my master for the third time and he himself would take the 500 rupees and be responsible for their being accepted by the banker.

When this land question had been finally settled and my junior teacher had given me leave to build a bungalow on a portion of it by the riverside, I sent my carpenters to start building. When I came back from school in the afternoon I found the carpenters in my garden. Their clothes were torn and stained with blood and they were weeping. On my asking them what was the matter they told me that they had just commenced to dig the foundations of the house when they were set upon by roughs and

o

driven out of the garden. These roughs had been paid by the banker to beat my carpenters and so prevent the building of the house.

I did not go to the Chief Judge for help this time, but I copied Nehemiah of old who appointed warriors to stand by the workmen who were building the walls of Jerusalem and, like him, I was successful, but my warriors were my school staff who were handy with their fists. The house was built in the garden which the banker had determined to snatch from the son of his old friend.

In the following May the river and canals were in flood after a day or two of heavy rain, and a visitor to Kashmir, Mr. Brierly, his wife and a lady friend, had hired a shikara in which they hoped to see something of the city of Srinagar.

They had been down the river and were returning by the Kuta Kul canal. They had just approached a dangerous spot in the canal, which was a right angle bend close to a bridge. As the boat turned at the right angle it met a very strong stream and in an instant overturned. Unfortunately, it overturned just above a big barge. The strong current swept the boat and all its occupants clean underneath this barge, washing them in all directions.

One of our school teachers, Nand Lal Bakaya, was sitting at the upper window of his house overlooking this particular spot on the canal and saw the accident. Others did so too, and they began to shout and wave their arms according to the usual custom. Not so our teacher; he immediately sprang into the foaming torrent and was soon joined by a mission school boy who was on the bank not far away. These two managed to take the drowning sahibs to their upturned boat where they joined the boatmen who had saved themselves by holding on to their boat. As they were being washed away, the canal boats put out from the shore and brought them to dry land. A tonga was procured for them and they were driven off to their camp some two miles distant.

Next morning the boatmen presented themselves at the sahib's camp and told him that they were the persons who

had saved their lives the day before. Mr. Brierly and the
ladies had been so upset by their prolonged ducking that
they had not noticed who had or had not saved them from
drowning. But being thankful that they had been saved
and wishing to reward somebody, they gave these lying
boatmen 500 rupees. When later Mr. Brierly came to
know who it was who had saved them from a watery grave,
he presented Mr. Nand Lal Bakaya with a watch, on
which was a suitable inscription.

On September 8th, 1926, I was elected Master of the
Masonic Lodge Takhti-Sulalman No. 3043 E.C.

One advantage of joining a lodge in India is that one
meets a good assortment of brethren which I think has
more advantages than disadvantages. I had been a member
of this lodge for over twenty years as I joined soon after
its foundation. Takhti-Sulalman or Throne of Solomon, a
rocky hill close to Srinagar, is a most appropriate name for
a Masonic Lodge.

One day I received an order from the Governor of
Kashmir, who was a Hindu, to visit him at his office.

On my arrival he told me that he had been ordered by
His Highness the Maharajah to ask me if it were true that
I was teaching Christianity in the mission schools. I
looked at him with great surprise, asking him if he did
not know that it was for this very reason that I had left my
own country and come to Kashmir. That it was my hope
that some day all Kashmir would be a Christian country
and that I would not mind seeing him, the Governor of
Kashmir, a Christian if he became a decent one. The
Governor looked a bit stupid, not knowing what to say
next, so, as he happened to be second in command of the
scouts in Kashmir next to the Maharajah, who was *Chief
Scout*, I told him that General Sir Baden Powell had asked
me to pass on his message about "quality not quantity",
which meant that he preferred a few true scouts to hundreds of worthless ones. The Governor turned round to
the officer sitting next to him on the dais, and asked him
who this gentleman was whom I had just named. The

officer answered: "Don't you know that he is the fellow who started scouts?"

There before me sat on the dais the Governor of Kashmir who was second in command of scouts and yet he did not know who Baden Powell was. So even Governors have something to learn.

In April 1927 the Viceroy, Lord Irwin, and his lady, with Sir John Maffy his secretary, and Lord and Lady Iveagh arrived in Kashmir. They came up the river through the city in the state barge with His Highness Sir Raja Hari Singh, his great officials and the Resident, Sir John Wood, and British officials. As the state barge passed our school we gave our usual salute and the same "Welcome" that we had given to Lord Reading.

Later on the Viceregal party did us the honour of visiting our school where we gave them our usual athletic show. Lord Irwin and party cheered us up much by their visit.

Extract from *Courts and Camps in India* by Yvonne Fitzroy:

"Concerning H.E. the Viceroy's tours in Native States. ". . . no mention of Srinagar but must include the name of the missionary who for the last thirty years has dedicated his life to the education of young Kashmir, and has fought every conceivable prejudice as well as the slackness and cruelty which seem the birthright of its people. His success is a matter of history, his boys are athletic and courageous, and I was specially struck by one tiny creature who was presented to the Viceroy as having won the year's prize for the kindest action to an animal. This midget— he was really about three feet high—had pulled a bone out of a pariah dog's throat, an action which demanded a stout heart, not only a kind one, and little short of miraculous, coming from small Oriental hands to a beast, and an outcast beast at that. And how it proclaims the power of personal influence in this country."

Mr. Shanker Koul, our school staff, and certain old boys, had been anxious for some time to have the marriage

age raised in Kashmir, as so much suffering was continually being caused through young girls being married to elderly men.

Fortunately, we had in Srinagar at this time an Englishman named Mr. G. E. C. Wakefield, who had been appointed by His Highness to help in state matters. He was a strong and kind-hearted man and had full sympathy with our desire to see the marriage age raised. So he kindly sponsored the deputation that went from our school to see His Highness with the result that their request was granted, up to a certain point. The marriage age of girls was raised to fourteen. We were thankful for small mercies, but we certainly were not satisfied, as no true man could be satisfied with such a law.

Unfortunately, girls continued to be married under the age of fourteen, contrary to the law, and we found it very difficult to stop this because, as the law stood, no one could be prosecuted until they had broken the law, i.e. after the girl of tender age had been married, and punishment could only come when the little girl had been victimized.

We were able, however, to save one girl who had not attained the required age, from being married. On arrival at the school one morning I was told that a girl of twelve was about to be married to a man of forty. So I sent one of my staff off at once to the city magistrate, asking him to stop the marriage. His answer was that he was sorry, but he could not stop it nor could he punish anyone, as no law had been broken. I sent off to the police officer asking him if he could prevent the marriage and he sent back the same answer as the city magistrate, that as no law had been broken no one could be punished. I then asked if any of the police officers in this part of the city had been a student of ours. To my joy I was told that one of them was, so I at once asked his help. He said he could not help us lawfully, but that he would do his best to put the fear of God into the scoundrel. In this he was successful, with the result that the little girl was saved from great pain and misery, and possible death.

Although I have been in this country for such a long time, I have never yet discovered why it is that Indians have so little sympathy for their women and girls. I fancy it is that their love of money is greater than their natural affection. A girl is worth so many rupees.

Major H. W. Hogg was invited by the Maharajah to come to Kashmir to get the Kashmir boys to become boy scouts. Major Hogg had been successful in the scout movement in the Punjab and he wanted a great jamboree to be held on a maidan near the city of Srinagar. He asked me to build a small gun-boat which was to be supported on hidden bicycles. This gun-boat was armed with guns which were to attack forts made of inflammable material. These would be set on fire by direct shooting from the gun-boat. This was the set piece which was carried out according to plan.

Major Hogg asked the Inspector of Schools if he would kindly arrange for the Government school band to play the royal salute when His Highness the Maharajah arrived on the field. So the Inspector ordered the Government school bandmaster to do this. The bandmaster asked what the royal salute was, as his band did not know it. So Major Hogg asked me if the C.M.S. band could play it. I answered "Certainly", for our band played it every day at twelve o'clock, before we began our gymnastics. But when the Inspector heard this he said that our band must not, the Government school band must play it. Again he was told that they couldn't. As the Inspector seemed much upset, Major Hogg asked me if I would agree to allow the Government school band to stand in front, holding their musical instruments to their mouths, while the C.M.S. school band stood behind and played the tune. I answered that we should be delighted. So, when His Highness entered the ground the Government school band marched proudly to the front, with their musical instruments to their mouths, whilst the mission school band played the royal salute in the rear.

Soon after this great jamboree my wife and I left Kashmir to visit our son Harold and his family in Burma. He was at this time stationed at Shwebo. We enjoyed every minute of our time in that delightful country, in the winter season. The dawns and the sunsets were a great delight.

Harold took me for a trip in his forests and we stayed for the night at different forest bungalows. He and I rode ponies, our tent equipage being carried on five elephants. What specially delighted me was watching elephants at work in the teak forests, as they pushed, lifted and dragged in a most successful manner, using their trunks, tusks and foreheads, seeming to know when to use the various parts of their heads, to deal with the heavy loads.

On our return journey we were most kindly entertained by the Metropolitan, the Rt. Rev. Foss Westcott, at Calcutta, who delights to have his house full of guests.

Then at Palwal, near Delhi, Mr. F. L. Brayne was holding his huge "uplift" gathering and had erected quite a small town of huts, booths and tents. Mr. Brayne is an indefatigable worker and has been most successful in waking up the villagers in the Punjab to a healthier life in every respect. We just revelled in seeing this truly great man at his work.

We had only just returned from our visit to Burma in time to see the preparations being made by the Kashmir state to receive Sir Harcourt Butler and the Indian State Commission delegates. Amongst the preparations for their reception there was to be a great scout rally.

The headmaster of the Government High School at this time happened to be a friend of mine and he told me the following story. He received a telephone message from the Prime Minister that Sir Harcourt Butler was much interested in scouts and therefore there must be over one thousand scouts ready within three weeks to welcome Sir Harcourt Butler and the Commission. He was to order all his school staff to become scoutmasters, and all his students to become scouts, without delay.

When the headmaster told his staff that they were to be scoutmasters they asked him how much extra money they would receive, when he told them that their pay would not be increased, they all refused to take on this extra work. When the boys were ordered to become scouts, they also refused. So the headmaster phoned up to the

Prime Minister to say that none of his staff was willing to become scoutmasters nor his boys to be scouts. The answer that came back over the phone from the Prime Minister was quite short. "If your school staff are not ready to be scoutmasters at once and your boys to become scouts, you will be relieved of your headmastership." So the headmaster ordered his staff to become scoutmasters, under penalty of dismissal, and the boys were told that they would not be allowed to enter for the Punjab public examinations unless they had become boy scouts. This order had the desired effect. All the staff became scoutmasters and all the boys became scouts that day.

A meeting was called at the palace at which all the heads of departments had to be present. I also had the honour of being invited.

The educational official was in the chair and he started off by telling us that within three weeks Sir Harcourt Butler and the Commission would be in Srinagar and there must be at least one thousand scouts to welcome him, and therefore within three days the scout troops must be ready with their scoutmasters to practise drilling and other scout activities. I said that it was impossible to have one thousand scouts with scoutmasters within three days. The educational official answered that there were many tailors in Srinagar and he felt quite certain that the necessary number of scout uniforms could be made in that time. I agreed that it was possible to make the uniforms, but clothes and badges did not make scouts.

However, the educational official answered that all that mattered was the proper clothing. So, on the great day, when Sir Harcourt Butler and the Commission were marching down the parade ground between the serried lines of Kashmir boys they saw them dressed in scout uniforms. In front of the boys were heaps, every ten yards, of articles of Kashmiri workmanship, papier mâché, embroidered clothes, carved boxes, and products of all the various arts of Kashmir. Sir Harcourt Butler was told that the scouts had made them. They had, in fact, all been brought from the Technical School.

Six weeks later a copy of *The Times* was sent to me from

England containing a long article stating that the Kashmiri scouts were the best in India, for no other scouts could make such beautiful artistic work as they had.

A week later I heard from General Baden Powell, who congratulated me on the scouts of Kashmir. I, of course, wrote back to my old friend to prevent *him* at least from being fooled.

I went to see my friend, Colonel Hugo, the Chief Medical Officer of Kashmir, to talk over this scout business and all the tomfoolery. He said: "I have had my share of it, for I received orders to dress up my hospital assistants as scouts, so that when Sir Harcourt Butler and the Commission visited the state hospital, scouts would be seen standing by the beds of the patients with pen, ink and paper, writing letters for the poor sick people to their friends who could not read in their villages. But", said Colonel Hugo, "I, of course, ignored the order." I asked him if he thought Sir Harcourt Butler would be taken in by all this eyewash. He answered: "Sir Harcourt is no fool."

I could write much more of the comic opera displays arranged for Sir Harcourt Butler and his Commission, but will finish with this last scene.

I had been asked to attend an official scout meeting. When all business was finished, I asked if I might be allowed to speak. My request was granted, and my speech was short. It was to this effect. "I wish to protest against the deceit that was practised by all those that were connected with the scout movement in Kashmir. When Sir Harcourt Butler visited this country, it was a disgrace to the Kashmir educational department. It was a disgrace to all the right-minded people in Kashmir, and it was a disgrace to General Baden Powell, the founder of scouts."

I sat down amid dead silence and the committee meeting ended abruptly. I need hardly say I have never been invited from that day to this to attend another meeting.

On November 8th, 1928, my wife, Eric, Frances and I motored from Kashmir to Jhelum, about three hundred miles distant, to the house of our old friends, Col. and

Mrs. Underhill, who had very kindly arranged to receive us for Eric's marriage with Phyllis Long, who was arriving from England that week. As the church at Jhelum was under repair and had no roof, the marriage took place in the Presbyterian church. It was one of the quietest weddings at which I had ever officiated.

Eric and Phil desired a quiet wedding, their desires were certainly fulfilled for there were not more than half a dozen persons present.

The bride and bridegroom had met one another at Wanganui, New Zealand, where one was teaching in a boys' school and the other at a girls' school.

CHAPTER NINETEEN

The Murder of Chimed

ON May 1st, 1929, our son Julian with his wife Yvonne and their little girl Renée arrived from Tanganyika, East Africa.

They attended the weekly school regatta on the Dal Lake and Julian swam across that part of the lake, a distance of nearly one mile. He had already done so when only seven. From the day Julian swam that distance at such an early age, I have always held this feat up to the Kashmiri boys, asking them if they could beat that record, but no Kashmiri boy of seven has yet succeeded, although a few have nearly done so.

When Julian was at school in England, aged twelve, he sent me ten shillings of his pocket money as a gift to the Kashmir schools. With that money I had a wooden fish made with a silver head, and that has been the school trophy for the best swimmer of the year.

One day in June I had a letter from an old pupil, Chimed Gergan, an officer in the Forestry Department and only a week later came a telegram from his father: "Chimed murdered, find murderers."

The story of these two is remarkable. In 1880 a Tibetan monk lay dying in Lesser Tibet. He sent a message to a Moravian missionary fifty miles away in Leh, asking him to come. He answered the S.O.S. immediately, crossing an 18,000 feet pass. On arrival the monk said he had heard him telling about Christ, that he believed that his teaching was true and he wanted to entrust his son to him so that he might become a real Christian. The monk died and the missionary brought the boy home, baptizing him as Yusuf.

Typhoid broke out and two missionaries, a doctor and

a padre, died after being nursed by their wives, Yusuf, and another Christian boy. The two widows, their children, and the two Christian Tibetans travelled two hundred miles to Srinagar and Yusuf was handed to me and became my first boarder at the mission school.

Yusuf was a quiet, shy youth, dressed in picturesque Tibetan costume, a prettily ornamented cap with ear flaps, a long dressing-gown like garment, held together with a broad red sash, and thick felt boots. He was the only Christian pupil bar one amongst about one hundred Brahmans. Going to school he had to walk two miles from his quarters to the school.

It was reported to me that the Brahman boys were giving him a rough time on his walk from school, abusing him and pelting him with mud and stones. Yusuf walked steadily on, ignoring their insults and never told me. I told him how sorry I was about this, but, although I could soon have stopped the cowards, I thought it better for Yusuf that he should himself deal with them.

I gave him two boxing lessons daily, and marked a circle on his bedroom wall, with a spot in the centre. He had to practise every night before going to bed, stepping out with his left foot, toes straight to the front, hitting straight from the shoulder at the spot in the centre, as I myself had been taught at Bradfield. After a month's intensive training Yusuf was ready for the fray and I gave him my blessing. As usual, as he left school next day, the mob of cowards started their insults, but not for long. As the leader of the gang came near, Yusuf followed my instructions to the letter. He sent his left straight from the shoulder into his opponent's wind-bag which brought down the tall boy's face and the next blow was given on the jaw. There was no need for more, the bully had had the shock of his life and his followers melted away. That ended Yusuf's trouble and gained him the respect of his fellows.

Yusuf passed up through various classes, and was a hard worker in school and a plucky boy at all sports. Now the time came for him to return to his own country and as he would be the only Western educated boy, several lines of service were open to him. I asked him what he would like to choose. He could be a policeman, or revenue officer and would then become a man of power and riches. He answered: "I do not want riches or power. All I desire is to return to Ladakh and teach my people about Jesus Christ."

So Yusuf returned to Ladakh and was accepted by the Moravian missionaries and posted as a master in their mission school. He and another were ordained padres. They were the first Ladakhi ordained ministers. Later he took up the difficult task of translating the Bible into Tibetan. When at that long and difficult task he wrote me a letter saying: "I am writing in my house at midday by the light of a candle as my house is under the snow. When I wish to take exercise I have to get out by a hole in the roof in order to reach the surface of the snow and go for a walk." Not only was he a pastor and a translator of the Bible but he actually ploughed his fields with his yoke of oxen.

Some years later, he sent to his old school at Srinagar his son Chimed, aged twelve, and he too became a good boxer and did well as an all-round boy at school. Subsequently, he entered the Revenue Department and was appointed Naib-Tehsildar at Budgam district, where lived one of our school staff, Bhagwan Dass, a man of fine character. Unfortunately, honesty is not one of the virtues practised in Kashmir and every official is expected to accept bribes. But Chimed, like his father, was of a different breed and, because he refused to do as others did, the people of his town boycotted him. If it had not been for Bhagwan Dass he would have been starved out. Chimed never gave in and was a man marked for no promotion.

But the unexpected happened. In Kashmir there is a valuable plant called kuth which grows on the mountains at about 12,000 feet, and is in much demand for making joss sticks for the temples in China, and for Mr. Keating's insect powder. In Kashmir it is worth about one rupee per coolie load, but in the outside market, about ten rupees, so this encourages thieves to raid the mountains for it. As it is a Kashmir Government monopoly, the Forestry Department requires brave men to guard it and to fight the thieves, who are wild and savage frontier men, armed with rifles and knives. I was asked by Captain Sam Steane, Assistant Conservator of Forests, if I could supply him with two brave men who would be willing to do this. I asked Chimed and one of my school staff, both of whom had proved themselves energetic and brave men, if they were ready to face these armed rascals. They answered "Yes". They were accepted and sent off to the mountains about two hundred miles from Srinagar.

About a year later Chimed captured a party of five armed robbers with their pony loads of kuth, marched them safely down the valley, and handed them over to the official of that province. This official, however, accepted their handsome bribe and set them free. I received a letter from Chimed telling me of this, adding that he was now returning to his post of duty and would most surely be killed by them. He also said that this was the last letter he would write to me, so wished to thank me for all I had done for him when he was a boy at my school, for we should not meet again on this earth. The week following I received the telegram already quoted.

I at once reported this murder to the Kashmir officials and asked them to catch the murderers. But they were not in the least interested. So I wrote to the political secretary of the Government of India. I received a reply by return of post expressing his desire to help. Some months later the Kashmir state sent police to investigate but they did nothing except loot the villagers in the area where the murder had been committed.

A year later the police were sent again and fortunately one of our old students was the officer in charge. He did not permit his constables to loot and *wished* to catch the murderers. He told me that when Chimed returned to duty he found, near a village, a party of thirty-six robbers with several thousand rupees of loot, packed on ponies. With the help of the villagers, he captured them, and placed them under guard. That night Chimed's servant, who had accepted a bribe of five hundred rupees, told him that the robbers offered to give him (Chimed) one thousand rupees if he would let them escape. If not, they would

kill him. Chimed refused the bribe and sent back an answer
that he certainly would not allow them to escape.

Next day he arranged the caravan, secured the robbers
and set off on his march to the political headquarters. After
some miles they came to a dangerous part of the road cut
out of rock, with a precipice on one side. All of a sudden
rocks came bounding from the heights above them and
immediately he and his party were attacked by another
band of robbers who shot his servant. Then he was shot
from his horse with seven bullets through his body. The
robbers threw both corpses over the precipice.

Thus died Chimed, preferring death to dishonour.

The police officer told me that he had traced three of the
murderers out of Kashmir to a native state where one had
been hanged, another imprisoned but the third had made
his escape.

At this time a Bengali gentleman had been appointed
Director of Education in Kashmir. He sent me notice that
he would inspect the C.M.S. school on a certain day.

Eric and I went down to the school in the motor launch
to greet him. Unfortunately, a heavy shower of rain came
on, which affected the carburettor, and put the engine out
of order, so we arrived at the school about ten minutes
late. Our headmaster had received the Inspector in our
stead and took him to the school hall. On the walls were
fixed our honour boards but he was busy examining the
boys in English. When our headmaster thought that it
was about time to draw his attention to the honour boards
on the wall, he asked him if he would not like to see the
names of those boys who had risked their lives for others.
He said he would not, as he preferred examining the boys
in English.

When I arrived I found him rather cross, because I had
not been present to receive him at the school, although I
apologized and told him the cause. I took him to my study.
To enter it he had to pass under a low door over which
was written "humility", so he had to bend low to enter. I
do not think he liked it.

I asked him if he would like to look at our "character

form" books. I told him that there was a page for every
boy in the school showing the marks gained for body,
mind and soul, and that we were out for "Character building". To my surprise he asked: "What is character building?" I said we were trying to make men out of these boys.
"Is it done at other schools?" said he. I said I did not
know, but that it was done in this school. Then he said: "I
do not want to hear about it, I will go away." I said: "You
have not yet seen the boys at gymnastics; they are ready
to come down from their classrooms and from the roof
in twenty-five seconds." He answered: "I do not wish to
see them. This is a very bad school and I will go away."
He left and a few days afterwards he wrote to say that he
had cut the school grant by five thousand rupees as it was
a bad school.

A week or so later a great flood was expected, so our
staff and boys were busy getting their boats ready for
rescue work. It was pouring in torrents. At a certain spot
about forty masters and boys were hauling the twelve-
oared cutter over a twenty-five-foot embankment when
the Maharajah and some army officers were passing. He
asked me what we were doing. We told him that we were
getting our boats ready for rescue work. He said it was
very good work and passed on.

When the scare of the flood was over, the Maharajah
called a meeting of all his chief officers of state and
said: "During the preparations for the flood I was out
with my military officers both night and day watching
these preparations. Wherever I went I found the mission
school boys hard at work, but my Government school boys
were conspicuous by their absence. Therefore I command
that my educational officers and headmasters shall go to
the mission school to learn what true education means."
Next day we had a visit from the Government education-
alists to whom we showed our character form books, &c.
But the Director of Education himself did not obey the
orders of His Highness to visit our school and learn our
system of education.

Fortunately for the good of education in Kashmir, His
Highness made a change. The Bengali gentleman returned

to his home in Bengal and Mr. MacDermott, who had been the Principal of the Government College, was, to our great joy, appointed instead. He was a true educationist and a MAN, and at once restored to us the five thousand rupees. While Mr. MacDermott remained Director, many crying evils were swept away and he did his best to teach his junior officers the meaning of education.

When I visited the C.M.S. school at Islamabad, which is thirty-four miles from Srinagar, I was told the following sad story by the headmaster.

A certain Gujar woman who lived at a village named Aish Makam, seventeen miles from Islamabad, was in trouble as she had lost her buffalo. The police were sent to her house to inquire how the buffalo had died. There is always a good deal of money to be made if any of the cow tribe die owing to the chance of working up a case of "cow killing". Evidently the poor woman did not satisfy the police, as she was ordered to appear before the law courts in Islamabad.

She was kept walking between Islamabad and her village for some weeks and then the case was removed to Srinagar, a distance of fifty-one miles from her home. This long journey she had to accomplish on foot, as she was poor and could not pay for transport. By the time this story was told to me she had walked 1,600 miles to and from the courts. The school staff was so sorry for her that they always paid her lorry fare to and from Srinagar.

I, of course, began to move in the matter. I first of all visited the law court to see the Judge, but he had no sympathy for the woman. I then told a high police officer, but he seemed to think it a joke. I thought to myself how splendid it would be to see him change places with the old woman. I then visited the Governor of Kashmir and he promised to help, but it was not until I found a police officer who was one of our old students that, finally, the poor Gujar woman's persecution ceased.

Then my old friend Sam Steane was again in trouble. In carrying out his duties he had discovered more forest

P

officers looting the state. These rascals had a friend at
court who poisoned the ears of the Maharajah. So Sam
Steane was served with an order to leave Kashmir within
a fortnight.

I was not successful this time in finding any British
official able to help him. But fortunately General Sir William Birdwood was again visiting Kashmir, so I went to
him to ask his help as I knew him to be a sportsman and a
MAN.

After hearing my story he said: "Biscoe, of course I
should like to help your friend but I have nothing to do
with Kashmir." I agreed, but asked whether, with his
great name in Australia, he would be prepared to write to
his friends out there and ask them to find a suitable job
for Sam Steane. He said: "Certainly, I will write at once
to the Government of Australia and pass on your suggestion and will let you know when I receive the answer."

After about two months the General placed a letter in
my hands. It was the offer of the Conservatorship of
Tasmania to Sam Steane. Our joy for his sake was mixed
with regret for the great loss his departure would mean to
Kashmir.

Next it was my turn to get into trouble but, fortunately,
only in a small way. My sister-in-law, Helen Burges, who
lived in a little cottage in our compound, put up a wooden
shed in which to do her carpentry. She was a very busy
lady, never giving her fingers any rest and thereby bringing in rupees to our school funds which, long ago, reached
four figures.

A few days after the erection of the wooden shed I
received a letter from the Public Works Officer, saying
that he had heard I had built a house in my garden without permission and that I must therefore pull it down at
once. I did not answer the letter but called my carpenter
and ordered him to fix six wheels to the hut.

I then visited the Public Works Officer to ask him if
there was any objection to my having wheeled vehicles in
my garden. He said: "Certainly not." I told him that the
building to which he objected was on wheels and I should
like him to see it. He said that of course there was no

objection to my hut on wheels, so it remained in my garden.

On November 7th, 1930, we left for England. From Bombay we sailed for Venice in the S.S. *Pilsna* of the Austrian Lloyd Company. This ship actually landed us at the house of my cousin, Walter Roop Tyndale, who was standing on the steps of his house in Venice as we looked down upon him from the top deck.

We spent some happy days with him as he showed us the beauties of Venice. From there we took train to Bordighera where we spent the winter. One of our friends on board the S.S. *Pilsna* came to our pension, a delightful police officer named Arthur Warburton, who told us the following most interesting story of his grandfather.

Lieutenant Warburton, R.A., was with the British Army at Kabul, and while there he somehow or other got in touch with one of the Amir's daughters, who was married and had a baby boy. They fell in love with each other and she begged him to take her away with him to India. This is how he managed it.

One Friday, as she was carried in her palanquin to the mosque, he sent a party of his men to waylay her; she had with her the baby boy and an ayah. They were all three brought to the British camp and hidden. The kahars on their return to the Palace reported the matter. In a short time some Afghan officers visited the General commanding to demand the return of the princess. The General, not being in this plot, would not believe their story, so they asked him if he would allow them to search his camp. He said "Certainly". They soon returned with their soldiers and searched the British camp, but without success. That was not surprising, for Warburton had disguised his princess in the uniform of a British subaltern. When the General commanded all the officers to be paraded before the Afghan search party the princess was standing in line with the rest of them.

After the search party had left the camp the General called for Warburton. The story does not relate what frame of mind the General was in when Warburton faced him, but he ordered him to leave Kabul at once. This he did with his princess, her baby and the ayah, and they all reached India in safety and lived there happily for many years. The Afghan baby grew up and became Warburton the famous police officer in the Punjab. He had several children and our friend Arthur was the youngest of them.

While we were at Bordighera we went over to Monte Carlo to see our old friends, Cecil and Mrs. Hadow, who had taken up their abode there, also my cousin, Canon Tupper Carey, who was chaplain at Monte Carlo. He and his charming wife were there carrying on a most useful, though difficult work, among the visitors.

I discovered that an old school friend of mine was also living there. We had not met since we were boys at Bradfield together in 1880. After knocking at the door of his flat a stout white-haired old gentleman opened the door, and the greeting I received was this: "You are that young Biscoe I knew at Bradfield! I always remember you on account of your cavern of a mouth, for I can never forget how you opened it when you were singing in the choir in church." He spoke the truth for our music master rightly insisted on his choir boys opening their mouths wide.

While in Italy I noticed that certain changes had taken place since my last visit. An important one was that one could travel by train without having one's luggage stolen, and people were kept very much in order by the police, who were everywhere in evidence. The fear of Mussolini had fallen upon them. No one dared to speak of him in public unless it were to praise him. Even foreign visitors had to be careful. A certain lady who was talking inadvisedly about him in a railway carriage, soon found herself in prison.

When we reached London I visited Sir Walter Lawrence. He told me that a Maharajah, who had been dining with him the night before, had asked him to persuade the Indian Government to do away with British Residents from the native states as they were expensive and the Rajas could manage their states without any help. Sir Walter Lawrence answered: "Let me tell you a piece of ancient history. Long before you were born I was in Jammu with your father when his Kashmiri troops meant to kill him. What did he do? He went for help to the British Resident, and what did the Resident do? He wired to the British military station (Sialkot) with the result that at once a regiment of cavalry galloped to the danger spot and saved your father's life. History may repeat itself. So I advise you not to ask for the removal of British Residents."

Later you will see that Sir William Lawrence was no mean prophet.

"Now listen to me," continued Sir Walter Lawrence, "there are three chief sins into which Rajas are apt to fall, love of vengeance, love of money and love of self, and the worst of these three is love of self, and that, Raja Sahib, is your sin, for if you love yourself you cannot love your people."

Ere long I found myself again on deputation work for the C.M.S. and, in order to get about the country more comfortably, I purchased a car and my daughter Frances acted as my chauffeur. Our first journey was from Exmouth to Liverpool, where we were entertained by the Rev. Bob Howard and his wife. At Liverpool College Bob Howard had always taken an interest in our schools and his boys adopted our schools as their special missionary interest. They sent us, yearly, the generous gift of twenty pounds.

Amongst the many schools and colleges I visited were Bradfield, my old school, and Jesus College, Cambridge, where I always received a very warm welcome. The headmaster of Bradfield was Eric Whitworth. Both he and his wife gave us a very happy time. The headmaster's house had been built in a copse just outside the college gate. This copse had been a great joy to me and my friends in the days of "hell" for we had constructed a tiny hut of branches in which we kept some food. Directly school was over we would escape out of the classroom *with* our master, before the bullies could catch us, and slip away to the copse singly, and never the same way, so that we should not make a trodden path and our hut be discovered; in fact we copied the ways of foxes.

We remained in our secret lair until the school bell summoned us back to work. Our hut was never discovered. This was the only spot where we had peace. Whitworth was very much interested to hear that his house was on the site of our lair.

At Jesus College, besides preaching in the college chapel, I was asked to address the rowing men in the college hall, where I felt thoroughly at home and imagined myself back at college again.

At Westminster School, also, the headmaster was kind, he said I need not climb into the pulpit but could stand or walk about in the main aisle while talking to the boys. This service was held in Westminster Abbey so I had plenty of room, and I felt at my ease, not being boxed up in a pulpit. The headmaster, the Rev. Costley-White, took me all over the school. There were two objects that specially interested me, one was an oil painting hung in the school hall, of the headmaster of Westminster during "the great fire of London". He had taken out his boys to fight the flames to save property. This, I felt, made an interesting link between Westminster School and the C.M.S. school in Srinagar.

The second object which roused any interest was the birch which lay on a table in the hall. The headmaster, to my surprise, told me that it was never used for giving a birching, but instead, the boy who deserved to be birched was called up before the assembled school. The headmaster then took up the birch and laid it on his hand. This was considered a very great disgrace. I had never heard of this being done in any school before and I must say that I think that, in most cases, this form of punishment would be very effective.

I was invited to Ireland again by my old friend Bishop Godfrey Day, and preached in many places. I preached at one church at Carlo where there were three times as many men as women in the congregation, which I should imagine to be almost unique.

CHAPTER TWENTY

Communal Riots

ON our return to India in 1931 we motored through the city where that Raja lived who was saved by British cavalry fifty years previously.

On arrival we found the streets littered with bricks, stones and broken furniture showing that severe rioting had been in progress. Furthermore, *British* soldiers were picketing the streets, so Sir Walter Lawrence's prophecy had come true sooner than any of us expected.

Trouble broke out in various towns in Kashmir where martial law was proclaimed and rioters shot. Trouble soon began in Srinagar and our schools were affected because the Government college and schools were empty, whereas our boys remained loyal to us. Their loyalty made the others angry and they picketed our schools to prevent our teachers and boys entering. So I ordered our boys to come by boat. The rioters did not expect this and were unable to prevent it. Then I gave orders, secretly, that the school next day would be held in my garden. The picketers went as usual to our school in the city only to find it empty, whilst our boys were comfortably doing their work in our garden.

Next day our boys were doing their lessons in Major Hadow's garden, outside the city, while the picketers came to our garden expecting to carry on their tomfoolery there. The next day our boys were back in their school again.

The following day when Eric arrived near our school, he found the street littered with recumbent figures, which is one of the ways used in India for blocking the streets. He pretended that they were lying there on account of illness, and in sympathy kneeled by the side of them and grasped the wrist of "the poor sick man", took out his watch and felt his pulse. The result of his chaff was instantaneous. Seeing that they were being fooled they got up one by one and departed, with the result that the masters and boys who had been held up by the liers-down were able to enter the school.

A similar game was played upon those blocking a street in a town in India. A young British policeman, hearing that there was trouble in a certain street, went to the spot where would-be travellers were held up by some young women lying on their backs, whom no one had been able to remove. He noticed that there was a space between two of them so he himself quickly lay down beside them, with the result that all of them immediately jumped up and ran away.

On June 26th, 1932, Miss Elizabeth Newman, to our great grief, passed from us. She had come to Kashmir in the year 1888 with the first lady doctor to Kashmir, Miss Fanny Butler. As there was no hospital for women in Kashmir in those days, they tried to minister to the sick women in the city, but only three houses would let them in. One of the excuses for exclusion was that, as they were unmarried they could not be good women. But they were able to enter some of the boats on the river where the women lived in squalor in the little cabin in the stern. On returning home from these visits they had to have a bath and change all their clothes to rid themselves of the "creepy crawlies".

The lady doctor within two years succumbed to typhoid. Miss Newman carried on and gradually won her way by her life of unstinted service. She saw the great need for a hospital for women. So, in her spare time, she continued for many years writing to her friends in England, obtained about a lac of rupees, and joyfully succeeded in getting it built. I have written a short account of her life entitled *Florence Nightingale of Kashmir*.

Communal riots broke out in Srinagar in September. Hindus killed Mohammedans in the name of Shiva and Rama, and Mohammedans did the same in the name of Allah. The riots began from a very small spark.

The Inspector of Schools arranged for a procession of

scouts. Our headmaster, Shanker Koul, tried to prevent this, for he was well aware that the city was in a highly disturbed state. During this procession the Hindu scouts of the state school insulted some Mohammedans. This set the city in a blaze.

Our mission school boys had just finished playing their usual games and the masters were going to their homes in the city. Hearing that the city was in a turmoil, I offered to take them down the river in my launch, but they felt quite certain that they would be safe. I doubted this and decided to accompany them. We had hardly gone half a mile when we found ourselves in the midst of the battle. They were stoning and clubbing one another. It was a very bloody affair and the Mohammedans were getting the better of it.

My teachers were at once attacked and I do not know why they were not killed. I myself was not attacked until I was trying to get them into a house which was shut against us, we had to turn our backs to the wall and face the mob with our fists. One of my teachers was left for dead underneath a shop. Eric and an old schoolboy turned up unexpectedly in the midst of the row and I asked them to fetch the police. When the police arrived the Mohammedans assaulted them with their clubs. They thereupon took to flight, and ran like hares down the gullies and anywhere to escape the clubbing.

I managed at last to get my wounded men into a house and gave them first aid. When it was dark, I guided them secretly through the narrow lanes to the canal to put them in boats. But the boatmen, being Mohammedan, refused to take them, as my lot were Hindus, but I got them at last to the state hospital.

I myself had a remarkable escape. I had only my fists against clubs, when an old grey-bearded Mohammedan rushed from somewhere and took the blows intended for me. Later I was able to get recognition from the Kashmir Government for this brave old Mohammedan.

For the next few days my launch came in very useful by carrying the wounded to the hospitals. As my launch proceeded up the river with the wounded men, we had to run the gauntlet. When I carried Mohammedan wounded, the Hindus threw stones at us, and when the patients were Hindus, then the Mohammedans threw the stones. I then carried Hindu and Mohammedan wounded at the same time, and had wire netting put as an awning over our heads, so that if anyone dropped stones from the bridges we should remain unhurt.

News reached us that the Mohammedans were attacking the Hindu women, so Eric and I hired a lorry and after dark rescued a Hindu family being besieged by Mohammedans, bringing them to our garden, where we housed them over the stables. They remained there until the city was quiet once more. I do not know how many people were killed but 400 were admitted to the hospitals.

An instance of gallantry in that riot occurred when one of our staff, Neranjan Nath, who was being clubbed and blood was pouring from his wounds, saw one of our scouts, a boy of twelve, being clubbed, while he lay on the ground. Neranjan Nath rushed to save him and bent over his body, thus receiving fresh blows on his shoulders and back, until I was able to go to his help. Why he was not killed was a miracle!

At this time the college students and all the schools, except the C.M.S. school, were on strike. Strikers invaded the Government offices and the law courts, destroyed papers and did other damage and generally enjoyed themselves.

Eric and I had been called by the Prime Minister to hear the order from His Highness that no schoolboys were to be punished. We naturally were astonished at this order, when all authority had vanished. But something had to be done to preserve discipline. When Eric arrived at the school, a boy refused to obey his order, so as he was not allowed to punish him himself, he sent for the boy's father and persuaded him to come to the school and give his son a sound thrashing before the whole school! By this means the C.M.S. boys learnt that in the mission school authority had not gone to pieces.

I left Kashmir for Lahore in order to be present at the

Cathedral on November 1st, when George Dunsford
Barne was consecrated Bishop of Lahore by the Metro-
politan, the Most Rev. Foss Westcott, assisted by the
Bishops of Bombay, Lucknow and Nagpur.

At a garden party in the Close that afternoon, Bishop
Barne asked me to accept a canonry. I felt honoured that
he should offer me such a dignified position, but was reluc-
tant to accept it, as I did not consider myself fitted to be a
canon. However, as many friends stressed that this
honour would be helpful to our Kashmir schools, I
accepted it gratefully.

The first act of our Bishop was to attend the Church
and Mission Central Council meeting. The Bishop was
in the chair and he said: "Before we begin business I will
ask the secretary to read out the minute recorded at the
last meeting of this committee concerning the Kashmir
schools." After it had been read out, the Bishop suggested
that the minute should be deleted before commencing the
business of the day, and this was agreed to. That minute
was to the effect that the C.M.S. schools were not truly
mission schools because there were so few Christian
masters, therefore they did not deserve the help they had
received formerly.

A month or two previously I had received a letter from
the secretary ordering me to close the Islamabad school as
it lacked a Christian staff. As soon as I had read the letter
a picture came into my mind of Lord Nelson at the battle
of Copenhagen, when he received an order of which he did
not approve. I did not possess a blind eye or a telescope,
but there was a waste-paper basket conveniently at my feet.

I do not know who had told our Bishop of the desire of
certain missionaries to see the C.M.S. schools in Kashmir
closed down. His action was naturally a great surprise and
comfort to me, and to all those who were working in
Kashmir for the extension of Christ's kingdom. I never
discovered the reason for Christian workers wishing to
close our schools, but I fancy it was because there were in
the Punjab a number of young men, some of them B.A.s
and M.A.s, who could not find employment and they
naturally expected their missionary friends to secure jobs

for them. I had had, in the past, unfortunate experiences with those Indian Christians sent up from the Punjab to be masters in our schools, so I preferred to have as masters those who were Christian-hearted rather than those bearing only a Christian name. In the same way I had always preferred to employ men of character rather than those who were merely graduates from the Punjab, and who, incidentally, expected double the wages of our Kashmiri teachers, with extras for lodging and firewood.

On February 3rd, 1933, we had the great pleasure of welcoming Mr. Fred Jacob on our school staff. When at Cambridge, he played rugger for England for several years. While at the Varsity he also became a Sunday school teacher. Some other undergraduates did not think it proper that such an athlete should undertake Christian work. So one day when Fred Jacob was not in his rooms they went there to smash his furniture. Unfortunately for them, he unexpectedly returned and these young gentlemen departed quicker than they came.

Mr. Jacob was an assistant master at Bradfield and Cheltenham Colleges before he went to be headmaster of the junior school at Felsted, which post he held for many years. When I visited Felsted several years earlier Fred Jacob became interested in our schools and gave me a cheque for £50 and, later on, when the time arrived for him to give up his headmastership, he decided to come to Kashmir to help us. He has been a tower of strength to us ever since. For what Jacob does not know of education, and how to impart it, no one else knows, and few know the joy of giving as he does. That many do not share this joy the following incident will show.

I was visiting a chief judge, a Bengali Brahman, when I happened to mention "the joy of giving". He at once asked: "What did you say?" I repeated it and he said: "Please say it again," which I did, when he exclaimed, holding up his hand: "The joy of giving! I have never heard of such a thing."

The Wular swim this year was notable for the fact that

Phyllis Tyndale-Biscoe, Eric's wife, was the first woman to swim across that dreaded lake.

About this time the school received rather a shock when it was announced that the state education department had cut our school grant to the tune of seven thousand rupees. They gave as the reason that Eric was not a capable teacher as he did not possess a teaching degree, and was only a B.A. of Cambridge University.

My sin was that I spent more time in supervising the six mission schools than teaching in the classrooms. Some unknown friends heard of the decision and wrote an amusing article about it in the *Civil and Military Gazette*, the most widely read paper in the north of India, which resulted in His Highness the Maharajah ordering the grant to be restored at once.

In the month of February the next storm blew up from another direction. The Mohammedans were once more on the buzz against the Government, and amongst the orders that they issued to the city was that the schools were to join in their hartal and close down. Although we had much sympathy with the Mohammedans in their aspirations, we did not see why we should be ordered about by outsiders so we refused to obey, just as we had refused the Hindus a year or so before when they ordered us to join their hartal. We were warned that our schools would be picketed again, and were kept on the alert whilst the Mohammedan mobs went marching about the streets, chasing the police and amusing themselves in various ways until the military were called in to take control.

Our real anxiety was that a communal war might start, as it did two years earlier. It is remarkable how quickly blood begins to flow in the name of religion. Each party pretends that its god or gods have been insulted so has an excellent excuse to show its devotion to its deity by breaking somebody's head, or looting the shops owned by those of the opposite religion.

Or they show their love to their god in a less militant manner by blocking the public thoroughfare, holding up the traffic and dislocating business. As Mr. Jacobs and I were walking to school, we found the main street, outside a mosque, absolutely blocked by the mullah's congregation, squatting on the road in their hundreds.

Well, all this tamasha, day after day, was hardly conducive to discipline among the Mohammedan scholars.

The storm, however, soon subsided, possibly because Kashmir had now got its first Legislative Assembly, where all parties could let off steam. Six of our old boys were members. All honour we give to this first sitting of the Assembly, for their first act was to pass a law to suppress the immoral traffic in women and girls. Kashmiri women being fair, fetch a good price in India. Every autumn lorries carry this human merchandise down the road to India. The "cat" has been added to the punishment of fines and imprisonment, so we trust that this devilry will be lessened, for it is the "cat" that traffickers in the bodies and souls of women and girls fear.

CHAPTER TWENTY-ONE

The Tragedy of Wular Lake

ON April 11th there fell upon us a terrible blow, the tragedy of the Wular Lake. Five of our teachers and two old students were sailing on the lake when they were overwhelmed by a specially heavy squall, and not one was left to tell the tale. All seven were strong swimmers.

You can understand the shock to me on hearing such news, but, within a second or two, through the blackness that surrounded me I saw light, and said to myself: "Out of this disaster will come blessing. Defeat will somehow become a victory," and it is of this I now write. The truth of the words of the Psalmist have ever been my experience in dark hours: Ps. 18, 29. With the help of my God I SHALL leap over the wall. Ps. 27, 1. The Lord is my Light and Salvation; whom then shall I fear.

It took us ten days of search before we found the seventh body. It was grim work sending these bodies thirty miles by boat to Srinagar. We did so because their relatives wished to have the funeral rites performed by their own particular priests before cremation.

The body of the captain was sent up first. When it arrived it was met by a relation of his, a retired Government clerk, who had been trying for the last year to ruin him and turn him and his family out of their house. When he received the body he called together about three hundred Brahmans, in order to make a demonstration against me. (Mr. Jacob and I had been trying to help the captain to save his house.)

They intended to organize a procession and carry the body round the city to show the citizens how "Biscoe kills his teachers", and they would have done so had not the leader of the Brahmans heard of it, and, with a party of his men, appeared on the scene and prevented it. Moreover, he wrote a strong article in the newspaper which he edits, giving a true statement of the facts, and distributed 3,000 free copies throughout the city with the beat of a drum. He then came down to the lake, thirty miles distant, bringing some of his party to sympathize with us and to offer his help.

Later, when I returned to Srinagar he brought several members of the Bar to see me and to sympathize, and begged me not to give up taking the teachers and boys to the Wular Lake to face the storms, saying: "For the last forty years you have taken your boys to the lake, to face storms, and have turned Kashmiris into men."

Now, to get to the point and to what really matters. He said: "We have not always seen eye to eye in the school's efforts for social uplift, but now we understand and intend to work with you."

You who have visited our schools or have read our school logs will have learned that we are out for things that really matter; to set wrong right, to defend the weak against the oppressor; in short, knight-errantry. In doing this we have bumped into all sorts of people, and got ourselves disliked, especially by the religious crowd, for it is through them that the women suffer; early marriages encouraged—old men marrying little girls—widows not allowed to re-marry—babies murdered. Naturally, the old school of Brahman has not loved us and has fought us continually, anywhere and everywhere.

Eric with his family were in England on furlough. On hearing of this Wular tragedy he was inspired to write the following:

WE'LL FACE THE STORMS TO-DAY

The clouds are banked on the mountains, the Wular is
    sullen and grey,
"We'll hoist the sail and brave the gale. Come! Out and
    launch away.
        We'll face the storms to-day."

The white-winged gulls are wheeling, they glint in the
    murky air,
As far below they see them go, the waves of the Wular
    to dare.
        To face the storms out there.

How did it happen? There's none can tell, save the gulls,
    the wind and wave
"Oh Shukr-U-Din![1] Had you ever seen such a fight
    'twixt the strong and the brave?"
        "Come fight, for there's none to save."

The flimsy craft is swallowed up; they're whipped with
    the spray and the rain.
With gasping breath they face their death, as they tussle
    and wrench and strain.
        "Come, heave her up again."

At last the task's accomplished, the boat's afloat once more.
But out of the crew remain but two; no rudder or sail or oar.
        They fought, but they fight no more.

"Come, what shall we do, my captain? Can we reach the
    shore alive?"
"I care no more to reach the shore. We only two survive."
        "But what of the other five?"

"No, perish the thought," he answered, "for this we were
    not born,"
"They fought our fight, have we the right to leave them
    alone forlorn?"
        "Come, meet them beyond the dawn."

When the wild wind lashes the water, and life is a stormy
    sea,
"In all things Men" is our watchward then. And may it
    always be,
        "Come face the storms with me."

[1] Shukr-U-Din is a Mohammedan saint whose tomb is on a hill top on the lake side,
the protector of those who cross the lake if money is given to the priest in charge. Our
fellows had not paid the fee.

Q

Let the thunder crash in the mountains. Let the lightning
    hiss in the rain.
We'll never forget the example they set in our sorrow, our
    trouble and pain.
          But we'll face the storms again,
          And again.
          We'll face the storms again.

Now, through the loss of our seven brave fellows, salvation for the women has dawned, for those men who were
against us are now for us. The younger spirits among the
Brahmans had been for the last year or so trying to alter
the custom of ages, and it is they who were able to see in
our lake tragedy something inspiring, viz., seven Brahman youths who went forth to conquer the Wular storm.
They could have run before the gale, but they did not,
they wanted to try their skill and strength against it. As
the Brahman barrister said: "Sir, they did what Britishers
do when they try to conquer mountains. That spirit is
coming to Kashmiri. That is the true spirit, as we now
realize, and hence we wish to join up with you."

Two Indian Christians were coming up the road to
Srinagar from India on a motor-cycle and were knocked
down by a lorry. One had his arm broken, which had to
be amputated at the shoulder, and the other his leg severely
smashed.

They were taken to the state hospital where they remained for two months. The state hospital was unable to
supply them with nurses to look after them, so I appealed
to my school staff. Two Brahman teachers offered to take
on this job and notwithstanding their caste they looked
after the two patients day and night, doing everything for
them, even the work of sweepers. The one who had his leg
broken succumbed to his injuries. His father, who had
come up from India to be with him, told me that while he
was laid up he had found his Saviour on account of the
wonderful kindness he had received, day after day, from
those who had nursed him through so many painful days
and nights.

On February 28th my wife and I left Srinagar for Jammu, as Harold and his mechanic were bringing two autogyros to show to His Highness the Maharajah.

The Rev. John Alexander and his wife most kindly invited us to stay with them. John Alexander was the Presbyterian minister at Jammu, a man much beloved both by British and Indians. The autogyros arrived in due time and flew all over Jammu city before landing on the polo ground. The airmen remained for two days giving joy rides to many of the officials and their friends. From Jammu they were flying us to Pindi. My wife and I were looking forward to this trip to see the forests and mountains from above. Harold took his mother in his plane and I took my seat in the other, piloted by the mechanic. We were off first, but only reached the height of about two hundred feet when we suddenly dropped on to some trees. The pilot steered the machine successfully between them and then came to a very high hedge and I thought we would charge it, but fortunately we just cleared the top and came down plump among the cabbages in a kitchen garden. The pilot apologized to me for this unfortunate landing, earnestly expressing the hope that I was not hurt. I assured him that I was not in the least hurt, saying that it was not his fault, perhaps he had never before taken up a canon, and cannons are very heavy things. This remark comforted him!

The autogyro was extricated with the help of many soldiers, and later the two autogyros flew, without us, to Pindi. Harold thought we should be safer travelling by road in our car. When we arrived at Pindi, Harold took us separately for a joy ride over the city and we both reached earth again without any mishap, canon or no cannon.

While in Jammu I was told a very pleasing story about Her Highness the Maharani.

The River Rawi which runs through Jammu was in spate. Some pedestrians who were crossing the river found themselves marooned on one of the islands in the centre of the river and as the water was rising, the island became smaller and smaller. Her Highness was on the roof of her palace, and saw them through her binoculars, whereupon she phoned to the Governor of Jammu, telling him of the plight of these people, and asked him to send relief. In the evening Her Highness was on the palace roof again, and saw that the people were still on the island, and in great danger. Her Highness naturally became angry at the callousness of the officials, so she phoned again to the Governor asking why nothing had been done. Darkness had now fallen and it was raining heavily. It was impossible to use boats in such a turbulent river and the only means of saving the marooned party was to find men who could swim on mashks (inflated skins). Such swimmers lived several miles away from Jammu and had to be fetched.

The Maharani sent blankets and brandy to the spot on the river where the survivors would be likely to arrive. It was not until midnight that the mashk men were able to come down the river to the island to rescue those in distress. They did it by putting one at a time on the mashks.

We were cheered by a visit to the school by Lieutenant Henry George Allen Percy, Duke of Northumberland, a delightful young fellow who was most interested in the school and its efforts to help the people of this country. He continued to subscribe to our school funds until he gave his life for his country in the 1939–45 war.

About this time we had another interesting visitor to the schools, Miss Cornelia Sorabji, who had done most difficult and useful work for the women of India. When she was a schoolgirl she happened to be with her mother when an Indian widow came for help. It was the case of a lonely woman being oppressed by the relations of her late husband, with no one to defend her. Cornelia was so much impressed by this widow's story that she determined to become a lawyer, so that she might be able to tackle such cases.

After finishing her education in India she went to London and became a barrister. Soon she was back in India intending to join the Indian Bar at Calcutta, but the Bengali barristers would not admit her. After about ten years she won through and was able to defend India's women in the law courts. Her law cases often took her to the houses of the rich and she has been able to succour, in their distress, many ranis and maharanis. On some occasions she was in great danger of being poisoned. Thank God, her life has been preserved to continue her fight against unscrupulous men.

In the summer months cholera broke out in the valley, but it was checked owing to the energy and enterprise of the head of the medical services in Kashmir, Colonel G. M. Millar. He secured from India all the medicine for inoculation that was available, that not being sufficient, medicine was brought from Germany by air, so that he inoculated 125,000 people and thus saved the country from another threatened epidemic.

A certain maulvi arrived at the mission hospital and Doctor Cecil Vosper wished to inoculate him but he refused, saying that the inoculation was against his holy book, the Quran.

Now it so happened that some of our ladies had gone to his village in order to inoculate the women and they were successful in entering the house of the maulvi, as he was away in Srinagar, and inoculated his wives and family. When he returned, to our surprise, instead of being angry with his ladies for permitting this wickedness, he allowed himself to be inoculated. I guess his women used more persuasive means than Dr. Cecil Vosper.

The Prime Minister of Kashmir, Colonel Elliot J. D. Colvin, C.I.E., unearthed the Wood-badge which had been presented, some three years previously, to Neranjan Nath Misri by Major Hogg who was then in charge of the scout camp in India.

On one occasion we sent down two of our scoutmasters to compete at a scout camp at Murree. A few days after the scout camp had broken up, Major Hogg wrote to tell me that Neranjan Nath Misri had proved himself the most efficient scout in camp, and that he had sent a Wood-badge to the Kashmir scouting authorities to be presented to him. About three months afterwards he wrote to me asking if Neranjan Nath Misri had received the badge. I answered "No". After two months he again asked the same question and still I answered in the negative. After two or three months he asked a third time and again my answer was "no". So he wrote yet another letter to the head of the scout movement asking why the badge had not been handed over. He sent this letter to me asking me to hand it in person to the officer, which I did, but nothing happened even then. About three years afterwards when a British Minister, Colonel Colvin, was appointed, I went to him and through his help the badge reached the owner.

I made it my business to discover the reason why this Wood-badge had been withheld. I discovered that the clerk in charge of the Kashmir Scouts Association had himself won the badge some years previously, and wished to be the only scout in Kashmir with this honour. This will give you some idea of the difficulties of instilling the true scout spirit into the people of Kashmir and why Lord Baden Powell asked me to tell the scouts in India that he wanted "quality and not quantity".

Sometimes visitors ask us why we have trees for our goal posts. The explanation is simple. We used to put up the usual wooden posts, but our football ground is quite close to a village and the villagers want firewood, so repeatedly we found that the goal posts had disappeared. After enduring this nuisance for long, we used trees instead. On these trees we have now fixed brass plates bearing the names of those gallant men Samuel Bakkal and Chimed Gergan of whom I have written. We trust that these two names will remain for many years on those mulberry trees, which live for about two hundred years. Thus one generation of boys after another can "read, mark and learn" of two heroes whose lives, we trust, may ever inspire them to follow their example.

CHAPTER TWENTY-TWO

A Journey to Africa

ON December 1st, 1936, my wife and I started for our furlough to England, but intended to spend some time visiting our daughter at Ranchi, our son Harold at Madras, and our son Julian in Northern Rhodesia.

We found at Ranchi a very pleasant climate. Our son-in-law, Captain Alec Best, was Political Officer there. He took us to the Christmas shooting camp in the jungles of Jashpore, for there was a tiger there which he wished to kill. It had already killed forty persons so it was about time its career was ended. We sat up in machans while a hundred coolies or so were beating the jungle, but unfortunately, the tiger did not arrive within the range of the rifles as he broke back through the coolies and got away. Later, Alec was successful in shooting the tiger which had by then killed about eighty persons.

We were interested in the aborigines of that district. They were a very cheery people and they treated their women like civilized folk, for the women mixed freely with the men and did not hide their faces from Europeans as women do in so many parts of India.

I went with Alec Best to visit the jail. There were about seventy prisoners in all and they seemed to me to be a happy lot. I was told that they were so comfortable in prison that they would commit crimes in order to be received again within those hospitable walls. We then visited the law courts, but found that they were empty and the judges had no work to do. On my inquiring the reason, I was told that no lawyers or barristers were permitted to remain in the state and, therefore, there was no one to encourage litigation.

During our stay there our daughter drove us three hundred miles to Calcutta where we spent some pleasant days with the Metropolitan of India, the Most Rev. Foss Westcott, who kept open house. He certainly followed the teaching of St. Paul that bishops should be hospitable.

Just to give one instance. H.M.S. *Impregnable* had arrived in port, whereupon the Bishop invited thirty-six apprentices to dinner, and he played games with them as if he were a boy again. Those young fellows, I should think, would never forget that rowdy evening under the roof of the Bishop.

On January 31st, 1937, we arrived at St. Thomas Mount at Madras to stay with Harold, who was a pilot at the Madras Flying Club. He took his mother and me for a joy ride four thousand feet above Madras in his Moth plane, a very enjoyable little trip.

While in Madras I went to Bangalore to visit our old friends Sir Charles and Lady Todhunter. Charles is Controller of Accounts to His Highness the Maharajah of Mysore.

As they were off next day to their beautiful house at Mysore, they asked the Prime Minister, Sir Mirza Ismail, to take me in his car to Mysore. On our journey through the state he showed me various places of interest. At every village we stopped at the village folk crowded round the car, putting garlands of flowers on our necks and greeting us with gifts of oranges. I was greatly impressed by the way the old people and children welcomed the Prime Minister for I saw at once, by the expression on their faces, that they had the greatest regard and affection for him. He kept me with him all day until half-past ten at night. He finished up by showing me a most wonderfully laid out garden, called Shalamar, which the Maharajah had copied from the Shalamar garden in Kashmir.

I was delighted with all the interesting things he had shown me and felt not unlike the Queen of Sheba after Solomon had shown her the wonders of his kingdom. What impressed me particularly, was that there seemed to be no eye-wash; everything I saw was genuine, so when I wished him good-bye I said: "Sir Mirza Ismail, you must have many enemies?" He looked me straight in the face at this rather unexpected remark and answered: "Yes, Canon! I have many enemies, but your Lord Jesus Christ also had many enemies." "True," I answered, "Mirza Sahib. Let us thank God for our enemies." I made this remark in all seriousness, I had not lived in a native state for nothing and had learnt that a man who does his duty makes numberless enemies.

I spent two delightful days with the Todhunters. They showed me some of the excellent social work in which they were engaged in Mysore, such as schools for the blind, schools for the deaf, crêches for the children and a hospital for sick animals.

In all this social work His Highness the Maharajah has always taken the greatest interest. He is a wonderfully humble man to whom one can talk quite freely. He has always lived for his people and therefore welcomes all those who work for the good of his country.

Our ship, the S.S. *Inchanga*, which was due to take us to East Africa, was scheduled to leave port early on Sunday morning. It did not arrive and we heard, when we reached the docks, that she had stuck on a sandbank in the river. We could not go back to Harold's house for he had flown off to another part of India, so we drove to the house of the Bishop. As it was very early in the morning, Bishop Waller was still in bed, but Wilfred Sell, who was living with him, came down in his dressing-gown to see us. I told him that we were stranded, would he kindly ask the Bishop if he could put us up. I told him to be careful to look at the Bishop's face when he asked the question; if he looked distressed we would go elsewhere but, if he looked happy, then we would stay. Mr. Sell, on his return, announced that the Bishop looked pleased at our request, so we went into the house where we spent a very pleasant twenty-four hours. We had the pleasure of entertaining him in Kashmir many years earlier when he was a young C.M.S. missionary at St. John's College, Agra.

We had a very pleasant voyage to East Africa, first calling at Mombasa, which interested me much from the fact that I had hoped to be sent to Africa after offering my services to the C.M.S.

The next port we stopped at was Zanzibar. As we steamed into the harbour we saw a fleet of dhows. I pointed them out to my wife saying that if we had come into Zanzibar harbour fifty-odd years before, those dhows would probably have been full of slaves, but there were no slaves on board, and why? Because of the British Navy. I thought of the days when my brother Edward was a middy, with the East African Fleet, chasing the slave dhows and releasing their cargoes. Thank God for the British Navy!

There were friends at Zanzibar Island to greet us and to show us the places we wanted to see. The first place we visited was the old slave market where the slaves had been treated like cattle, about which I used to hear when a boy. The slave market is no more, and in its place stands the Cathedral, but there are two trees, one marking the spot where the auctioneer stood to hand over the slaves to the highest bidder. The other tree marks the spot where the executioner stood to torture, or kill, those who objected to being torn away from their families.

Who has changed all this? My fellow-countrymen! Thank God!

The Director of Education very kindly took me in his car to a Government school on high land some twenty-five miles away. When we arrived there we saw the boys playing cricket. On my asking who those boys were, I was told that they were the grandsons of the slaves and the grandsons of the slave dealers, playing happily together as friends and brothers.

Who has been responsible for this wonderful change? My fellow-countrymen! Again thank God!

From Zanzibar we sailed to the port of Beira, in Portuguese East Africa, where we disembarked, and from there we went by train to our son in Northern Rhodesia. We broke our journey at Salisbury where we were met at the station by our nephew, Ronny Tyndale-Biscoe, who is on the staff of the Geological Department and there we made the acquaintance of his wife and two dear children. It was

a great joy to me to be in Salisbury because of the part
my sailor brother Ted played when, with the Rhodesian
Expedition in 1890, he was in charge of the guns and was
selected to hoist the Union Jack at Fort Salisbury. The
house that he and Frank Johnson built with their own
hands is still standing as a memorial. His name is still
remembered in Salisbury, and around, for he spent many
years there gold digging and fighting in the Matabele and
Mashonaland wars. He developed a great affection for the
Africans.

At Gwelo we again broke our journey to stay with an
old friend, S. de I. Lenfesty and his wife. Lenfesty had
done splendid work for education there. They entertained
us right royally for a week before we proceeded to
Mazabuka.

After another day in the train we reached Mazabuka
where we had a great reception from Julian, his wife and
two children Renée and David. Julian is Director of African Education in Northern Rhodesia. He has no wish to
give top-heavy education as in India, with a B.A. and
M.A. dangling in front of their eyes, but is out to make
them true men, fit to take on any work that is useful to
their country.

One afternoon I was walking with Julian when I heard
tom-toms, and asked him what the row was about. He said
that the villagers were having a dance. We were soon in
the village and saw both men and women dancing together and thoroughly enjoying themselves.

As I watched these Africans, happy and free, my
thoughts went back to my childhood, I pictured what a
different scene it would have been in this village fifty years
or so ago. I should have seen them being chased by Arab
slave-dealers, the old people being killed because they
were of no use, and the rest, women, men, boys and girls,
bound with chains, with the slave sticks on their necks,
being marched off to the sea coast, and their villages
burnt.

I enjoyed my visit to North Rhodesia immensely; the
days were full of interest, as my son showed me some of the
grand work being done in the country.

One of the many things which appealed to me when being shown the technical school was the athletic sports, as I had seen so many in Kashmir. You will understand my keenness in watching the boys, and especially the school staff, to see if they allowed their boys to cheat or not.

I watched the competitors most closely, those who started them, those who received them at the winning post, and also whether anyone was allowed near the running track to trip up or to obstruct the competitors. Towards the end of the sports I felt thrills running through me, for after many years I had seen athletic sports carried through without any cheating. I went up to the Principal to tell him how delighted I was to have seen no one attempting to cheat in any way. He answered in surprise: "But why do you think that they should cheat?" My answer was: "In all my forty-odd years in Kashmir I have never been to any Indian sports meeting without having to see several cases of cheating." I asked him if he could tell me the reason why Africans do not try to get the better of one another by unfair means. He said: "I think the reason is that from their youth they have been taught to obey their chiefs without question."

Julian took me to visit the U.M.C.A. mission about 130 miles distant, where excellent work is being done in schools, hospitals and agriculture. We found the fathers a very pleasant lot.

On the way we picked up the medical officer of the district. He and his wife lived on a small outstation. I asked him if they were ever able to attend a church service. In answer he said: "We have a visit from a padre about every month or six weeks, and he kindly gives us a service. On the last occasion my wife and I stayed for the celebration of the Holy Communion when the padre came up to us and asked if we were members of the Church of England. On our answering that we were Scots and Presbyterians, he said that he was afraid he could not administer the Holy Communion to us." This answer naturally shocked them, as it did me when I was told, but I fear that padre does not stand alone in this matter, for about three weeks later I happened to meet one of the Cowley Fathers, a very delightful man, to whom I told this incident and asked him if he thought that our Lord would have acted thus. He did not speak for some time and looked down on the ground and answered as if he were ashamed: "I am afraid that I should have had to act in the same manner."

I felt very sorry for him, for I knew that in his heart he was a follower of Jesus Christ, but he felt that the Church had the prior place. This incident made me extremely sad because I was told that there are scores of different Christian sects in Africa. The poor African must become utterly muddled when he goes from one station to another and finds that nearly every Christian padre whom he meets preaches something different.

As our son Julian's job is concerned with African schools of every denomination in Northern Rhodesia, he naturally wishes them all to pull together as Christian friends, instead of allowing themselves to be fooled by the Devil over doctrines and dogmas.

We, of course, have the same trouble in India as we have many varieties of Christian missions. I was reminded of Bishop Lefroy's answer to the chaplain who reported to him my wickedness at having partaken of the Holy Communion in a Presbyterian church. "You had better leave Biscoe alone."

The time came for us to leave Mazabuka and, on our way to Cape Town, we stopped at Livingstone in order to see the Victoria Falls. Quite a long way before we reached Livingstone, we could see the great column of white spray shooting up into the sky and glistening in the sunlight. The sight of the Falls when we arrived at the Zambesi was far more wonderful and awe-inspiring than I had ever expected. One had the feeling of repletion. The breadth of the Falls I was told was two miles. The river above them was full of wooded islands, a most beautiful sight.

That evening we were entertained at dinner by Doctor and Mrs. West. They were kindness itself and had invited Mrs. Clay, the daughter of Lord Baden Powell, to meet us. They came to the station and gave us a good send off in the train bound for Cape Town.

We arrived at Southampton on May 31st and drove

straight from the ship, in a taxi, to the house of my brother at Swanage. It was a lovely drive; England was looking its best, like one continuous garden.

The first item of our programme was to attend the Dean's garden party at Westminster Abbey, where we met many old friends; among them the Right Rev. Winnington Ingram, late Bishop of London, about whom I have already written when telling of my Whitechapel days. He looked very well and was still able to lead a busy life.

To our surprise we saw Colonel Gore-Brown whom we had lately met in Northern Rhodesia. He had come with others from the Rhodesian Government to be present at the Coronation of George VI. Colonel Gore-Brown and his wife are owners of an estate in Northern Rhodesia, over four hundred miles from the nearest railway. They are both devoted to the welfare of the African. They have schools for boys and girls and a hospital for the people on their estate. They must be a great blessing to all around. The wife of the chief of their village was taken away when a girl in a slave ship, but was rescued by the British Navy and restored to her country. Now she is an old woman and delights to tell the story of her deliverance.

My wife and I were invited to stay with our old friends General Sir Walter and Lady Cayley at Crowthorne in Berks. and they drove us to my old school, Bradfield College, to see the Greek play performed in the chalk pit. The last time that I had seen a Greek play was when I myself was one of the actors in the year 1881.

Our next garden party was at Lambeth where again we met many old friends, among them Bishop J. E. Palmer of Bombay and Bishop Eyre-Chatterton of Nagpore who, when I had last seen them, were taking part in our school regattas on the Dal Lake at Srinagar. His Grace, Archbishop Lang, when greeting my wife, said to her: "I hope your husband is behaving himself." Unfortunately for me the Archbishop was a bachelor, so I was unable to put the same question to his wife.

One day I was called up to London to the B.B.C. headquarters from where my wife and I were driven to the Alexandra Palace to be televised. It was a new experience for us to be fellow-passengers with popular actors and actresses and film stars.

I found the B.B.C. staff an exceptionally pleasant crowd and they made me feel at home at once. I was first of all taken to the dressing-room where a lady touched up my face with rouge and powder and in other ways tried to turn me into a handsome man. I was then conducted to a hall with very powerful lights hanging from the ceiling, such powerful lights as I had never seen before.

When all was ready an interviewer came forward to ask me questions about Kashmir which I answered to the best of my ability. It was certainly an ordeal, I knew that thousands of people were watching the expression of my face, as well as listening to my answers. I happened to know that in one of the hotels in London were some important Kashmir officials, possibly listening, as I was endeavouring to speak the truth, and nothing but the truth, and I wondered how they liked my answers.

Whilst in London I visited Sir Walter Lawrence who very kindly drove me in his car to Ascot to see our mutual friend Sir Neville Chamberlain who, in the early nineties, was in charge of the Kashmir troops. This brave and charming officer we found utterly crippled with arthritis. Although he was continually in pain he never showed it or complained. It was delightful to hear these two old friends reminding one another of those early days in Kashmir.

On the return journey Sir Walter Lawrence told me many stories of his life in Kashmir. On one occasion when he was in camp about thirty miles from Srinagar by the side of the river, he heard an agonized voice. Looking in the direction of the cry he saw a man running towards him, wringing his hands and crying out: "Oh my hands! Oh my hands!" Lawrence told the sais who was with him to bring the man to him. He noticed that his hands were covered with blood and asked him the cause. He, like many other farmers, had been ordered to bring his rice to the Tehsildar's camp, for in those days the farmers paid their taxes in kind, instead of cash. After he had delivered all his pony loads of grain, the Tehsildar asked him where his (the Tehsildar's) share of the rice was. The farmer said

that he had given all his rice to the Government and had
nothing left. The Tehsildar said: "I will teach you!" and
called one of his servants to bring the torture irons into
which his fingers were forced. Blood was squeezed out of
them and the joints broken.

Lawrence was horrified at this story and told the man to
come back to the Tehsildar's camp with him. When they
arrived, the Tehsildar came out to greet Lawrence. Lawrence asked him if the farmers were paying up well in
rice or if he had had to punish any of them. He said he had
not had to punish anyone: his word was always sufficient.
Lawrence then brought the tortured man before him and
asked him how it was that his hands were covered with
blood. The Tehsildar answered that he knew nothing
about it. Lawrence found out from the wounded man that
the torture irons were kept in a box in front of the Tehsildar's Hindu clerk. He asked the Tehsildar if he might
look into this box. The request was granted and the torture
irons were found at the bottom of the box below some
papers.

Lawrence held the blood-stained irons before the
Tehsildar's eyes and asked him if he had seen them before.
He received an answer in the negative. "Well!" said
Lawrence, "how is it that these irons are covered with
fresh blood and this man's hands are running with
blood?" The Tehsildar again said that he did not know
anything about it. Lawrence then said to him: "I do not
want any more lies from you, and I will teach you never to
lie to me again. Take off your coat and stand on this
spot." He was standing in his own court at the moment.
Lawrence handed his riding-whip to one of the servants
telling him to continue to beat the Tehsildar on the back
until ordered to stop. So this high official received a sound
thrashing in his own court.

As I remained in England only a few months I did not
do much deputation work, but I paid a very pleasant
visit once more to the Green Isle, to my old friend Godfrey
Day at Kilkenny. I had a pleasing experience after preaching in one of his churches. After the evening service many

of the congregation were taken to a large barn where supper was prepared and where rich and poor, high and low,
all sat down together on wooden benches round the tables
to enjoy a friendly meal. The Bishop sat amongst us and
kept us all lively with his interesting talk.

This mixed gathering for a common meal made one
think of the early days when Christians of all classes met
together for their love feasts. This happy gathering I am
not likely to forget.

I visited a few schools, amongst them Liverpool College, where I received, as usual, a most hearty welcome
from Bob Howard, his wife and family.

I drove over to Huyton College to address the girls,
where my old friend Miss Potts is headmistress. It is an
excellent school and I was struck by the friendliness of the
teachers. I returned rather late to Bob Howard's house,
and as he wished me to give yet another talk to his boys,
he went up to their dormitories and brought them all
down, in their night wear, into the drawing-room. There
was no room for them on the chairs and sofas so they
spread themselves on the floor in all directions. It was just
the sort of congregation that anyone would wish to
address.

Mr. Spenser Leeson, Headmaster of Winchester, invited me for the week-end to the college. I stayed with my
cousin Harry Tyndale, one of the housemasters, where I
had a happy time. I then went to Bedford School. The
headmaster, Humphry Hodge, had been in the I.C.S. and
had served with the Corps of Guides on the North-West
Frontier, so he was naturally glad to hear what I had to say
about our schools in Kashmir.

I was specially glad to meet him for when I was a curate
in Whitechapel I had known his father who later was at a
C.M.S. gathering in London which I had to address. I
was comforted by his presence, for during my talk at this
meeting there sat before me a very popular preacher,
Rector of a well-known church in London. I noticed that
my talk on our work in Kashmir had shocked him much,
as his chin suddenly fell upon his breast. I feared I had
caused him to have a fit, for apparently I had dropped a

R

good many bricks. However, when I left the hall, I met Canon Hodge outside and he immediately came up to me, grasped both of my hands and thanked me for my address, saying: "If only missionaries on their return to England would speak out, as you have done, it would indeed be a blessing." His kind words cheered me, here was one man, at any rate, who appreciated what I had said.

CHAPTER TWENTY-THREE

An Unholy Traffic

MY wife and I left England on October 20th, 1937, and arrived at Srinagar on November 8th when we received a hearty welcome from the assembled schools, with their bands playing cheerily. Eric showed us over the beautiful new school building which he had built in a corner of the Sheikh Bagh Hostel ground.

I was delighted to find that Colonel Glover Thompson was British Resident of Kashmir. When he was here as the Assistant Resident, he had always been most helpful when I sought his advice on difficult questions. He had lately been British Political Agent in Kashgar, where he had saved many Indian subjects from being murdered by the Bolsheviks.

At this time I was introduced to a very brave Kashmiri.

An insignificant looking little Mohammedan, a barber, whose trade is considered a low caste one, lived in a street in Srinagar in which were situated many houses of ill-fame. This man, like his neighbours, was continually disturbed at night by the ribald songs accompanied by musical instruments such as the harp and zither, and also by men wrangling. But what really upset him were the cries of anguish from the unfortunates recently forced into this cruel life, many of them quite young, who had been sold by their relations under the pretence that marriages had been arranged for them.

The cries of these poor creatures went to his heart and prompted him to action. He went to some decent men he knew, and asked their help to fight this evil. He wrote pamphlets to show up this cruel traffic, and distributed hundreds of them in the city. He would stand up in the streets and preach, and at night, with some of his friends, would stand outside those houses trying to dissuade the men visitors from entering.

The keepers of these houses soon became active, and with the help of the police, ran him into the police courts. Their trumped-up charges were continual, so that by degrees he was ruined and had to sell up in order to pay the law costs.

But he still had one source of income, which was as barber to His Highness's state band, with seventy or so heads to shave. His enemies, however, brought false charges against him to the officer in charge of the band, so he was dismissed. He was now utterly ruined, but still fighting. One night he and his friends were picketing a certain house of ill-fame, when who should enter, under cover of darkness, but a police officer who was the son of a high official of Kashmir, a Sikh. The barber begged this officer not to enter, but without avail.

At this, the barber ran off to the phone and told the high official where his son was, whereupon he came down and was met by the barber. To the high official's surprise the barber did not ask for hush money but something very different. He said: "I do not ask for money, but if you wish me to keep the matter quiet regarding your son, you must have all this traffic stopped." The official agreed, so the order went forth that all such places be removed from the municipal areas of Srinagar.

Of course this has not cured the evil, but it has put temptation at a distance instead of being right under the eyes of every passer-by.

Now this gallant little barber cuts the hair of 100 British boys and masters in Eric's Prep. School. He has not even now ceased to fight. Only the other day, with the help of the police, mark you, he saved a girl who had been sold for Rs400. Why this change in police behaviour? Because some of our mission school old boys are now officers in the police force.

During 1938 Eric and his wife, Fred Jacob and Muriel Millanson, took one hundred schoolboys and forty schoolgirls, to climb the Mahadey Mountain, 13,000 feet high.

The remarkable thing about this climb was, that the Kashmiri girls were with the Kashmiri schoolboys in such an outing. Only a few years before, no male folk were ever permitted to enter the girls' school compound. When I myself wished to speak to the mistress of the school, notice had to be given, and all doors and windows had to be closed, so that my eyes should not fall upon the faces of the girls.

Now, they were not only going on an expedition together, but had their camp on the mountain side. The girls' camp, which had been placed in hollow ground, was flooded by a cloudburst, with the result that their tents were about one foot deep in water. The cloud burst about midnight, so the boys came from their tents on higher ground to rescue the property of the girls and helped them to find shelter in the huts of the herdsmen which, fortunately, were not far away.

To Westerners this episode would not seem peculiar, but to us, who had been accustomed for years to Eastern habits and customs, it was very remarkable, and a cause for great thankfulness.

A certain Inspector of Schools, after he had inspected the C.M.S. school at Islamabad, wrote out two reports, one for me to see, and the other for the Minister of Education, who he knew would not like to see a good report of our school.

By mistake his clerk had sent me both reports. In the report intended for me, he wrote: "This is a good school" and then described our activities, but there was one drawback and that was that the school building was hired, not ours. (We were not allowed in those days to build our own school house.) In the report intended for the Minister of Education, he wrote: "The C.M.S. school at Islamabad is a bad school and the reason for boys attending that school is that many scholarships were given (which was quite untrue) and the only redeeming point about this school is that the house in which it is situated is satisfactory."

These two reports I placed in the school museum as

objects of interest. I also sent a message to the Inspector saying that when I next met him I would pull his ears; in consequence the Inspector never wished to inspect our schools again and always succeeding in avoiding me. Some years afterwards he sent his two sons to our school, and on being asked by the headmaster the reason, he replied that his sons would be disciplined there.

"Honesty is the best policy," but not yet in Kashmir.

This is one of the mottoes that hang on the wall of our school and under it the photo of Chimed who, as has been related earlier, preferred death to accepting a heavy bribe of dishonour.

An old student, Ram Chand Dhar, was being dismissed from a Government department of the Kashmir state by his superior officer because he would not loot the villagers for him. This old student implored his superior officer, a son of Belial, to have mercy on his wife and family, but to this appeal he turned a deaf ear. Later, he called him back, saying: "I will reconsider your case if you bring a pretty girl to my boat to-night." Fortunately, there was another old student of ours near at hand, a brave fellow, who gave him the following advice: "Dress up my manservant, who is a hefty fellow, as a nautch girl and put him in the boat to-night, and we shall see what we shall see." All turned out according to plan. The son of Belial went to the boat at night and received a sound thrashing which so cowed him that he promised not to dismiss his subordinate officer if he promised not to let this disgrace be known.

You can understand that I do not wish to leave the country while our old students are putting up a gallant fight against the world, the flesh and the devil.

Every visitor to our school does not approve of the motto, "Honesty is the best policy". An Indian Babu said of it: "This is not good, it teaches boys to disrespect their parents. You should take it down." I guess it touched him on the raw.

An old student of mine, who once came to me for advice, handed me a document accusing one of our old boys, in the Forestry Department, of bullying the villagers in his division and preaching against the Maharajah. The document was signed by some fifty heads of villages and prominent persons.

He had been ordered by the Prime Minister to go to this particular division to discover the truth of these allegations. He told me that a police officer of the C.I.D. Department had already been sent to the division for this purpose, and had reported that the statement was absolutely true. The Prime Minister wished to be quite certain so he had ordered this man, who was a senior officer in the C.I.D., to make a final inquiry. This senior officer asked me for my advice. I said: "Go ahead with your inquiry and if you find that our old student is a rascal, say so, and if you discover that he is an honest man, say so. Do your duty and trust in God," and I dismissed him with my blessing.

After two weeks the officer returned with the following report: He had visited every village in the forest range and had interviewed every one of the signatories of that paper. They told him that the document which they had signed was entirely false, but they had been forced to sign it by the District Forest Officer.

Now the reason why this D.F.O. wished to get our old school boy into trouble was, that he did not like a strong and honest man who would not allow the men under him to loot the villagers. It had been the custom for the forest guards to collect for their superior officer about twenty or twenty-five rupees a month, and as each of these officers has twenty to thirty guards under him, it meant much addition to their monthly salary. They in their turn were expected to give a few hundred rupees every month to their superior officer. Our old student, being an honest man, did not allow his subordinates to loot the villagers. Hence he had no hundreds of rupees to present to his superior officer every month, and consequently this D.F.O. wanted him dismissed.

The second report was sent to the Prime Minister but nothing happened. Fortunately, God intervened and called the D.F.O. to another world where, we hope, he will learn to be sorry for his sins. It was specially unfortunate that this honest man should have thus suffered, for his wife, a very charming lady, is a trained nurse and, wherever he was posted, the sick and suffering were cared for.

On December 30th I left Kashmir, bound for India under doctor's orders, to escape the cold of another Kashmir winter. During the previous winter I had spent two months in my bedroom and had had to sit up in a chair for three weeks at night, on account of uninterrupted coughing.

I had been asked by my old friends, Major and Mrs. Bill Sykes, to their home in the native state of Bundi in Central India. While there I was taken to see a group of tombs of former Rajas which were beautifully carved temples. Over the doorway of each tomb was inscribed the virtues of that particular Raja. On one of them was inscribed the fact that fifty of his wives had been burnt alive with his corpse.

At Delhi, my old friend, the chaplain, P. F. N. Young, kindly invited me to stay. He had just received a letter from a brother padre who was in a famine-stricken part of the Punjab, telling him that the money collected by His Excellency the Viceroy for distribution amongst the sufferers had not been issued. It was still in the hands of the Deputy Commissioner of that district who happened to be an Indian, and he was wondering what to do about it.

He told me that His Excellency the Viceroy would be attending the morning service next day in his church, so I suggested that he should read out the letter in church, so that the Viceroy would come to know of the trouble and its cause. He hesitated a little before accepting my advice until I told him of the time when the people of Srinagar were starving, and I was able to tell the Viceroy of those days direct from the pulpit what the trouble was, and who was the cause of it. This decided him, so next day when His Excellency the Viceroy, Lord Linlithgow, and all his staff were in church, he read out the letter from his missionary friend, and thereby acquainted the head of the Government of India with the truth.

Another matter which pleased me that Sunday morning was that P. F. N. Young and his wife, with helpers from his congregation, had tables outside the church on which were light refreshments for those who had attended the early service. There I saw people of all classes meeting together to partake of a love feast such as had happened to me in Ireland.

Before leaving Delhi I was introduced to a very brave lady, Miss Millicent Shepherd, who is the chief worker in the field of moral uplift. One day she received news that a certain girl, in whom she was interested, had been taken to a house of ill-fame in the city. She went in search of her and found her there. While she was talking to her, she suddenly realized that they were not alone and, on looking round, she saw two men with daggers in their hands who savagely ordered her to leave the house at once, otherwise they would kill her. This instance of the danger in which she was apt to find herself, will show you what courage is needed in tackling this very difficult business of rescuing young girls from the clutches of devils.

I heard later that this same girl's parents tried to force her (aged fourteen) to marry a man of seventy. She refused, so her parents, to punish her, sent her to Delhi, pretending that she was to go to a boarding-school. But this "school" proved to be where Miss Shepherd found and rescued her. She was sent to a school where she was properly cared for and, as soon as she was old enough, she entered the W.A.C.S. To-day she is a senior officer over seventy girls.

We were at our holiday hut at Nil Nag, in the month of August 1939, when two of our teachers, Govind Razdan, a widower, Sham Lal and his wife, and an old boy, Kashi Nath and his wife, asked me to baptize them. They had for years been very keen on all kinds of social service, so I knew by their lives, as well as by their words, that they were truly fit persons to be received into the Christian Church. On Sunday morning I took them to the lake and baptized them.

We, and they, of course were well aware that when they returned to Srinagar, they would have to suffer persecution from the Brahmans, and they did.

About a month later we were at school again, when the old boys of the school arranged for a dinner in honour of our revered friend Bishop Barne of Lahore. On that occasion 150 old boys sat down to a meal. They were of various religious castes and classes. It was a great joy to all of us who had been striving for so many years to break down caste prejudices, to see this great number of old boys entertaining our Bishop. My thoughts naturally went back to the days when the Brahman members of my school staff had to throw away all their food because my shadow had fallen upon it.

Not many days passed before we heard that the teachers whom I had baptized, were in danger from their fellow-Brahmans.

Govind Razdan was the first to be attacked by hooligans while crossing one of the city bridges. Fortunately for him, one of the policemen near by was an old boy of our school and he rescued him from the angry crowd. A few days later Sham Lal was going from my house to his home in the city, after dark, when he was attacked and so badly hurt that he had to be taken to hospital. The man who was the cause of this attack was a Brahman policeman. Then came Kashi Nath's turn. He was employed by a motor omnibus company and was taking a bus full of Brahmans to one of the most holy places in Kashmir named Tula Mula, where a goddess is supposed to live in a tank. After landing his party at the holy spot, he was attacked by the worshippers, but fortunately there were Mohammedans at hand who came to his rescue and saved him.

Shortly after my first arrival in Kashmir I was about to start for school when a tall, handsome Kashmir Brahman called to see me, bringing with him a delicate-looking boy of seven years of age. He asked if I would admit him into the school. This man belonged to the official class. The highest posts in Kashmir were filled by members of the family. In those days Sir Walter Lawrence was Land Commissioner, and he was having a titanic struggle to save the farmers from the persecution of the Brahman officials.

I happened, in 1896, to visit a fort on the road between

Srinagar and Leh, with the British officer concerned, in order to see how the grain was stored. There was a threatened famine in Baltistan and Ladakh and the Kashmir Government had arranged for many thousand sacks of grain to be stored there. Members of this Brahman family had been given the contract. One of them was asked to show his store. He made all sorts of excuses to prevent our visiting the fort, but they were of no avail. The truth was out, the storerooms were empty, there was no grain.

The grain had been secretly exported to India instead of sending it to the country threatened with famine. This is just one instance of how this family used its power.

Now, a few days ago, I received a visit from the head of the Kashmir Uplift Department who described to me some of the work he had been able to accomplish to lighten the burdens of the Mohammedan farmers.

(a) Better health through cleaner houses and surroundings.

(b) Improvement of roads so that their merchandise could travel more easily and cheaply.

(c) Keeping them out of the law courts in the city by arranging courts in their own village.

(d) Saving their money by starting co-operative societies and in every way teaching them to help themselves and become free men.

Who is this head of the Uplift Department of this state? He was a boy of seven when he was brought to me by his rich Brahman father in the year 1892.

As I listened to that Kashmir Brahman official speaking with enthusiasm of his efforts to raise the oppressed, I looked back to that day forty-eight years ago when he was brought to me as a child, and thanked God.

On Sunday, August 18th, 1940, ten of our school teachers arrived at Nil Nag when we were on holiday and asked me to baptize them. They had all been students of our school from childhood, so that I knew them intimately and was delighted to receive them into our Christian brotherhood. They were baptized in the beautiful lake in

the presence of our camp and servants, and they all returned that same day to Srinagar rejoicing, but did not
realize the troubles that were awaiting them.

On October 6th, the Bishop of Lahore motored the
four hundred miles from Lahore to confirm these teachers,
and to attend on October 9th our Golden Jubilee Celebration which had been arranged without our knowledge by
Eric, the school staff and many friends, including our
Bishop, the British Resident Colonel D. Fraser, and
many others.

On that morning both the boys' and the girls' schools
assembled in the Residency garden, as well as a great
crowd of British and Kashmiri friends. The British Resident then presented us with a purse of 8,000 rupees and
a book most beautifully bound and inscribed with the
names of the several hundred donors.

Two days later, at the annual school display, the Bishop
of Lahore formally opened the beautiful swimming bath,
presented to us by our old friend, Major K. C. Hadow,
M.C., son of the late Cecil Hadow, the great friend and
champion of the C.M.S. schools.

On December 12th my wife and I went to Karachi
where we spent three happy months to escape the Kashmir winter. We found so many friends that we were almost overwhelmed by their kindnesses.

While we were enjoying ourselves at Karachi our newly
baptized teachers were having a very bad time. My
absence from Srinagar gave our enemies the opportunity
they wanted. They knew that it was useless making direct
attacks on them, so they persecuted their wives and relations.

It is difficult for anyone who does not know the manners
and customs of Brahman priests to understand fully what
it means to be attacked by this class of super religious
fanatics, but those who remember the attacks made on our
Lord Jesus Christ and on His disciples by the Pharisees
and Sadducees will understand in some degree those made
by the Brahman priests.

All sorts of lies were spread abroad in order to induce

the Hindu population to persecute these men. One amusing lie that was published in the press, was that I had forced their wives to eat beef.

The Brahman women in this country are strong believers in the teachings they receive from the Brahman priests. One can hardly picture the difficulties these men faced with their women relatives, wives, daughters, sisters, aunts, and cousins weeping around them, and who, when they held out against their entreaties, threatened to leave them and would certainly not take food with them. The result was, that six of the twelve gave in, and ceased attending our church services. But, of course, their hearts and their desires were not changed and we hope it will not be long before they will win over their families by their consistent lives. There was always the danger, too, of poison in the background, which did not exactly add spice to our lives. On my return to Srinagar from Karachi I met the persecuted teachers of our school staff. Poor fellows, they looked utterly miserable and dejected, for, not only had they suffered at the hands of the Brahman priests and their own relations, but many of the Christian congregation gave them the cold shoulder. These Christians were mostly from the Punjab, and were the sons or the grandsons of Christians and therefore did not understand what religious persecution was, or could be.

But, fortunately, there were several old boys of our school, both Mohammedans and Brahmans, who sympathized with them in their distress. Amongst them was our headmaster Shanker Koul, who went with them when they were called to face the Dharam Sabha, i.e. the Brahman Sanhedrim, and stood by them to give them courage. Abdul Karim, our brave police officer, visited me to offer his help in case violence should be offered them.

One bright exception in this persecution and seeming failure happened at Islamabad where lived Mustafa, the Mohammedan teacher, whom I had baptized. He was the only Christian from Mohammedanism in that town and, naturally, came in for slander and reproach. Fortunately, he had a strong and brave father who sympathized with his son and from whom he received protection. This is the first time that I have ever heard of a father standing up for a son who had left Mohammed for Jesus Christ.

I firmly believe what one of these men said to me, that "before long they will win through", and I believe his words were true for I have so often been permitted to see victory after defeat and I say with Joseph of old, "God meant it for good".

Britain having given India self-government, our British Resident, Colonel W. F. Webb, C.I.E., closed the Residency, and that ended protection of British subjects. Transport was arranged for any British who wished to leave Kashmir.

I had no wish to leave as long as I could be of some help to those old students who were honest men putting up a continual fight against the Devil and all his beastly works in this fair land of Kashmir. But in certain quarters it was thought that my presence might cause difficulties for the new Principal, Dr. Phil Edmunds, Ph.D., who indeed is a man and able to tackle the disciples of the Devil.

So Blanche and I left Srinagar on October 9th, when all was quiet and peaceful in the Valley of Kashmir. We left our home, after fifty-odd years, in grand style as thirty of the school staff hauled our car to the P.O. bus stand, preceded by the school band, and the road was lined for a quarter of a mile by the boys and old students.

After crossing the Jhelum river at Kohale, a distance of 133 miles, we were in Pakistan where we met armed men searching for Hindu or Sikh travellers, whom they dragged out and shot at sight. They had already killed 300 of them. At Rawalpindi we found the town absolutely cleared of Hindus and Sikhs, for in the first fortnight of India receiving the gift of "Home Rule", they managed to slaughter one another (in North Punjab alone) to the tune of over 400,000, which was a greater number than all the British soldiers killed during the five years' war.

At Pindi we met our son-in-law, Lt.-Col. Dick McGill, D.S.O., who, dear fellow, had brought a military truck with a Gurkha guard 200 miles from Lahore to take our heavy luggage. He had intended to carry it right from Kashmir, 400 miles. He arranged seats for us and Miss Mary Grove (who most kindly took us under her wing) in a military Dakota plane to Delhi, while he took our luggage by road to this entirely Hindu city. Dick had been for the last two or three months with his Gurkha battalion striving to save from slaughter tens of thousands of refugees fleeing by road and rail to possible safety. Over a thousand refugees were slaughtered on one train alone. It was a ghastly job and Dick was pretty well tired out.

At Delhi General Sir Arthur Smith and his lady gave us shelter with much kindness. A few days previously the General, with his aides-de-camp, had to guard night and day, with revolvers loaded, their Mohammedan servants with all their families crowded into his house, from the Hindus and Sikhs anxious to slaughter them.

From Delhi we travelled by mail train to Bombay where we were kindly entertained by Canon L. B. Butcher at the C.M.S. house for a month, until we secured passages for Beira on the S.S. *Tairea*. Dick and Frances McGill, with their two little boys, joined us, so my wife and I were again well looked after and cared for during the month's voyage.

On the twenty-four-hour journey from Beira to Salisbury, Southern Rhodesia, Blanche was taken seriously ill and removed by ambulance from the station to hospital where she was made comfortable, but on the 26th December she passed peacefully into life more abundant. Thank God she was granted an easy crossing.

The Bishop, Edward Paget, an old friend, kindly took the service in his Cathedral and at the cemetery which is near the house which my sailor brother Ted built soon after he arrived with the pioneers in 1890. My nephew, Ronald, and his wife Margaret, who live here, were kindness itself so that we had many friends around to help and cheer us.

It was not until we had reached Bombay that we heard the terrible news of the invasion of Kashmir by Afridi tribesmen and other devils who came up the 100 miles of road, bound for Srinagar with 500 lorries, burning, looting and slaughtering. But fortunately, the Hindustan

troops from Delhi flew to Srinagar just in the nick of time
and saved the city. You can understand my anxiety for the
scores of my old students who were at work on that 100
miles of road.

Just after the invasion the Maharajah, with his officers,
fled to Jammu. He handed over the country to Sheikh
Abdulla whom he had just released from prison. Fortunately Abdulla is a friend of the C.M.S. hospitals and
schools (his children attend our boys' and girls' schools).
He has appointed as his ministers fourteen of my old
students, who are patriots and honest men, and also
Kshyup Bandu who has worked with us to save Hindu
widows, etc., and has made him Minister for Women! ! !
So I have cause for thankfulness that my friends are safe
at present. But what is going to happen to our hospital
and school, and to this beautiful land of Kashmir?

CLOSING DAYS—BY THE CANON'S SON

It was a little more than eighteen months after his
arrival in Rhodesia that my father passed away on August
1st, 1949. He told me that in writing his memoirs he
had mentioned misfortunes and apparent disasters which
had turned out, in the end, to be blessings, in the hope
that his experiences would help others who might be
down on their luck, to take heart. He certainly faced his
own uprooting from Kashmir, and the loss of his compan-
ion of fifty-six years, with remarkable fortitude and cheerfulness.

He took a lively interest in his new surroundings at
Salisbury where his brother first hoisted the British flag
in 1890: the same year that he himself first set foot in
Kashmir. He much enjoyed meeting new friends and it
was a special pleasure to him to hear stories of his brother
and of the early days from that grand old man Mr.
Rudland. Also from Mrs. Edmunds, herself the wife of a
pioneer. She passed away on the same day as he did.

He was greatly struck by the cheerfulness of the
Africans and the vigour with which they rode their
bicycles. During his illness he was impressed with the

care and thoroughness with which the native servants swept and tidied his room.

The sunsets were a constant delight to him and the cloud effects often reminded him of the snow-capped mountains of Kashmir.

On his eighty-sixth birthday he christened his grand-daughter in the Cathedral. His voice was still powerful and compelling. He enjoyed the cheery party afterwards at the McGills' house, where a joint toast to him and baby Julia was drunk. About a month later he was laid low with a severe heart attack and was taken to St. Anne's Hospital staffed by Roman Catholic sisters. He could not speak highly enough of their wonderful kindness and happy dispositions. After three weeks he left, to con-valesce at the home of his nephew and niece, Ronald and Margaret Tyndale-Biscoe. His old heart, however, did not improve as was hoped, and there he remained, gradu-ally weakening, during his last three and a half months. He was full of admiration for the ingenuity of Sister McInnes, who was called in towards the end, in contriv-ing ways to make him more comfortable. She had served with the Navy during the war. He said: "She must have acquired this special skill in nursing those poor fellows in the Naval hospitals." He also enjoyed the visits of that kind man Doctor Holiday who looked after him.

Knowing he had not long to live, it amused him to think of the many friends he would be likely to meet again, and also some of his enemies! He also wondered what his next job would be.

He spoke of the pleasure it had been to him getting to know so many British soldiers in Kashmir during the latter years of the 1939 war, My parents and sister started a small camp for them in their garden. Others followed suit, with the result that a great number were able to afford a holiday in Kashmir. Over 900 of them visited the schools, some taking part in their activities. My father was surprised and cheered by the keen interest they showed in all they saw. I mention this episode because it happened after my father had written his book, and he continued to enjoy, up to the time of his death, letters

8

from a number of these men and several of their parents.

He did not speak much of his one anxiety which was for his old and faithful staff who were trying to carry on in Kashmir, but one knew that it occupied his thoughts. Should there be any profits from the royalties of this book they will be devoted firstly to swell the small fund which Miss Mallinson has kindly undertaken to administer for such of them as may be in need, and, thereafter, to help in the splendid work Miss Mallinson is doing for the girls of Kashmir—a work always very near to my father's heart.

Up to the last he enjoyed chats with friends and relations, among whom was his old friend, the Rev. Herbert Pegg, who also had recently come to live in Rhodesia.

His passing was in keeping with his life. His last words were to tell the sister who had come in to give him something for his breathing and was standing by, that he felt easier and she should go off and get some sleep.

The funeral service was taken by his friend Rev. St. John Evans, who had served in West Africa before coming to Rhodesia. And so the old warrior passed on to his next assignment, and his body was laid near the grave of his wife.

> *Impatient of cant or dogma,*
> *He helped the weak and those in trouble,*
> *His dauntless life on the pattern of his Master*
> *Helped others to live like* MEN.

C.J.T.-B.

INDEX

INDEX

Printed in Great Britain
Latimer, Trend & Co., Ltd., Plymouth
1951